THE RANDOM
WALK AND BEYOND

THE RANDOM WALK AND BEYOND

An Inside Guide to the Stock Market

Mark A. Johnson

WILEY

JOHN WILEY & SONS

New York   Chichester   Brisbane   Toronto   Singapore

To my father,
who has always claimed to be
my toughest critic and my most enthusiastic supporter.
He has proven it.

Library of Congress Cataloging in Publication Data:

Johnson, Mark (Mark A.)
  The random walk and beyond.

  Bibliography: p.
  1. Stocks.   2. Investments.   3. Stock-exchange.
I. Title.

HG4521.J645 1988   332.63'22   87-31602
ISBN 0-471-63223-6

Printed in the United States of America

10 9 8 7 6 5 4 3 2 1

Author's Note

A great many months pass from the time the text of a book is completed to the time that the book is finally manufactured and distributed. Intervening events can sometimes render an idea or argument obsolete, leaving the author wishing he could take back or change his words. In my case, the text was completed in early 1987. Subsequent market events have been dramatic by any standard. Wherever the market stands when you read this, no one will forget the events of the fall of 1987. So, the question is: Would I write the book differently if I had it to do over again?

The answer is "No." If I were writing the book today, I might include references and illustrations from the upheaval of 1987, but the ideas and conclusions would be the same. In fact, the events of 1987 reinforce, not diminish, my major points. As you shall see, I emphasize that the stock market is primarily a risk/reward system and that the key to successful investing is to understand and manage risk. In addition, risk is a function of time. There is a clear relationship between short-term risk and long-term reward. The events of 1987 prove the need to understand that relationship.

An event such as the crash of 1987 tends to focus our attention on predicting the future, because the potential rewards from success are so obvious. After a major market upheaval, the news media report enthusiastically on the people who forecasted the event, making them instant heroes and celebrities. Some predictions will be so accurate they will be described as "uncanny." But there is nothing that happens in the stock market—no matter how unusual—that is not predicted by someone. Thousands of professional analysts and millions of amateurs continuously predict the future. Some inevitably will be correct, simply as a matter of statistical probability. Finding and extolling the winners can be harmless fun, but assuming that they or their methods will win again the next time may be both foolish and expensive. Both logic and evidence indicate that the chances of forecasting with enough accuracy and consistency to significantly outperform the market over time are extremely remote. A major theme of this book is that long-term investment success does not lie in predicting the future. Unprecedented market volatility does not contradict that idea; it strengthens it.

October 30, 1987

Preface

The most disastrous investment strategies are those based on hope rather than knowledge. James Thurber once wrote, ''A pinch of probably is worth a pound of perhaps.'' The simple goal of this book is to provide you with a pinch or two of probably.

This book is aimed at nonprofessional investors and doesn't require a technical or academic background. I've included mathematical formulas for the sake of completeness, but if you suffer from math anxiety or the last time you did any algebra was in high school, don't be dismayed. The formulas are not crucial. The ideas are what matters, and I trust that they, at least, are clear.

Nothing worthwhile is accomplished without help and support. I would like to thank a fellow author, Jean Ross Peterson, for her unwavering empathy, enthusiasm, and encouragement. I would also like to thank Kenneth Fisher for providing unpublished research data as well as some stimulating conversation, Theresa Lobdell for assistance in locating research material, and Charles Anderson and William Ayer for their comments. Thanks to my editor, Karl Weber, for his insight. His suggestions led to a better book. Thanks also to my literary agent, Richard Balkin, for representing me not because he foresaw huge commissions but because he felt the book was important. Finally, thanks to my family for putting up with me, and especially to my father for his devotion, support, and ideas.

I hope you will find this book useful and informative. But no matter how much you may learn from reading it, I am sure that I have learned more from writing it. I have tried to write from your perspective and thus my greatest thanks must go to you. I would be pleased to hear from you, with praise, criticism, arguments, or suggestions. You may write to me at the following address:

Mark Johnson & Co.
3817 42nd Ave. N.E.
Seattle, WA 98105

Contents

Part One
Approaching
the Market

1

What's the Problem?

This guidebook to modern individual investing is both theoretical and practical—theoretical, because investors need to know the principles that govern the stock market and determine results, and practical, so that investors can use those principles to formulate workable and successful investment strategies. Don't expect a quick fix here, or a one-sided argument for a single strategy. There is no single best market strategy. I am not attempting to predict the future, to tell you that a new era has dawned or that a second Great Crash is imminent. I do intend to separate sense from nonsense, to show you that investing can be both simpler and more rewarding than you imagine, to take you beyond wondering what you should buy or sell Monday morning, and to show you what works in the market, why it works, and how you can apply it.

Is this book for everyone? Not quite. If you are a confirmed short-term trader, I cannot help you, except perhaps to disabuse you of some of your ideas. If you are in the stock market for the money, not the thrills, then this book is definitely for you. Whether you are investing $5,000 or $5 million, some of the practical problems and solutions may be different, but the principles are the same. Experienced investors will gain insight into the causes of their past results, good or bad, and learn how they can avoid losses. Relative newcomers can perhaps be saved from walking too far down the wrong paths, though at least one chastening failure in the market seems almost inevitable. Are you staying away from individual stocks and investing in mutual funds? You have turned over some of your decisions to the fund managers, but you have no less need to understand the market, if only to determine which funds are appropriate for you.

What qualifications should you have, to profit from this book? I assume that you have had enough exposure to the market to know what common stocks are and, at least generally, how they are traded, and that you are familiar with the kinds of research and analysis conducted by the Wall Street community. Beyond those basics, you need only a desire to understand the market, a healthy skepticism, and an insistence on being persuaded by evidence rather than by rhetoric. (A few nagging doubts about the traditional ways in which Wall Street provides advice and sells investments to the public wouldn't hurt, either.)

This book is simple, not simplistic. It is written for the layperson, but it deals with the most sophisticated ideas and issues in modern investment practice. A professional investor once pointed out the biggest problem with individual investors: They spend more time and effort on researching the purchase of a $10,000 car than they do on a $10,000 investment. I assume that your investments are important enough for you to spend a few thoughtful hours reading about them.

THE USUAL GAME

Recently I received an advertisement that offered a challenge: "As a serious investor, we dare you to match wits with Wall Street." I was invited to enter a contest that involved predicting the level of the S&P (Standard & Poor's) 500 stock index at some future date. The only cost would be the price of a stamp, and so matching wits carried no dangerous risk. (I didn't win.) The ad was a perfect illustration of how most people view investing: as a game of forecasting, stock picking, and timing—the matching of wits. This is the game most investors play. Most of them lose. The real stock market is not what they think it is.

The outcome of any investment depends on future events and developments, and so it is natural for investors, analysts, and advisors to focus their efforts on predicting the future. Since it seems more difficult to predict the distant future, they focus on the near term. As a result, they invest an enormous amount of money in the market, for relatively short-term gains. Probably most investors are playing at prediction, particularly institutional investment managers, who must compete with each other under the most nerve-wracking circumstances: Every quarter, their performances are calculated and rated for all the world to see. They are continuously evaluated by their clients, too, often on a simplistic basis: "What have you done for me lately?" Like it or not, most professional investment managers are forced into short-term performance; they just don't have the luxury of patience.

Individual investors, of course, are not forced into the short-term prediction game. They do not have to consider themselves in competition with other investors, and their results, fortunately, are not made public. But most individual investors still choose this game anyway. John Maynard Keynes, famous as an economist but equally astute as an investor and observer of human nature, noted, "There is particular zest in making money quickly, and remoter gains are discounted by the average man at a very high rate" (p. 157). Keynes also suggested (pp. 149, 155) that a short-term orientation is a natural reaction to uncertainty:

> Our knowledge of the factors which will govern the yield of an investment some years hence is usually very slight and often negligible.... Thus the investor is forced to concern himself with the anticipation of impending changes, in the news or the atmosphere, of the kind by which experience shows that the mass psychology of the market is most influenced. It is not sensible to pay 25 for an investment, of which you believe the prospective yield to justify a value of 30, if you also believe that the market will value it at 20 three months hence.

The overwhelming majority of Wall Street's resources and efforts, virtually all of what we normally think of as analysis, is devoted to the short-term prediction game—the battle of wits. Its ultimate purpose is to get an edge on the market, to gain some advantage. Over whom? Other investors. The prediction game is essentially a competitive struggle among investors, a game of winners and losers: I am buying and you are selling; one of us will be right and one of us wrong.

Over time, the returns from owning stocks are positive. Thus it is possible for everyone to be a winner in the sense of making money. The prediction game, however, is not about achieving positive returns; it is about beating the market. Do brokerage firms and advisory publications advertise that they can keep you from losing money, or that they will help you *match* the market? Of course not. They're going to help you *beat* it. Merrill Lynch will help you; E.F. Hutton and Smith Barney will, too, along with other firms, large and small. Joe Granville will help you, and so will Martin Zweig and Stan Weinstein and a host of other subscription advisors. You can hear from astute, informed professionals every Friday on "Wall Street Week," and you can read their views in *Barron's*, *Forbes*, *Fortune*, and so on. With all the expert help available, you'd think that beating the market would be easy, that everyone would be doing it. There's the problem. Everyone can't beat the market.

If you are going to beat the market, you must do so at somebody else's expense. It is as mathematically impossible for everyone to beat the market as it is for every team in the National League to play better than .500 ball.

In terms of beating the market (rather than simply earning a return), prediction is a *zero-sum game:* The gains (outperforming the market) of the winners are equal to the losses (underperforming) of the losers. In real life, unfortunately, the situation is not even this good, because it costs something to play: commissions, bid/ask spreads, fees to advisors, subscriptions to magazines, market letters, and data services. In reality, prediction is a *negative-sum game*—a fancy way of saying that the odds are against you from the start.

When costs are considered, winning in this game is extremely difficult. We don't have to be better than average; we have to be *much* better than average. It is impossible for everyone to win; it is *not* impossible for everyone to lose. As one wag put it, not only is there no free lunch, there may not be any lunch at all!

Ample evidence shows that there is very little "lunch" in the prediction game; many studies have been conducted on the performance of professionally managed investment funds and subscription advisory services. If any group has the tools, training, and motivation to beat the market, it is the pros. Yet, as a group, they almost never beat the market. Individually, they sometimes do and sometimes don't, but none of them beats the market with any consistency. Indeed, the pattern looks suspiciously as if luck, not skill, is controlling the outcomes.

Most investors take it as an article of faith that skill, intelligence, and effort will be rewarded, but the evidence shows that these virtues will not win the Wall Street prediction game. Why not? Because in our competitive system, in which tens of thousands of people, controlling hundreds of billions of dollars possess these virtues, they are not at a premium. The market doesn't reward qualities that are not scarce.

THE REAL GAME

The short-term analysis/forecasting game is an odds-against proposition. Skill is not likely to overcome the costs of playing, because skill is not the primary determinant of the outcomes. What is? Risk. Investing is primarily a risk/reward system.

Investing in common stocks is risky. No matter how much analysis we conduct, the results are uncertain. Few people are willing to make risky investments unless they know that *on average* they will get higher returns than they would get from, say, insured savings accounts. The riskier the investment, the higher the average or expected return must be to entice people.

The key word here is *average*. The market rewards risk, but not consistently. That's why we call it risk. In the short run, risk may or may not be rewarded. It simply represents uncertainty. The more risk you take, the more likely it is that your results will be far from average. Thus the reward for risk taking is only a long-run prospect.

The idea that stocks are risky and that investors expect to be compensated for taking risk is not big news. What many investors don't realize, however, is that there are several different types of risk in the stock market. Some risks are rewarded, but others are not. You can eliminate one type without reducing your returns, but you cannot avoid another unless you get out of the market altogether. Still other kinds of risk are specific to particular investment strategies. The key to investing is understanding these risks so that you can take acceptable, rewarding risks and eliminate those that are useless.

Over time, stockholders are rewarded not for being smart, but for taking risk. Risk taking alone, however, is not enough to ensure rewards. For all the brainpower that investors and analysts apply to evaluating stocks, there are still some deep-seated and apparently inherent biases in the way the market values companies. Some characteristics are habitually undervalued, while others are overvalued. Thus certain categories of stocks have strong tendencies to outperform or underperform the market. We can create strategies to take advantage of these tendencies.

Such strategies have a singular virtue: They do not require us to match wits in the short-term prediction game. They don't depend on our correct estimate of next quarter's earnings, and we don't need to know whether interest rates or the dollar will rise or fall. These strategies don't require forecasting at all. They are based on the fundamental nature and behavior of people and markets, and this is a more plausible basis for most private investors than reliance on an ability to predict the future.

Successful investing is a three-step process. First, we must have *knowledge* of the theory and the facts of how the market really behaves. This knowledge leads to our finding, understanding, and evaluating workable, effective *investment strategies.* Finally comes *risk management,* in which we implement our strategies to ensure that our positive *expected* returns become positive *actual* returns.

As we cover these three steps, we will see how professional investment managers operate and what we can learn from them, where they have advantages over individual investors, and where and why individual investors have an advantage over the professionals. We will see why most reported investment results are not what they appear to be, and why they are unattainable in the real world. We will examine the most controversial of all investment ideas, the *efficient market hypothesis.* This disconcerting theory suggests that there are no undervalued stocks and no overvalued ones (at least none that we can expect to identify), and that efforts to identify them are both costly and futile. We will see how this idea may be true and what investors can do about it. Finally, it will become clear that time is on our side in the market. The risks of investing are not nearly so great as is commonly believed.

Investing seems highly complex, but once we cut through the jargon, the fancy mathematical models, the intimidation, the hype, and the cult of expertise, we find a surprisingly simple and logical situation. Our challenge is to let go of traditional and habitual modes of thought and behavior. Most investors who are losing in the stock market are not stupid; they are just playing the wrong game. As a serious investor, I dare you *not* to match wits with Wall Street.

A STRATEGIC APPROACH

When a football coach prepares for an upcoming contest, he prepares a game plan. He already knows the rules of the game, and he uses his knowledge of the two teams to create an overall strategy for victory. He analyzes what the opposition is likely to do in various circumstances, but only after his strategy is formed does the coach select specific formations and plays—his tactics. A strategy, then, is an overall plan to achieve some goal, and tactics are the specific decisions and actions that implement the strategy.

In the stock market, strategy involves the types and numbers of stocks in which you invest, their riskiness, whether you seek short-term or long-term gains, and so on. Tactics have to do with selecting individual stocks and with timing transactions. Buying stable blue-chip stocks and holding them for many years is a strategy. Choosing the stocks, replacing them, and timing these actions are tactics.

The roles of strategist and tactician are different; indeed, they may be performed by different people. On most football teams, for example, one person develops the game plan while another calls the plays. The distinction between strategy and tactics is crucial in investing, too. In effect, there are two fundamental jobs: strategy selection and portfolio management. In many institutional settings, these jobs are entirely separate. They are usually performed not only by different people but also even by different firms. Individual investors, however, must be both investment strategists and portfolio managers.

Unfortunately, most investors have not considered the distinction between these two roles. They are portfolio managers who buy stocks on the principle that the stocks will go up. But how can we know whether to buy or sell a particular stock unless we know what we are trying to accomplish and how to go about it? Until we have a well-developed strategy, our tactics will be a hodgepodge of isolated actions leading nowhere in particular—except, perhaps to disaster. We need a game plan.

Wall Street and the investment business may change, but some things stay the same. Unfortunately, one of those things is the kind of advice that investors receive. Whether it comes from brokers, publications, radio and television, or subscription market letters, advice is almost always either someone's opinion about the future of the overall market or someone's recommendation of particular stocks to buy or sell. But these are tactics, not strategies.

The entire industry is structured to keep investors focused on tactics, and this is the major failing of Wall Street. Any stockbroker can tell us at any moment whether IBM is rated *buy*, *sell*, or *hold* by his firm's research department, as if that were all there is to successful investing. We shouldn't be surprised. Tactical advice puts commissions and fees in the hands of brokers and advisors. It is immediate and tangible, and it touches basic emotions—the desire for action and profit, to compete in the game. Tactical advice can gratify those desires, but when the time comes for our most important decisions—the strategic ones—we are on our own.

Wall Street's focus on tactics is ironic because once there is good strategy, tactics usually come naturally and rather easily. Most investors, because they haven't stopped to develop strategy, have to spend much time, effort, money, and emotion on tactics. Developing strategy is not easy or fast, but it is essential to successful investing. It demands sound theory as well as facts, and it even requires some introspection: Not only must you understand the market and your competition; you must also know yourself. The goal of this book is to help you be both a better portfolio manager and a better investment strategist.

2

Measuring
the Market

The American stock market consists of every publicly traded company in the United States, and there are thousands of them. They range from small companies, with values of less than $1 million, to such giants as Exxon and IBM, whose sales, assets, and profits are all counted in the billions. Their combined value approaches $3 trillion. Roughly 1600 companies are traded on the New York Stock Exchange (NYSE), a few hundred more on the American Stock Exchange, and a few score more on various regional exchanges. Tens of thousands more companies are also traded over the counter. They form a heterogeneous group—about the only thing they all have in common is that they are common stocks—yet, taken together, they are what we call *the market*, the largest, most open, most active capital market in the world.

MARKET INDEXES

The condition or the action of the stock market at any time mirrors the condition or the action of its individual issues. For many purposes, we may want a general picture of the market—a summary view instead of a huge collection of individual prices and price changes. An average, or index, combines and distills these thousands of bits of information into a concise measure of the market. It tells us where the market stands and, more importantly, it keeps track of changes over time.

This process seems straightforward enough, but devising a suitable market index is not easy. An index must be derived from a formula that combines data from individual stocks. There is no "correct" formula: Stocks are very different, and the formula depends on what we want to know. Several measures of the market are available. They are widely cited, and so it is important to know how they are constructed and what they measure.

We could make up market indexes based on any number of common characteristics. We could make an index of dividend yields, for example, or of price-earnings (P/E) ratios. Let's say we are interested in stock prices and values. Having decided that, we still face some important choices. We must find a basis for combining the various nonidentical stocks into an index. That basis is called *weighting,* and it determines how much individual stocks will count in the index. How stocks are weighted has a profound effect on the way their changes are reflected in the indexes.

Three commonly used weighting systems lead to three types of market index. These systems are *value weighting, equal weighting* (also called *unweighting*), and *price weighting*. (You may be surprised to learn that the least logical system is the basis for the best-known index.)

Price-Weighted Indexes

The Dow Jones averages are a set of three averages, of which the Industrial Average is the most famous. They are based on 65 large, established companies, most of which are considered blue-chip issues. The construction of the average is very simple: The sum of the prices of all the component stocks (30 Industrials, 20 Transports, and 15 Utilities) is divided by a second number, called the *divisor.*

The divisor keeps the average on a mathematically comparable basis when component stocks split or are replaced by others. It is changed so that the average will not reflect changes that are unrelated to the stocks' price performance.

For example, suppose that on a given day the sum of all the prices of the thirty Dow Industrial stocks is 2000. At this writing, the divisor is 0.889. Dividing 2000 by 0.889 yields 2250, which is the Dow Jones Industrial Average for the day. Now suppose that one of the component stocks splits 2 for 1, reducing its price from 100 to 50. The sum of all the component prices will now be 1950. If some adjustment is not made in the divisor, the Dow will be 2193 (1950 ÷ 0.889). It is nonsensical to have the average drop 57 points just because one of the stocks has split. Thus the divisor is reduced to 0.867, and the average is maintained at 2250.

Stocks in the Dow averages are seldom replaced, but stock splits are common. As a result, the divisor has decreased steadily over the years. Only a few years ago, it was around 3; decades ago, it was around 15. At one time, a combined 15-point change in the underlying stocks was required to move the average by a point. Now all it takes is a combined change of less than a single point. This circumstance has led to a widespread and widely published misconception: that the Dow average has become inherently more volatile.

It is easy to show why this is not true. Let's return to our previous example. Suppose that every stock in the Dow Jones Industrial Average splits 2 for 1, and that the sum of their prices is reduced to 1000. The divisor is then reduced to 0.4445 to maintain the average at 2250. Now it takes only a 1-point change in a component stock to create a 2.25-point change in the average, whereas before it took a 2-point change. On a percentage basis, however, nothing has changed: a 1-point change in a $50 stock is equivalent to a 2-point change in a stock worth $100. No matter what you may read, reductions in the divisor do not make the Dow averages more volatile.

The key decision in creating an index is how much weight to give its individual stocks. In the Dow system, a stock's importance is a function only of its price— the higher its price, the more weight it has. Suppose that Kodak sells for $80 per share and Sears for $40. If Kodak goes down 10 percent (from 80 to 72) and Sears goes up 10 percent (from 40 to 44), then the Dow Industrial Average will decline, because the 8-point loss in Kodak is greater than the 4-point gain in Sears. Kodak is more important than Sears—not because it has greater assets, more market value, more shareholders, or more of anything else, but simply because its stock is priced higher.

This is certainly a strange weighting system. You can see how illogical it is if you consider the effect of a stock split. Suppose that Kodak splits 2 for 1 and its price drops from 80 to 40. Two things happen. First, Kodak now has less weight in the Dow average, simply because it has a lower price. Second, the divisor is changed to keep the average on a comparable basis. This change affects all the component stocks, not just Kodak. The weightings of the other twenty-nine industrial stocks have now increased, to balance the decrease in Kodak. Magically, Sears and Kodak are now equally important.

Value-Weighted Indexes

The Dow Jones averages may be the most famous, but value-weighted indexes are the most common and, according to most experts, the most useful. Value weighting defines importance very straightforwardly: as the total market capitalization of all a company's stock. This is not the same as the capitalization shown in a company's financial statements. Rather, it is the number of shares outstanding, multiplied by the current price per share— the total market value of the stock.

The market performance of large companies, whose values are measured in the tens of billions of dollars, is certainly more significant than the fortunes of much smaller companies. Thus a value-weighted index is appealing because a company's capitalization is a realistic measure of its importance to investors.

The most useful characteristic of a value-weighted index is that it is a *market value* index. Changes in the index are directly proportional to changes in the market value of the underlying individual stocks. For example, if the index is up 2 percent, we know that the total market value of all the stocks in the index is also up 2 percent. The same thing cannot be said of price-weighted indexes like the Dow Jones averages.

Value-weighted indexes now in use include the New York Stock Exchange indexes (all common stocks on the NYSE), Standard and Poor's indexes (S&P 500, etc.), the Amex Market Value Index, and the over-the-counter NASDAQ (National Association of Securities Dealers Automated Quotation System) indexes.

Equally Weighted Indexes

Unlike price- and value-weighted indexes, an equally weighted index is based on the assumption that all stocks should be counted as equally important. This type of index is constructed by calculating the average *percentage changes* in the stocks. For example, if on a given day the average price change is + 1 percent, and if the index at the previous day's close was 108.00, then the new index will be 109.08 (108.00 × 1.01). Since a 2 percent fall in a tiny stock will offset a 2 percent rise in a huge one, the changes shown in an equally weighted index do not represent changes in the combined market value of its stocks.

The most popular equally weighted index is compiled and published by Value Line, an investment advisory firm. The index is based on about 1500 stocks, mostly of New York Stock Exchange companies, and it is quoted daily in the *Wall Street Journal*. Some other equally weighted indexes are also compiled, primarily by writers of market letters, but these indexes are not readily available to nonsubscribers.

A Tool for a Purpose

There is no such thing as either the perfect or even the best index. Our choice of index depends on the information we seek. Broad, value-weighted indexes, such as the S&P 500, give the best measure of the experience of investors *as a group*. An individual is extremely unlikely to hold a broad, value-weighted portfolio, but investors as a group *must*—by definition, since all investors taken together must hold all the stock in all the companies.

For some purposes, though, an equally weighted index, such as Value Line's, may be preferable. First, many investors tend to put roughly equal funds into each stock they buy, thus creating equally weighted portfolios. Second, equally weighted indexes reflect the performance of smaller issues, which scarcely show up in value-weighted indexes. For example, at the end of 1984 the 50 largest companies accounted for more than one-third of the entire New York Stock Exchange Composite Index. Value-weighted indexes may indeed be the best way to measure the performance of investors as a group, but they are by nature blue-chip, large-stock indexes. Equally weighted indexes are better at showing the performance of smaller stocks.

The Dow Jones averages, of course, give a very specialized view of the market, a purely blue-chip view. Despite their elite focus and the peculiar way in which they are constructed, the Dow Jones averages give us a basic and generally useful view of the market, or at least of one part. In the short run, the Dow Industrials are highly correlated with the S&P 500 and the NYSE Composite. (Over short and long periods alike, the latter two are virtually indistinguishable from each other and represent little more than brand-name marketing.)

Different indexes reflect the behavior and performance of different market segments. Indexes can vary considerably, as in their reflection of action in the market during 1984. For the entire year, the S&P 500 and the NYSE Composite were up roughly 1 percent, suggesting that the market was essentially flat. Nevertheless, the Value Line and Amex indexes both declined more than 8 percent, and NASDAQ's lost more than 11 percent. In 1984, large-capitalization and blue-chip issues held their own, while the majority of stocks—the so-called secondary stocks—suffered significant losses, a fact that investors might not know if they looked only at the most widely cited indexes.

THE SCORES

Predicting what the market will do next week or next year may be difficult, and the past is not necessarily prologue, but we should take at least a brief look at history. It is impossible to have any perspective on investing if we have no idea of how the market has behaved over time.

We have just seen the many choices available for measuring and assessing the market's performance. For now, we will look at only one measure of the market, the S&P 500. This is a value-weighted index consisting of 400 industrials, 20 transports, 40 utilities, and 40 financial issues. These are not precisely the 500 largest companies in America, but they come close. The S&P 500 represents well over half the total value of all common stocks

traded in the United States. In professional as well as academic circles, this
index is the most widely recognized measure of the market.

Table 2.1 shows the year-by-year performance of the S&P 500 from 1926
through 1986.* For the sake of comparison, the performances of some other
investment securities—long-term corporate and government bonds, and U.S.
Treasury Bills—are also shown. In each case, the table displays the total
return, consisting of dividend or interest income plus capital gains or losses.
No allowance is made for taxes or transaction costs. Annual changes in the
Consumer Price Index are also given.

Jumping right to the bottom line, we see two summary measures—the
average annual rates of return and the compound rates of return. The difference between them is important. For example, suppose that an index went
up 30 percent in one year and lost 10 percent in the next. If we simply averaged these two figures, we would say that the average return is 10 percent
(30 − 10, ÷ 2). If the returns were compounding at 10 percent per year, the
total gain in two years would be 21 percent ($1 \times 1.10 \times 1.10 = 1.21$). But in
this example, at the end of two years the index actually would have gone
up only 17 percent ($1 \times 1.30 \times .90 = 1.17$). The compound rate of return
would be 8.2 percent. The compound rate is the rate that, if achieved in
every period, would result in the observed total return over several periods.
In this case, $1.082 \times 1.082 = 1.17$, the ratio of the ending index to the beginning. Compound rates of return are *always lower* than average rates.

By either measure, the stocks in Table 2.1 far outperformed the other
investments. Stocks were also the only investment to outstrip inflation. It
is interesting that the average return on Treasury Bills, or T-Bills, has been
almost equal to the inflation rate—not on a year-to-year basis, of course, but
over the long haul. In a way, this should not be surprising: T-Bills are the
classic risk-free investment; there is no possibility of default, and since the
maturity of a T-Bill is a year or less, there can be no year-to-year capital gains
or losses. But the fact that after inflation they provide virtually no real return
should give us pause. It is even more interesting to observe that Treasury
Bonds have performed almost identically. These bonds are scarcely free of
risk; there is no default risk, but there is a great deal of price risk.

Some other facts deserve comment. An investor in T-Bills will never lose
money, almost by definition of the investment, but investors in government
and corporate bonds suffered net losses in 16 and 14 of the 61 years, respectively, and stockholders suffered losses in 19 of those years. The extremes
in returns show great variability in stocks, as compared to bonds. The great
disinflation of the 1980s brought a tremendous fall in interest rates, and so

*The S&P 500 was actually introduced in 1957, but it has been extended back to 1926, primar-
ily by the Center for Research in Security Prices at the University of Chicago.

there were a few years with very high total returns in bonds. Otherwise, however, in their best years bondholders had a total return of less than 20 percent. The best year for the S&P 500 saw a return of 54 percent, and there were several years when returns exceeded 40 percent. The same pattern can be seen on the downside. The worst performance for government bonds was a 9 percent loss; in corporate bonds, the biggest loss was 8 percent; and in the stock market's worst year, the losses hit 43 percent. If volatility means risk, then stocks were not only more profitable but also much riskier than other investments.

Table 2.2 shows the same information in a different form. Instead of presenting annual returns, it gives cumulative returns in the form of *wealth ratios*. A wealth ratio is an investment's terminal value divided by its initial value, a measure of how much an investment has multiplied. Table 2.2 is constructed as if one dollar had been invested at the end of 1925 and left for accumulation (with dividends and interest reinvested) through the years.

Through 1986, a dollar invested continuously in T-Bills would have grown to $7.93, a sum approximately equal to the cost-of-living increase during the same period. Like corporate bonds, long-term government bonds would have achieved only modestly better results. Stocks, however, would have grown 331-fold! Even on an inflation-adjusted basis, the value of the stock portfolio would have increased 52-fold. Such is the power of compounding on investment returns.

Using Table 2.2, we can calculate the wealth ratio between any two dates. For example, suppose we want to determine changes in value in the stock portfolio during the 1940s. The table shows that the ratio at the end of 1949 was 4.38; at the end of 1939, it was 2.01. The wealth ratio for this period is simply the ending ratio divided by the beginning ratio—in this case, 4.83 ÷ 2.01 = 2.40.

A glance back at Table 2.1 indicates that stocks did rather poorly in the early years (that is, during the Crash and the Depression) but have done relatively well in recent years. Remember, though, that these figures are nominal returns and are not adjusted for inflation. Table 2.3 presents the same information on an inflation-adjusted basis, and the picture changes considerably. The early 1930s look better because the cost of living was going down, and this situation ameliorated stock losses. In contrast, the inflation of the late 1960s and later ravaged the returns of investors. In real terms, an investor in the S&P 500 at the end of 1964 was still in the hole at the end of 1981 (the bull market of 1982 finally reversed this trend). Bondholders had the same experience.

If you enjoy rummaging around in statistics, you can find many other interesting items in these tables. The most important conclusions are already clear, but they will bear repetition. The returns from owning stocks are much

TABLE 2.1 Year-by-Year Total Returns 1926–1986

YEAR	Common Stocks (S&P 500)	Long-Term Corporate Bonds	Long-Term Government Bonds	Treasury Bills	Consumer Price Index
1926	11.6%	7.4%	7.8%	3.3%	1.5%
1927	37.5	7.4	8.9	3.1	- 2.1
1928	43.6	2.8	0.1	3.2	- 1.0
1929	- 8.4	3.3	3.4	4.8	0.2
1930	- 24.9	8.0	4.7	2.4	- 6.0
1931	- 43.3	- 1.8	- 5.3	1.1	- 9.5
1932	- 8.2	10.8	16.8	1.0	- 10.3
1933	54.0	10.4	- 0.1	0.3	0.5
1934	- 1.4	13.8	10.0	0.2	2.0
1935	47.7	9.6	5.0	0.2	3.0
1936	33.9	6.7	7.5	0.2	1.2
1937	- 35.0	2.8	0.2	0.3	3.1
1938	31.1	6.1	5.5	0.0	- 2.8
1939	- 0.4	4.0	5.9	0.0	- 0.5
1940	- 9.8	3.4	6.1	0.0	1.0
1941	- 11.6	2.7	0.9	0.1	9.7
1942	20.3	2.6	3.2	0.3	9.3
1943	25.9	2.8	2.1	0.4	3.2
1944	19.8	4.7	2.8	0.3	2.1
1945	36.4	4.1	10.7	0.3	2.2
1946	- 8.1	1.7	0.1	0.4	18.2
1947	5.7	- 2.3	- 2.6	0.5	9.0
1948	5.5	4.1	3.4	0.8	2.7
1949	18.8	3.3	6.4	1.1	- 1.8
1950	31.7	2.1	0.1	1.2	5.8
1951	24.0	- 2.7	- 3.9	1.5	5.9
1952	18.4	3.5	1.2	1.7	0.9
1953	- 1.0	3.4	3.6	1.8	0.6
1954	52.6	5.4	7.2	0.9	- 0.5
1955	31.6	0.5	- 1.3	1.6	0.4
1956	6.6	- 6.8	- 5.6	2.5	2.9

Year					
1957	−10.8	8.7	7.4	3.1	3.0
1958	43.4	−2.2	−6.1	1.5	1.8
1959	12.0	−1.0	−2.3	3.0	1.5
1960	0.5	9.1	13.8	2.7	1.5
1961	26.9	4.8	1.0	2.1	0.7
1962	−8.7	8.0	6.9	2.7	1.2
1963	22.8	2.2	1.2	3.1	1.6
1964	16.5	4.8	3.5	3.5	1.2
1965	12.4	−0.5	0.7	3.9	1.9
1966	−10.1	0.2	3.6	4.8	3.4
1967	24.0	−5.0	−9.2	4.2	3.0
1968	11.1	2.6	0.3	5.2	4.7
1969	−8.5	−8.1	−5.1	6.6	6.1
1970	4.0	18.4	12.1	6.5	5.5
1971	14.3	11.0	13.2	4.4	3.4
1972	19.0	7.3	5.7	3.8	3.4
1973	−14.7	1.1	−1.1	6.9	8.8
1974	−26.5	−3.1	4.4	8.0	12.2
1975	37.2	14.6	9.2	5.8	7.0
1976	23.8	18.6	16.8	5.1	4.8
1977	−7.2	1.7	−0.7	5.1	6.8
1978	6.6	−0.1	−1.2	7.2	9.0
1979	18.4	−4.2	−1.2	10.4	13.3
1980	32.4	−2.6	−4.0	11.2	12.4
1981	−4.9	−1.0	−1.9	14.7	8.9
1982	21.4	43.8	40.4	10.5	3.8
1983	22.5	4.7	6.8	8.8	3.8
1984	6.3	16.4	15.4	9.8	4.0
1985	32.2	30.9	31.0	7.7	3.8
1986	18.5	19.8	24.4	6.2	1.1
Average Rate of Return	12.1	5.3	4.7	3.5	3.1
Compound Rate of Return	10.0	5.0	4.4	3.5	3.0

SOURCES: Roger G. Ibbotson and Rex A. Sinquefield, 1982, 1987.

TABLE 2.2 Indexes of Year-End Cumulative Wealth 1926–1986 (1925 = 1.00)

YEAR	Common Stocks (S&P 500)	Long-Term Corporate Bonds	Long-Term Government Bonds	Treasury Bills	Consumer Price Index
1926	1.12	1.07	1.08	1.03	0.98
1927	1.54	1.15	1.17	1.06	0.96
1928	2.20	1.19	1.17	1.10	0.96
1929	2.02	1.22	1.22	1.15	0.96
1930	1.52	1.32	1.27	1.18	0.90
1931	0.86	1.30	1.20	1.19	0.81
1932	0.79	1.44	1.41	1.20	0.73
1933	1.21	1.59	1.41	1.21	0.73
1934	1.20	1.81	1.55	1.21	0.75
1935	1.77	1.98	1.62	1.21	0.77
1936	2.37	2.12	1.75	1.21	0.78
1937	1.54	2.17	1.75	1.22	0.80
1938	2.02	2.31	1.85	1.22	0.78
1939	2.01	2.40	1.96	1.22	0.78
1940	1.81	2.48	2.08	1.22	0.79
1941	1.60	2.55	2.10	1.22	0.86
1942	1.93	2.61	2.16	1.22	0.94
1943	2.43	2.69	2.21	1.22	0.97
1944	2.91	2.82	2.27	1.23	0.99
1945	3.96	2.93	2.51	1.23	1.02
1946	3.64	2.98	2.51	1.24	1.20
1947	3.85	2.91	2.44	1.24	1.31
1948	4.06	3.03	2.53	1.25	1.34
1949	4.83	3.13	2.69	1.27	1.32
1950	6.36	3.20	2.69	1.28	1.40
1951	7.89	3.11	2.59	1.30	1.48
1952	9.34	3.22	2.62	1.32	1.49
1953	9.24	3.33	2.71	1.35	1.50
1954	14.11	3.51	2.91	1.36	1.49

Year					
1955	18.56	3.53	2.87	1.38	1.50
1956	19.78	3.29	2.71	1.42	1.54
1957	17.65	3.57	2.91	1.46	1.59
1958	25.30	3.46	2.73	1.48	1.62
1959	28.32	3.77	2.67	1.53	1.64
1960	28.46	3.96	3.04	1.57	1.66
1961	36.11	4.27	3.07	1.60	1.67
1962	32.96	4.36	3.28	1.64	1.70
1963	40.47	4.57	3.32	1.70	1.72
1964	47.14	4.55	3.44	1.75	1.74
1965	53.01	4.56	3.46	1.82	1.78
1966	47.67	4.34	3.59	1.91	1.84
1967	59.10	4.45	3.26	1.99	1.89
1968	65.64	4.09	3.25	2.09	2.10
1969	60.06	4.84	3.08	2.23	2.10
1970	62.46	5.37	3.46	2.38	2.22
1971	71.41	5.76	3.91	2.48	2.29
1972	84.96	5.82	4.14	2.58	2.37
1973	72.50	5.65	4.09	2.76	2.58
1974	53.31	6.47	4.27	2.98	2.89
1975	73.14	7.68	4.66	3.15	3.10
1976	90.58	7.81	5.44	3.31	3.25
1977	84.08	7.81	5.40	3.48	3.47
1978	89.59	7.48	5.34	3.73	3.78
1979	106.11	7.28	5.28	4.12	4.28
1980	140.51	7.22	5.07	4.58	4.81
1981	133.62	10.37	5.16	5.25	5.24
1982	162.22	10.86	7.24	5.80	5.44
1983	198.74	12.64	7.29	6.32	5.65
1984	211.20	16.55	8.42	6.94	5.88
1985	279.12	19.83	11.03	7.47	6.10
1986	330.67		13.72	7.93	6.17

SOURCES: Ibid.

TABLE 2.3 Inflation-Adjusted Total Returns 1926–1986

YEAR	Common Stocks (S&P 500)	Long-Term Corporate Bonds	Long-Term Government Bonds	Treasury Bills
1926	13.2%	9.0%	9.4%	4.8%
1927	40.1	9.6	11.1	5.2
1928	45.1	3.8	1.0	4.2
1929	-8.5	3.0	3.2	4.5
1930	-20.1	14.8	11.3	8.9
1931	-37.2	8.4	4.6	11.6
1932	2.6	23.3	30.0	12.4
1933	53.2	9.7	-0.7	-0.4
1934	-3.4	11.5	7.8	-1.9
1935	43.3	6.4	1.9	-2.8
1936	32.3	5.4	6.2	-1.0
1937	-37.0	-0.4	-2.8	-2.7
1938	34.8	9.1	8.5	2.8
1939	0.4	4.4	6.3	0.4
1940	-10.7	2.4	5.1	-1.0
1941	-19.6	-6.4	-8.1	-8.9
1942	10.1	-6.2	-5.6	-8.3
1943	22.2	-0.4	-1.1	-2.8
1944	17.3	2.6	0.7	-1.8
1945	33.4	1.8	8.3	-1.9
1946	-22.9	-14.4	-16.0	-15.5
1947	-3.2	-10.6	-10.8	-7.9
1948	2.7	1.3	0.6	-1.9
1949	20.9	5.2	8.4	2.9
1950	24.6	-3.5	-5.5	-4.4
1951	17.2	-8.2	-9.3	-4.2
1952	17.4	2.6	0.3	0.8
1953	-1.6	2.8	3.0	1.2
1954	53.4	5.9	7.7	1.4
1955	31.1	0.1	-1.7	1.2
1956	3.6	-9.4	-8.3	-0.4

Year				
1957	− 13.4	5.5	4.3	0.1
1958	41.0	− 3.9	− 7.7	− 0.2
1959	10.3	− 2.4	− 3.7	1.4
1960	− 1.0	7.5	12.1	1.2
1961	26.0	4.1	0.3	1.4
1962	− 9.9	6.6	5.6	1.5
1963	20.8	5.4	− 0.4	1.4
1964	15.1	3.5	2.3	2.3
1965	10.3	− 2.4	− 1.2	2.0
1966	− 13.0	− 3.1	0.3	1.4
1967	20.4	− 7.8	− 11.9	1.1
1968	6.1	− 2.1	− 4.8	0.5
1969	− 13.8	− 13.4	− 10.6	0.5
1970	− 1.4	12.2	6.3	1.0
1971	10.6	7.4	9.6	1.0
1972	15.1	3.7	2.2	0.4
1973	− 21.8	− 7.1	− 9.1	− 1.8
1974	− 34.8	− 13.7	− 7.1	− 3.8
1975	28.3	7.2	2.0	− 1.1
1976	18.2	13.2	11.4	0.3
1977	− 13.1	− 4.8	− 7.0	− 1.6
1978	− 2.3	− 8.4	− 9.4	− 1.7
1979	4.6	− 15.6	− 13.0	− 2.6
1980	17.9	− 13.5	− 14.7	− 1.0
1981	− 12.8	− 9.2	− 6.7	5.3
1982	16.8	38.5	35.1	6.4
1983	18.1	0.9	− 3.0	4.8
1984	2.2	12.0	11.1	5.7
1985	28.4	27.1	27.2	4.0
1986	17.8	19.2	23.8	5.5
Average Rate of Return	9.0	2.2	1.6	0.4
Compound Rate of Return	6.7	1.7	1.0	0.3

SOURCES: Ibid.

23

more variable and much less consistent than those from government or corporate bonds and especially from Treasury Bills. Over the years, however, stocks have vastly outperformed all of these other investment vehicles and have provided undeniable opportunities for wealth, in the long run. Indeed, stocks are the only one of these investments to have provided substantial real returns over time.

3

Numbers *Can* Lie

Researchers, analysts, and other experts on the stock market continually subject us to their claims. Usually someone tries to convince us that his method, theory, or record is superior to someone else's, backing up this claim with statistics that presumably prove his point.

Here is where investors are most vulnerable. Most people have a great deal of faith in facts, but they do not fully appreciate how easily facts can be misused or manipulated. Furthermore, investors *want* to believe. Always looking for a better way, a chance to gain an advantage in the market, they are particularly susceptible to arguments that use statistics.

Mark Twain wrote that the three kinds of deception are "lies, damned lies, and statistics." An entire book could be devoted to the common statistical errors and pitfalls of Wall Street, but this book examines only the most common deceptions, those to which investors must be most alert. Our goal is to learn about the true nature of the market—how it behaves, which strategies work and which don't—and to be persuaded by evidence, not by assertion. We need a clear idea of what genuine evidence is. It may be far different from facts and statistics.

THE SETUP

Most statistical research goes wrong or becomes biased right at the beginning, in the way it is set up. It may set us up, too.

Suppose that someone proposes a theory about the market—for example, that stocks with low price/earnings (P/E) ratios outperform stocks with high P/Es (we will look at this idea in detail in Chapter 10). A statistical study will be needed to prove the point, with decisions on how performance will be measured, how prices and earnings will be determined (sometimes a surprisingly complicated matter), how to account for dividends (reinvested or not), what the assumed holding periods will be, how to deal with transaction costs and taxes, and how to treat stocks that are liquidated or acquired. These and other decisions will affect the results of the study. Right at the outset, one major decision may seriously undermine the research: the period of time to be studied. Whether or not low-P/E stocks generally outperform high-P/E stocks, we can be sure that the relationship won't be constant. Some periods will be relatively favorable to low-P/E stocks, and others will not. The chosen period may or may not be valid for making generalizations. If a study is conducted for the period 1972–1979, for example, we may ask ourselves why the range of years isn't 1970–1979 or 1965–1975 or some other period. The reasons are usually innocent, having to do with the availability and cost of data and processing—but not always.

You should be especially skeptical when someone with something to sell you presents evidence based on a very short time period. Why is the period so short, and why was it chosen? Probably because it is most favorable to the promoter and his methods.

Not long ago, I was mailed an outrageous but amusing advertisement for a market letter that reviewed and digested the recommendations of other market letters. The ad even promised that this letter would tell me which advisors I should follow. Suggesting that I could profit handsomely by having access to these recommendations, it stated, "How much better are these advisors? As a group, they performed 670% better over the Dow in a 19-month period and 950% better in a recent three-month period." There was no mention of which nineteen-month or three-month period was covered, nor was there a statement on the way the Dow had performed during these comparison periods. Suppose that a period had been carefully chosen, one in which the Dow's total gain was 0.1 percent (certainly not difficult). To have beaten the Dow by 950%, these advisors would have had to average only a 1 percent gain, hardly a brilliant achievement.

THE LAW OF SMALL NUMBERS

If I told you that I was going to study whether low-P/E or high-P/E stocks perform better, and that my research would consist of tracking one stock in each category for 10 years, wouldn't you find this proposal ridiculous? I couldn't possibly reach any valid conclusion by tracking the performance of just two stocks. But suppose I tracked 5 stocks in each group, or 10. Would that satisfy you?

In most statistical research, it is impossible to study all the cases, what mathematicians call the *population*. Gathering and processing all the data is simply too expensive and a time-consuming task. We do what George Gallup does: use a sample. If we're trying to determine some difference in performance between low- and high-P/E stocks, then once we've seen the returns from each group, we need to know whether the difference is significant. In a rigorous academic study, mathematical measures of statistical significance would be presented. These measures basically would tell us whether the phenomenon we have observed is valid and important or just random.

Statistical significance depends in great part on the size of the samples. According to the Law of Large Numbers, the larger the sample, the more confidence we can have in the resulting estimates. Unfortunately, much of the so-called research aimed at individual investors—especially sales-oriented research—is based on very small samples and very few cases. This kind of research does not deal with such niceties as statistical significance, and so we can easily become victims of what we'll call the Law of Small Numbers: The smaller the sample, the less reliable the estimates. There is no magic number that represents an adequate sample, but if it feels small, be skeptical. As a very rough guide, expect legitimate studies to include at least 25 stocks.

SPARE THE ANECDOTES

Contrived or extremely short time periods and very small samples can bias or invalidate research at the outset. In the nonacademic world, an equally common and even more egregious fault is the anecdotal approach. Here, research results derive not from exhaustive testing or even from sampling, but rather from cases selected to make a point. In the right setting, anecdotes are useful and powerful, but they are not research.

Let's return to discussing low-P/E stocks. To show that they outperform high-P/E stocks, suppose that I told you the stories of several low-P/E stocks that yielded huge returns. You would rightly ask, "What does that prove? What about similar stocks that didn't fare so well? What about high-P/E stocks that also performed spectacularly?" Anecdotes can illustrate a point, but they can never prove one. Much of what passes for market information, wisdom, or research is really just anecdotes. Unbiased research requires us either to study all the cases or to use a random sample. Every case must have an equal chance of being selected; that's our assurance that the sample is representative. The anecdotal approach denies us that assurance. Anecdotes may be interesting and stimulating, but don't be taken in by stories.

THE UNATTAINABLE RESULT

Research on the stock market usually shows us the returns that have or would have accrued to following a particular strategy or method. These are shown sometimes as average or compounded annual rates of return over the period studied, and sometimes as cumulative returns. For example, in Chapter 2 we tracked the results of the S&P 500 over several decades. The information we discovered actually corresponds to a strategy of investing in the market, as represented by the S&P 500 index. Yet even if you had followed that strategy through the years, you could not have achieved the results shown in the tables. Why not? These tables and calculations did not make any allowance for transaction costs or taxes.

Almost all studies of the stock market have this shortcoming, and for a good reason. Different investors are faced with different circumstances. What you pay in transaction costs and taxes depends on your individual situation. If you are a round-lot customer of a full-service brokerage house, you may pay from 2 to 4 percent in commissions on a transaction. If you use a discount broker, the commission may average around 1 percent. If you are an institutional money manager, dealing in tens of thousands of shares at a time, the commission may be still lower. There is another transaction cost, too: the spread, the difference between the bid and the ask prices of stocks. A realistic look at costs has to include the difference between what an investor actually pays or receives and the last sale price. The cost of the spread varies considerably, depending both on the types of stocks being bought or sold and the number of shares involved.

Taxes present a similar problem: On interest, dividends, and short-term capital transactions, an individual historically could have a marginal tax rate beyond 50 percent by the time federal, state, and local income taxes were considered. For long-term capital transactions, of course, the maximum rates were much lower. The 1986 Tax Reform Act eliminated the preference for long-term gains and narrowed the differences in rates faced by different investors, but significant differences still remain. In addition, many accounts, primarily retirement accounts, are tax-exempt; a pension fund manager doesn't have to worry about taxes at all.*

Since circumstances vary so widely, there is simply no way to develop a good set of assumptions for adjusting returns to allow for transaction costs and taxes. We must resign ourselves to reading research that deals with the *gross* returns from various strategies, not the *net* ones.**

---

*There is no guarantee that the 1986 tax policies will last long. They may even have changed by the time you read this (see Chapter 13).

**Most serious research is directed at the pension fund market, because that's where the money is. Since such funds are tax-exempt and pay very low commissions, these costs are negligible for them—but not for the rest of us.

This is no small problem, and one relevant example of it is the reporting of mutual fund returns. Whenever you see an advertisement that reports on the cumulative returns a mutual fund has achieved, notice the small print: "Assuming reinvestment of all dividends and capital gains distributions" (this phrase reflects the way cumulative returns from the S&P 500 were calculated in Chapter 2). Let's think about what this means. For most individuals, every distribution of dividends is taxable, and so are capital gains distributions, at either ordinary or long-term capital gains tax rates. If you reinvest the distributions, where will the money to pay the taxes come from? From your pocket, of course. This means that the returns reported by the funds depend upon your coming up with more money—in effect, contributing more capital. Your original investment will not achieve the reported results on its own. Thus investment statistics are usually not what they seem to be. Most reported returns are not attainable in the real world.

Different strategies also imply vastly different trading patterns. Some strategies may require only infrequent trading, with low transaction expenses, long holding periods, and gains that almost always have been taxed at long-term rates. Others require much more activity, with high costs, and gains taxed at ordinary income tax rates. Even when there is no tax preference for long-term gains, comparing strategies on the basis of gross returns greatly prejudices the results.

DIGGING FOR TREASURE

Thousands of people spend their working and even leisure hours researching the stock market. Using computerized data banks, books of stock charts, and piles of old *Wall Street Journals*, people are looking for *correlations*. This term has a precise mathematical definition, but essentially it means the degree of association between two variables. In other words, people are looking for patterns in the market. Guess what—people always find them and always will.

There is a practice in the social sciences that I call "mucking around in the data." It works like this: If you have enough data on enough variables, and if you keep working long enough, you will uncover patterns of association. The problem is that they may not mean anything. When we search for correlations, what we're really looking for is not just association but *causation*. We want to know that a change in variable A causes a certain change in variable B, or that changes in both variables are caused by some third force. Only after we determine causation can we use our information for making policy. If we think A causes B, we may use one strategy; but what if B causes A?

A researcher discovered a few years ago that winning teams in professional football used running plays more often than losing teams did.

Armed with this information, many coaches and sportswriters drew the wrong conclusion: that teams would do better if they ran more and passed less. Running well is part of playing well, but a team that doesn't run well will not improve its results by running more often. What people failed to see was that successful teams don't win more because they run more; they run more because they win more! Because winning teams tend to take the lead, they adopt the conservative and time-consuming strategy of running. Losing teams find themselves trailing. They are forced to pass so that they can catch up. This example illustrates that there is more to research than correlation. We also need sound theory. While it seems likely that there is a real relationship between running and winning, it takes some thought to see what that relationship is.

There are also cases of correlation that offer no grounds for belief in any meaningful causal relationship. Mathematicians call this phenomenon *spurious correlation*. The rest of us call it coincidence. The best-known example of it in the stock market is also drawn from football. It is the famous Super Bowl indicator, discovered by Robert Stovall, an amiable investment strategist at 21st Advisers, Inc. Stovall's idea is that if the Super Bowl is won by the NFC team, or by one of the three AFC teams that started out in the NFC (the Steelers, the Browns, and the Colts), then the market will be up for the year; otherwise, the year will be a bear. This indicator has an almost flawless record—superior, as far as I know, to that of any other. Yet there is no even remotely plausible explanation for its success. We must assume that what we've observed is a coincidence.*

Unfortunately, things get still more complicated in the search for correlations. If we study the relationship between stock returns and some variable (such as P/E ratio), we may uncover an apparently clear relationship. Nevertheless, the variable we are studying, the one we think is important, may actually be a proxy for some other variable. This means that the proxy variable and the real one are themselves highly correlated. If so, and if we study the wrong variable, we will discover a relationship that doesn't really exist. As we will see, some of the most exciting market research has been challenged on precisely this basis.

TRENDS VERSUS TRUTHS

We have seen some of the problems and pitfalls involved in designing, conducting, and evaluating investment research, but an even more subtle

---

*Stovall published his indicator as an exercise in humor. It has since been taken seriously. Perhaps this enthusiasm reflects the desperate and frustrating search for a winning formula on Wall Street.

problem underlies all research, no matter how carefully it is constructed. If we test enough variables in enough different ways, we will always find patterns—in the *past*. Strategies that *would have been successful* in a given period are easy to discern.

One particularly seductive and dangerous practice is the search for a successful trading rule. A trading rule is a formula, simple or complicated, that guides buying and selling decisions. It is usually applied to overall market timing, rather than to individual stocks. An example of a simple trading rule would be to buy stocks after the S&P 500 has declined 10 percent from a high and to sell them after the index has risen 15 percent from a low. This rule is based on the premise that the market is cyclical. Another rule could be based on the premise that trends in the market tend to persist. For example, the rule might be to buy stocks after they have risen 5 percent from a low and to sell them after they have declined 5 percent from a high.

These are very simple trading rules, but much more sophisticated rules can be conjured up. Here's a set that ought to cover myriad market conditions: Buy stocks after a 5 percent rise following a decline of 12 percent or more, but buy immediately if a 10 percent decline occurs in a 30-day period; buy even without a 5 percent rise following a 20 percent decline; buy after a 10 percent gain in a 30-day period, even if there has been no preceding decline; sell stocks after any one-year period of gains of at least 15 percent without an intervening decline of 7 percent; sell after a 5 percent decline following a 35 percent gain in less than two years; and sell after any two-month gain of 20 percent.

Does this set of rules seem farfetched? It should. I made it up as I went along. Actual trading rules of similar complexity have been seriously proposed to investors. Why? Because the rules *would have worked* in the past. One problem of our newly computerized world is that people can sit with a historical database at the PC keyboard and play "what if" to their hearts' content. Perhaps buying stocks following a 10 percent decline in 30 days isn't the best strategy. What if we try 42 days? A few keystrokes, and the computer has the answer. With enough patience, enough "mucking around in the data," we're bound to discover a set of trading rules that seem like the key to the kingdom.

This process is called back-testing, and it's fine, as far as it goes. (Besides, it's all we have.) Still, it's one thing to find a strategy that would have worked in the past and quite another to find one that will work in the future. While back-testing can reveal important truths about the market, it may also reveal nothing but temporary trends or statistical aberrations. The test of a market strategy is how it performs *after* it is discovered, not before. At the very least, a strategy found through back-testing should be retested on a different time period. For example, if we find a successful strategy using trading data from 1975 to 1979, then we should verify the results—say, over the years from 1980 to 1984. Unfortunately, people too seldom take this simple precaution.

We must always remember that market research, no matter how well done, is based on the past. We are always susceptible to discovering a truth whose time has gone.

WHAT'S TO BE DONE?

I wish I could say that besides showing you all the problems and caveats, I can also show you the solutions; but I can't. The problems we have looked at have no practical solutions, at least none relevant to individual investors. Academics sometimes seem to spend as much time and effort criticizing each other's research methodologies as they spend actually doing research. We investors, however, lack the training, the resources, and probably the inclination to evaluate everything we hear or read. Besides, many of the problems we've been discussing are inherent and do not result from faulty or biased research. Is research useless to us? No. A great deal of excellent research has developed important new ideas and understandings about the stock market and created a knowledge revolution. We must simply face the fact that investing and investment research are not exact sciences: There are limitations on how research can be conducted and how results can be applied. Understanding those limitations can help us evaluate the claims and advice that surround us.

We may not be able to conduct our own market research or correct the flaws in the research we see, but we can do one fairly obvious thing: maintain a healthy skepticism. Confronted with some persuasive claim, we can ask ourselves, "Does this make sense? Do the conclusions seem to stem from the evidence, or does the evidence appear to have been hand-selected to prove the conclusion?" If we see evidence that a particular strategy has been superior, we must seek the cause or explanation. If the explanation makes sense, then we must ask whether the cause still exists or will persist. Perhaps it simply reflects the trend of a particular era. What if it is grounded in the fundamental behavior of markets and people? If so, we are much more likely to be on the trail of something important.

In the chapters to come, we will examine many studies relevant to our understanding of the market. I have selected these studies not only to prove or illustrate my points but also because they generally represent high-quality, unbiased research whose validity is widely accepted. The research was conducted by competent investigators, mostly academics, with nothing to sell and professional reputations to protect. It avoids the statistical abuse and flimflam I've warned against. Some of the problems we've looked at are unavoidable, of course; as we go along, I will point them out and discuss their implications. Because I want to give you an accurate, unbiased look *inside* the stock market, I have chosen studies to serve my purpose.

4

Concepts of Value

When you buy shares of stock, you are literally becoming part-owner of a business—very much a minority owner, but an owner just the same. You will share in the results, good or bad, that the business achieves. What should you pay for your share of the company? What is it worth?

To make sense of the market, we need to know what *value* is, how it is defined and measured, and the process by which it changes. Most crucial for investors, we also need to know if changes in value can be predicted.

INTRINSIC VALUE

All our economic decisions are based on the concept of value—value given and value received—whether we are buying stock or a can of sardines. In both cases, we seek benefits—returns—that are satisfactory in terms of what we are paying.

It seems obvious that the value of a business depends both on its current health and on its prospects for the future. These determine what business owners are seeking: profits. On the basis of current and future profits, shares of a company have what can be called an *intrinsic value*. Intrinsic value is not a matter of opinion. It exists on its own, no matter whether anyone ever uncovers it. In some sense, it is the true value of the shares.

Followers of this approach to stock valuation see intrinsic value as a sort of reference point around which stock prices fluctuate. It is like an anchor to which stock prices are moored. Because a mooring line is long, an anchored ship is seldom directly over its anchor. The ship moves one way and then another according to winds and tides. Stock prices, too, can move above or below intrinsic value. Over time, these excesses are self-correcting, because prices are ultimately tied to intrinsic value. Meanwhile, the fluctuations in price provide investment opportunities. The idea, of course, is to buy stocks that are temporarily undervalued and sell them later—ideally, when they are overvalued. Buy low, sell high.

On Wall Street, it is widely believed that intrinsic value can be determined, or at least closely estimated, with enough information and exhaustive, insightful, expert analysis. But analysis of what? The value of any financial or economic asset is established by what it produces: its returns. A bond that pays $2,000 per year is worth twice as much as an otherwise identical one that pays $1,000. A factory producing profits of $10 million is worth more than one whose profits are $5 million. To discover the intrinsic value of a company, we must analyze all the factors that affect its present and future profits and dividends.

Analysts consider many factors: the company's markets, its facilities and equipment, its research and development, its sources of labor and materials, its financial condition, its management, and so on. They analyze the same factors for the company's competitors, both actual and potential. This is called *fundamental analysis* because it looks at the basic elements that underlie success.

Discounting the Future

Mathematically inclined economists have demonstrated that a stock's intrinsic value is equal to the present value of future dividends, or what investors will receive from the company over time. The term *present value* reflects the fact that a dollar in dividends sometime in the future is worth less than the same amount today. Future payments have to be discounted at some appropriate rate to determine their present value. This process is represented by the Dividend Discount Model.*

For example, consider the way many contests and lotteries work. In my state, the minimum top lottery prize is advertised as $1 million, but it

---

*Returns come both from dividends and from price changes over the holding period. A stock exists in perpetuity, however, passing from one investor to another. Each owner has capital gains or losses, but the total return to *all* investors is simply the dividends, because "tomorrow never comes." According to this model, changing prices reflect changes in the present value of expected future dividends.

Alternatively, we can view returns as a series of regular dividends followed by a large final dividend when the company is liquidated and net proceeds are distributed to shareholders.

comes in the form of $50,000 annually for twenty years. It does not cost the state $1 million. The state buys an annuity contract to cover the payments. At this writing, such a contract costs about $500,000—in essence, the present value of dividends of $50,000 annually for twenty years. From the lottery winner's viewpoint, a $500,000 cash prize *now* would be equivalent to the deferred $1 million, because the winner could buy the annuity contract himself.

The Dividend Discount Model is not just a theory. It is a specific mathematical formula for determining the present value (PV) of a stock from the future dividends and the discount rate:

$$PV = \frac{(1 + G)D}{1 + R} + \frac{(1 + G)^2D}{(1 + R)^2} + \ldots + \frac{(1 + G)^nD}{(1 + R)^n}$$

where G is the growth rate of dividends from years 1 through n, D is the current dividend rate, and R is the discount rate. (The calculation is similar but more complicated if either the growth rate or the discount rate varies from period to period.)

This formula may seem complicated but is actually quite simple. The top half of the formula (the numerators) is a standard compounding calculation, similar to the one used for calculating compound interest. The bottom half (the denominators) discounts future value back to present value.

You don't need to memorize this formula. I have yet to meet an investor who actually views stock valuation in these terms or who tries to make these calculations. Nevertheless, all investors do understand that dividends—and profits, the source of dividends—are good things, and the more the better. Thus the future course of earnings and dividends is generally seen as the most important determinant of stock values. Research has clearly shown that they are the most important determinants of *prices*. As a result, most security analysis—fundamental analysis—is concerned with projecting companies' growth, usually in terms of earnings rather than dividends (the two growth rates will be the same if the proportion of earnings paid out as dividends remains constant). The relation of price to earnings—the price/earnings (P/E) ratio—is the most common standard of valuation in fundamental analysis.

As we have seen, the Dividend Discount Model is a mathematical truth, rather than a theory, but it is based on knowledge of the future. If we knew D, G, and R, we would know PV automatically. In real life, however, we don't know G and R. Nevertheless, we can't begin to determine the intrinsic value of a stock unless we can estimate its future earnings and dividends, and we have to decide how much those future earnings and dividends are worth to us now. In other words, whether we realize it or not, we already use the Dividend Discount Model, at least casually. When we look at a typical brokerage-house research report that recommends a stock, the bottom line shows estimates of the stock's earnings per share (EPS) for the coming year, perhaps for several years. The *buy* recommendation is based on these estimates in relation to the stock's current price. This is just an informal way of saying that the analyst believes the present value of future returns to be greater than the current price of the stock.

Most security analysts, at least those whose efforts are directed at individual investors, don't realize that this is what they are saying. They simply calculate the current P/E ratio and compare it to what they think the P/E ratio should be on the earnings estimated for some future period. A typical research report might look like this:

XYZ Corporation

Current Price: 10

	1987	1988 (EST.)	1989 (EST.)
EPS:	$1.00	$1.15	$1.40
P/E:	10.0	8.7	7.1

The analyst would then make a case for an estimated P/E ratio for 1988 or 1989. He or she might write, "We feel that this growth rate will justify a 1989 P/E of 12." From this estimate, a target 1989 price of $16.80 can be calculated, along with the corresponding rate of return (30 percent per year if the stock reaches $16.80 in exactly two years), assuming that the stock is purchased today at $10. (For simplicity, I am assuming that all returns take the form of capital appreciation).

This procedure may seem quite different from the Dividend Discount Model, but it is not. The analyst just takes some shortcuts. First, he or she estimates earnings, rather than dividends. Second, the analyst does not explicitly estimate earnings beyond 1989, although such an estimate is implicit (otherwise, there is no way to justify the expected 1989 P/E ratio, since the P/E ratio that investors will be willing to accept in 1989 is based not only on what the company did in the recent past but also on what investors expect it to do in the future). Finally, the analyst makes his or her recommendation on the basis of rates of return, rather than on the basis of intrinsic present value.

The analyst's projections can easily be worked into the Dividend Discount Model. If we assume a discount rate of 10 percent, the formula shows that the present value of the stock is $13.88 per share.

The user of the Dividend Discount Model recommends the stock because it has a value of $13.88 versus a price of $10.00. The security analyst recommends it because it offers a 30 percent rate of return. In both cases, the same data are used. The security analyst is actually applying the Dividend Discount Model.

Economists, finance professors, and institutional investment professionals are enamored of mathematics and financial models, especially if these promise clearly defined results and seem to impress and baffle the average person. Thus the Dividend Discount Model has enjoyed great popularity in some circles. Not only does it look scientific, it also yields a method for coming up with a specific value for a stock. An analyst simply takes the formula, plugs in the estimates and an appropriate discount rate, hits a few keys on the computer, and presto! Out comes the value—$48.036. Check the current price—26. *Buy!*

If only it were that easy.

Garbage In, Garbage Out

The computer, or the mathematical model you use in it, will not give you valid output unless you start with valid input. If your data is no good, all the processing in the world is not going to give you useful results. In the case of the Dividend Discount Model, there are only two kinds of data: the estimates of future dividends, and the discount rate. Estimating a company's future earnings may be difficult, but what about estimating the discount rate? The discount rate has to do with the time value of money (remember, a dollar in the future is not worth as much as a dollar today). The discount rate is related to interest rates; but what interest rates? Is the appropriate discount rate the current rate on T-Bills, long-term government bonds, corporate bonds? Should it reflect the prime rate, the commercial paper rate, or an inflation rate (of which there are several)? No one knows. We do know that as interest rates change, so must our discount rate. The people who really take this business seriously believe that the discount rate should also reflect the different risk levels of different stocks, with higher-risk stocks having higher discount rates. This factor adds still more complexity—and more judgment calls.

By now you probably have a headache and are beginning to wonder how important all these details are. Can a difference (or an error) of a point or two in the discount rates or dividend estimates really make much difference in value? The answer is an emphatic yes. The Dividend Discount Model does yield specific estimates of stock values, but, equally important, it can show us the consequences of using incorrect data and bad estimates.

Let's invent a stock (ticker symbol HYPE), one expected to achieve extraordinary rates of growth in earnings and dividends for a long time to come. The company has current earnings of $.50 per share and pays a dividend of $.10. A security analyst projects that earnings and dividends will grow at 25 percent annually for the next 5 years, at 15 percent for the following 15 years, at 8 percent for the next 30 years, and at 5 percent thereafter. (These estimates reflect his knowledge that growth opportunities diminish as a company gets bigger and bigger; growth inevitably slows as the company matures.) The appropriate discount rate is set at 10 percent. If the analyst plugs this information into the Dividend Discount Model, he gets the intrinsic value of HYPE: $17.79 per share.

So far, so good, but his results will be only as good as his growth estimates, and he has projected growth rates for a very long time—from now until forever. In this example, dividends to be paid more than 50 years from now account for fully one-fourth of the stock's present value. The so-called precise calculation of value depends on long-range projections whose accuracy is doubtful, to say the least.*

Of course, different projections yield different estimates of value. Suppose that another analyst has a slightly different view of HYPE. She projects 5-year growth at 23 percent, 15-year growth at 13 percent, and 30-year growth at 6 percent. After 50 years, she estimates, growth will be at 5 percent. If she uses the same discount rate, 10 percent, her projections yield a value for HYPE of $10.47, 41 percent lower than its value under the first set of estimates!

This two-part example has an ominous implication. The two different sets of projections yielded radically different estimates of HYPE's value, yet the projections themselves weren't very different. Neither of our analysts is likely to argue very cogently or vehemently for his or her position. Given the process and the uncertainties of estimating earnings, such argument would be mere quibbling. But this means that different sets of projections, all of them reasonable, can be used to justify almost any stock valuation. This fact can lead into a major psychological and financial trap. When an analyst or an investor wants to justify buying a stock, it will usually be easy to come up with the required projections, and they will not seem farfetched.

If such small variations in growth projections can cause such large discrepancies in value, we can see a reason for one of the market's most typical and disconcerting dynamics. When a company reports earnings that are below expectations (especially a company like HYPE, whose appeal is rapid growth), its stock price sometimes plummets. Analysts and investors usually don't adjust only their near-term expectations. They are likely also to lower the entire spectrum of their estimates for future growth, and in the process the stock price may be marked down dramatically. The Dividend Discount Model explains this phenomenon: There is great leverage in changing forecasts of earnings.

---

*It may seem preposterous to estimate dividends to infinity, but our only alternative is to assume that at some point the company will simply vanish (not liquidate, but vanish), which would be even more preposterous.

What about the discount rate, the rate used to value future dividends? Here, the effects are equally startling. Let's go back to our original set of growth projections for HYPE. At a discount rate of 10 percent, they yielded a value of $17.79 per share, but at a discount rate of 8 percent, the value shoots up to $40.78, while at 12 percent, it drops to $9.85—all with the same growth rate of earnings and dividends. Since the correct discount rate is a matter of judgment, this is another potential source of deception, self-induced or otherwise. Further, the correct discount rate is not static. It changes along with changes in inflation and interest rates, and very large changes are not at all unheard of. Wells Fargo Bank, one of the leaders in quantitative investment research, estimated the appropriate discount rate for stocks of average riskiness at about 8.5 percent in mid-1972, but more than 15 percent at the end of 1974. No wonder the market crashed during the period!

You may never again hear or read about the Dividend Discount Model. Almost no research or analysis of any practical value to individual investors uses it directly. Even your broker has probably never heard of it; if you asked your broker for an estimate of the present value of the future stream of dividends from a particular stock, he or she would consider you a lunatic.

The model is real, though. It won't go away just because it is seldom used explicitly. Fundamental security analysis is implicitly based on it. The model provides the scientific method for valuing a stock on the basis of what we expect a company's growth to be.

There is another and even more important reason why we have been considering the model here. Most of us would readily agree that stock valuations are no more accurate than the estimates that go into them, and the Dividend Discount Model demonstrates just how fragile, volatile, and arbitrary those estimates and valuations can be. What seem like small differences in expectations can create huge changes in values. Intrinsic value may exist, but finding it is an uncertain proposition. The Dividend Discount Model offers a lesson and a warning to all investors.

THE VALUE OF ANALYSIS

Can fundamental analysis be effective? Can intrinsic value be determined with reasonable confidence? If so, it is because security analysts have made very accurate projections of the future. But how successful are they? How accurately can they predict future earnings? There is good reason to be skeptical about the quality and effectiveness of most security analysis.

Professor Burton G. Malkiel, in his witty and thought-provoking book, *A Random Walk Down Wall Street*, reports on research that he and his colleagues performed at Princeton. They obtained old earnings forecasts from

19 leading Wall Street firms. The forecasts, made at several different times, were for the one- and five-year earnings trends of many different companies. After comparing the forecasts with the companies' actual earnings, Malkiel wrote: "Bluntly stated, the careful estimates of security analysts...do little, if any, better than those that would be obtained by simple extrapolation of past trends..." (p. 150). There was high degree of correlation between the forecasts and the companies' past growth—analysts may indeed be doing little more than simple extrapolation—but there was very little correlation between the forecasts and the companies' actual earnings. In addition, the experts proved less adept at estimating earnings for one year ahead than for five years: Analysts apparently make series of errors that cancel one another out over the long run. Little wonder, then, that the 19 Wall Street firms agreed to share their forecasting records only on condition of anonymity.

Another study surveyed the earnings forecasts of a major investment advisory service for 50 companies from 1971 through 1975. These forecasts were compared with others, which were obtained through mechanical projections of past trends into the future. The results are shown in Table 4.1, and the analysts emerge as the winners this time. For example, 63.5 percent of their forecasts were within 25 percent of the actual results, compared with a 54.5 percent success rate for the mechanical model. This is a rather marginal victory, however. It proves that analysis is not totally useless, but if fewer than two-thirds of forecasts come within 25 percent of actual earnings, we hardly can say that the efficacy of analysis has been demonstrated.

Michael B. O'Higgins, an investment advisor, has been conducting an ongoing study of the effectiveness of fundamental analysis as applied to the 30 stocks that make up the Dow Jones Industrial average. Working with consensus earnings estimates compiled by the Institutional Brokerage Estimate System (IBES), O'Higgins compares projected earnings changes to

TABLE 4.1   Errors in Earnings Forecasts

Forecasting Error as Percentage of Actual Earnings	PERCENT OF FORECASTS WITH A SMALLER ERROR	
	Mechanical Model	Analysts' Forecasts
5%	15.0%	18.0%
10	26.5	32.0
25	54.5	63.5
50	81.0	86.5
75	87.5	90.5
100	89.5	92.0

SOURCE: Brown and Rozeff, 1978.

the actual results for each of the 30 companies. The forecasts take their starting point as two weeks before the end of the year, covering that year and the year to come. (Thus a forecast made on December 15, 1980, would be for 1980 and 1981 earnings, even though 1980 is almost over.) His results are dramatic (see Table 4.2). The average margin of error for growth in the following year's earnings is 53.8 percent. Even more remarkable, estimates have been off by an average of 18 percent for current years, with only two weeks remaining in each current year, and with the benefit of already knowing the actual earnings for the first three quarters.

These and other studies strongly suggest that security analysts, despite all the resources at their disposal, are unable to forecast earnings with the degree of accuracy that we should consider satisfactory, especially since we've seen that earnings changes have highly leveraged impacts on stock values.

Still another study illustrates the consequences of inaccurate forecasts. In 1970, 150 stocks on the New York Stock Exchange were studied. Three groups of 50 were chosen: stocks that had shown the biggest price gains for 1970 (the year's winners), those that had shown the biggest price declines (the losers), and the rest, which were selected at random. The stocks in each group were compared to forecasts of changes in their earnings per share (EPS) and to their actual changes in EPS (see Table 4.3). (The earnings forecasts were consensus forecasts done at the beginning of 1970 and reported by Standard & Poor's.)

**TABLE 4.2 Consensus Earnings Change Estimates
Annual Average Margin of Error
(Dow Jones Industrial Stocks)**

	Current Year	Coming Year
YEAR	AVERAGE ERROR	AVERAGE ERROR
1974	9.5%	36.6%
1975	16.5	54.1
1976	24.9	46.7
1977	9.7	25.3
1978	12.4	24.2
1979	10.1	74.8
1980	16.3	42.5
1981	9.6	38.4
1982	14.8	153.3
1983	56.2	42.1
10 Year Average	18.0%	53.8%

SOURCE: O'Higgins, 1984.

TABLE 4.3   Forecasts of Earnings, Actual Earnings, and Price Changes Selected NYSE Stocks, 1970

	Median Price Change	Median Actual Earnings Change	Median Forecasted Earnings Change
	1970	1970	1970
Top 50	+ 48.4%	+ 21.4%	+ 7.7%
Bottom 50	− 56.7%	− 83.0%	+ 15.3%
Random 50	− 3.2%	− 10.5%	+ 5.8%

SOURCE: Niederhaffer and Regan, 1972.

The median expected increase in EPS for the group of stocks that turned out to be the winners had been 7.7 percent, while the actual increase was 21.4 percent. In other words, these companies showed surprisingly good earnings. In contrast, the median expected increase for the group that turned out to be the losers had been 15.3 percent, but these stocks showed an actual median *decrease* of 83.0 percent. In both cases, analysts had been far off the mark in their forecasts for the year: They had expected better earnings from what turned out to be the losers than from the stocks that actually turned in the best performances. Just looking at the top and bottom fifty prejudices the case against the analysts. It was precisely *because* of the earnings surprises that they ended up in these groups. What happens when we look at results for the random 50 companies? We don't find much solace here, either, since the analysts missed those actual earnings, too, by more than 16 percentage points.

Why is the performance of analysts apparently so poor? Numerous explanations can be offered, each with a certain plausibility. First, earnings themselves may be illusory. Accounting practices allow so much latitude that reported earnings can be created or destroyed almost at will. Items of both revenue and cost can be taken currently, be deferred, or be capitalized. Large write-offs can be taken more or less whenever management feels it would be most opportune to do so. Depreciation and amortization rates and inventory valuation methods can be changed. In this kind of situation, it is hard to be sure what the true past and current earnings are and even harder to predict future earnings.

Second, unforeseeable events can wreak havoc with even the most careful and thorough analysis. Myriad unpredictable events can affect a company, an industry, or even the national or world economy, embarrassing analysts through no fault of their own. (After all, there is a difference between analysis and clairvoyance.)

Third, even under the best of conditions, forecasting earnings may be too difficult to do accurately. The complexities are enormous, and no amount of information will necessarily improve the situation, especially when much of that information is contradictory and must somehow be balanced to allow an overall appraisal.

Do you feel guilty because a big pile of investment publications is sitting unread on your desk? Maybe you shouldn't. The error rates of experts in many fields are essentially constant, and increased information seems to improve the experts' confidence but not their judgments.*

Security analysts cannot now and probably will never be able to forecast the future of a company with great accuracy. They may be able to improve somewhat upon the assumption that whatever happened in the past will continue to happen in the future, but that's about all we should expect. The notion that we can calculate intrinsic value with any real precision is naive.

TRADING SARDINES

In China (so I've been told) there was once a lively market in canned sardines—not a consumers' market but a traders' market. It had operated for years and was not unlike our commodities markets today. Buyers never actually received their sardines; instead, cans of sardines were kept in a warehouse. This warehouse full of cans represented the trading supply of sardines. At any given time, the sardines were owned by various people, whose ownership was evidenced by warehouse receipts. A sale of sardines simply required the issuance of a receipt to the purchaser, who could then indicate his new ownership of some of the sardines. The market was lively and somewhat speculative. Everyone enjoyed the game.

One day, along came a man who wanted to take a large position in canned sardines. Being both practical and cautious, he decided to investigate before investing. He went to the warehouse, where he saw what looked like endless cases of sardines; they were unquestionably real. To inspect the quality of the sardines, he demanded that the warehouse manager open a few cans. This demand had never been made before, but the manager complied. The sardines turned out to be spoiled and inedible (not surprising, since they had been in the warehouse for decades). The investor was outraged. "This is a fraud!" he cried. The warehouse manager was unfazed. He drew himself up to his full height, and with the self-assurance of a French waiter dealing with a tourist, he intoned, "But you misunderstand, sir. These are not sardines for eating, they are sardines for trading!"

The story is apocryphal, but it concerns our discussion. In a way, the warehouse manager was right: Since they were spoiled, the sardines

---

*For an excellent discussion of this subject, see David Dreman's *The New Contrarian Investment Strategy* (New York: Random House, 1982).

obviously had no intrinsic value, but they did have trading value, and that was all the sardine traders cared about. They did not want to eat the sardines, nor did the people they were trading with. They just wanted to turn a profit. They actually wanted nothing to do with the sardines themselves; the receipts were sufficient.

Even if the story were true (and if the sardines were edible), the idea of their intrinsic value still could not be totally eliminated. If the price of sardines fell far enough below their intrinsic eating value, then consumers would buy the sardines and take them home from the warehouse, increasing the demand for sardines and driving their price up. If the price rose far enough above the intrinsic value, then outsiders would bring canned sardines to the market, adding to the supply and forcing the price down. Ultimately, then, the price of the sardines is tied to their intrinsic value (remember the analogy of the mooring line).

Investors in the stock market are a lot like those sardine traders. They have no real interest in the companies in which they invest (certainly no interest in running them); they are interested in the little slips of paper that prove their ownership of stocks in the "warehouse." Analyzing data and estimating intrinsic value may have a part in their decision making, but their goal is to turn a profit. John Maynard Keynes expressed this reality succinctly. Most people, he wrote, "are largely concerned *not* with making superior long-term forecasts of the probable yield of an investment over its whole life, but with foreseeing changes in the conventional basis of valuation a short time ahead of the general public" (p. 154). In other words, investors are interested not in intrinsic value but in market value.

The central premise of fundamental security analysis is that all stocks have some intrinsic value, which can be determined or closely estimated with careful study. Stock prices, in contrast, move above and below intrinsic value, sometimes by wide margins. This movement between under- and overvaluation creates profit opportunities for astute investors and analysts.

This premise is sensible (even if determining intrinsic value is a doubtful proposition), but it fails to answer a crucial question: Why and how do stocks become misvalued?

The fundamentalist has ready answers. Stocks become misvalued because of trends or fads that temporarily boost some stocks and punish others. Investors, in effect, overreact to perceived changes in the outlooks for various stocks and industries. Turnarounds presumably occur when such overreactions become severe enough to be generally recognized. Then again, stocks may become misvalued because of delayed or insufficient reactions to new developments. Intrinsic value may change markedly, but prices take time to catch up.

These explanations take no account of the dynamics of misvaluation. Fundamental analysis takes misvaluation as a given and fails to account for it as a process. To say that it results from misguided investor sentiment may be true, but that begs the question. The investor who has bought an under-valued stock will not be pleased if that stock becomes even more under-valued. For all real-world investors, the process—the dynamics—of misvalua-tion is crucial.

The stock market is not essentially different from other markets, whether they be the markets for canned sardines, pork bellies, or condominiums. Price behavior in markets is governed by the law of supply and demand—in the case of the stock market, supply and demand for stocks. An increase in demand (more buyers) will raise prices; an increase in supply (more sellers) will push prices down. Shifting patterns of supply and demand for particular stocks, or for stocks in general, may or may not have anything to do with value at any given time.

TECHNICAL ANALYSIS

This idea—that supply and demand for stocks governs the market's price behavior—does not contradict the notion of intrinsic value. It simply explains why stock prices swing from one side of intrinsic value to another. What it also does, however, is lead us to a method of analysis very different from fundamental security analysis. This second method is called *technical analysis,* and it bypasses the question of intrinsic value.

Like the fundamentalist, the technical analyst (or *technician*) recognizes that trends and fads are rampant in the market. The technician, however, does not relate these trends and fads to intrinsic value. If trends send stock prices swinging far above and below intrinsic value, then why bother to analyze value? Analyze trends! In other words, the fundamentalist looks at demand for IBM products, while the technician looks at demand for IBM stock.

Technical analysis of the stock market concerns the psychological and emotional characteristics of investors. These factors are undeniably impor-tant: If investors suddenly move from pessimism to optimism, then the market will rise. The problem is that there is no satisfactory way to measure sentiment and perceptions directly, at least not with the accuracy and timeliness needed to make exceptional profits in the market. Technical analysis must take an indirect approach.

The basic premises of technical analysis are that the changing opinions, expectations, and feelings of investors are reflected and can be identified in market action, and that past and current market action can accurately forecast future action. To technical analysts, the study of intrinsic value seems like a colossal waste of time, energy, and money; the only relevant study is study of the market. Stan Weinstein, publisher of the *Professional Tape Reader*, expresses the technician's viewpoint: "It isn't that fundamentals don't matter, it's that it's only *future* fundamentals that matter.... Future fundamentals and psychology—and neither of them is measurable...so the only way as far as I am concerned is to listen to the market's own message" (quoted in Scott, 1984b, p. 5). The masthead of his market letter is more succinct: "The Tape [the stock market ticker] Tells All."

For a confirmed technician, fundamentals are irrelevant. Technicians ignore interest rates, earnings, strikes, inventions, oil embargoes, and the like, not because these are irrelevant to stock prices, but because a particular development seems to matter less than the market's reaction to it. This reaction gives technicians clues to the future, because it reflects the mind and the mood of the market. For technicians, knowing the market's mood is the key to success, and mood can be determined from market action.

It is much easier to say what technicians believe than to describe what they do, because a bewildering variety of analytical methods and tools exists under the umbrella of technical analysis. Most of these involve the analysis of price and volume patterns, either separately or together; their description could fill a book. Here, a brief review will have to suffice.

The central concept of technical analysis is *trends*. Technicians believe that individual stocks (and the whole market, for that matter) have upward or downward movements that tend to persist over significant time periods and distances. The goal of technical analysis is to identify these trends and recognize when they reverse themselves.

The best-known approach to trend analysis is charting: literally making a chart of a stock's price action over time usually on a daily or weekly basis. The technician then studies the chart, looking for patterns that presumably will lead to an accurate appraisal of where the stock will go in the future. Some chart patterns are supposed to indicate that the current trend will continue, while others (*reversal patterns*) either portend an impending change or identify a change that has just occurred. The charts show where *support* and *resistance* levels are. Such terms as *broadening top, rounding bottom,* and *head and shoulders* are not anatomical descriptions; they are examples of the colorful lexicon chartists use to describe common reversal formations. Stan Weinstein claims that all stocks go through a repetitive four-stage process of price movement, from base building to uptrend to topping out to downtrend, and then back to base building. A careful reading of the charts reveals which stage each stock is in. Weinstein actually makes such a study for every stock on the New York Stock Exchange every week. (Warning: other chartists might disagree with his conclusions.)

Charting is widely known (and widely ridiculed by skeptics), but it is not the only form of technical analysis, especially for analyzing the entire market rather than individual stocks. Another form derives from the principle of confirmation (or, negatively, nonconfirmation). The idea here is that a market move, or trend, must be a broad-based move before it can be considered valid. The best-known example is the Dow Theory, based on the separate action of the Dow Jones Industrial and Transportation averages. Bull trends are considered to have been confirmed when both averages move above previous intermediate-term highs. If one average fails to confirm the new high in the other, a state of nonconfirmation exists (and the seeds of doubt are sown). If both averages later violate previous intermediate-term lows, the trend is considered bearish.

The principle of confirmation has been expanded far beyond these two market averages. Many technicians look for confirmation from broader price indexes on various markets, from *advance-decline lines* (the cumulative plurality of advancing versus declining stocks), from the numbers of new highs and new lows, and from *on-balance volume* (the cumulative difference in trading volume of advancing versus declining issues). Technicians use all these methods and many more to determine whether the market is in gear, ascertain the likely strength and longevity of any market move, and detect possible turning points.

A vast number of technical indicators are based on the concept of *momentum*. These indicators are usually defined in terms of rates of price change (e.g., the 12-day rate of change). Strong momentum usually implies continuation of a current trend. Other measures are designed to determine when the market is oversold or overbought (excessive moves that can't be sustained without a correction).

Still other indicators are based on the market activities of particular participants. For example, various measures are developed from statistics on odd-lot trading, specialists' buying and selling, and big-block trades. These indicators are all based on the assumption that some groups of investors are smarter than others—for example, that specialists know what is really going on, while odd-lotters do not.

Finally, some technical analyses are based on the idea that the market is governed by defined time cycles. People claim to have discovered cycles ranging in length from a few hours or days to several decades. Since these cycles operate simultaneously, the trick is to understand how they all interact, either cancelling out or reinforcing one another.

These are only some of the more common approaches to technical analysis (there are many, many more). They seem quite disparate, but they have a major premise in common: that past market action, broadly defined, provides the best and perhaps the only reliable clue to the market's future.*

---

*Three representative and well-regarded books on technical analysis are Robert Edwards and John Magee's *Technical Analysis of Stock Trends* (Boston: John Magee, 1966), which concerns

BUT DOES IT WORK?

As we have seen, it is difficult to determine the effectiveness of fundamental analysis. The basic goal of that approach is to determine the intrinsic value of stocks (even though the analytical results are usually not expressed that way). If they were, we still could not make valid direct judgments on how effective such analysis is, because only time can tell whether the original appraisal was accurate. As time passes, intrinsic value keeps changing, and so we are forced to attempt judgments from indirect evidence, such as the accuracy of earnings forecasts.

With technical analysis, the problems are even worse. We can try to evaluate the recommendations of technical analysts, but they give us only hypothetical results, even though their recommendations are no less real. We have to make assumptions about the timing of purchases, sales, prices, transaction costs, number of shares involved, and so on. These assumptions can dramatically affect results (see Chapter 3). Many technically based recommendations are also surprisingly vague and do not provide clear guidance either to potential investors or to people trying to evaluate the quality of the advice. While fundamental analysis at least uses concrete estimates of earnings as a benchmark, in technical analysis no standard output can be defined or measured; there is no technical equivalent of earnings. Technicians have their own individual constellations of indicators, and the output of their work often shows nothing more than their individual judgment, which is very difficult to test scientifically.*

One way to test technical analysis, at least partially, is to test commonly used indicators. In essence, we try to determine whether using a given indicator will yield investment results superior to those of a simple buy-and-hold strategy. For example, will trading on the basis of the Dow Theory result in better returns than simply holding a representative stock portfolio through thick and thin? Many tests of this sort have been performed, and we will look at some of them in Chapter 6. For now, I will just offer a preview. The results aren't encouraging.

A SIMPLER WAY?

Technicians do recognize that fundamentals affect stock prices. Likewise, fundamentalists recognize that trends and fads can take prices far above

charting; Gerald Appel and Fred Hitschler's *Stock Market Trading Systems* (Homewood, Ill.: Dow Jones–Irwin, 1980), which puts emphasis on cycles and momentum and "mechanical" trading rules; and Joseph Granville's *Granville's New Strategy of Daily Stock Market Timing for Maximum Profit* (Englewood Cliffs, N.J.: Prentice-Hall, 1976), which takes an eclectic approach.
*Independent efforts to measure and evaluate technical recommendations have provoked endless arguments and even lawsuits.

or below intrinsic value. Nevertheless, these two analytical methods are diametrically opposed, and their proponents fight with relish and spirit, not least because each side considers the other such an easy target. The argument has been going on for a long time. It is not going to be resolved anytime soon, and certainly not here. People who see the stock market as a market for investment capital will find the fundamental approach more congenial, and those who see the stock market as a trading market will tend to find technical analysis more plausible. Each approach has intuitive and theoretical appeal, as well as practical difficulties. With either one, value still has to be determined. In fundamental analysis the search is for intrinsic value, while in technical analysis today's value must be determined essentially by forecasting tomorrow's price. Both are difficult, time-consuming, and expensive methods. Neither has any guarantee of success.

Is there an easier way? Can we abandon both fundamental and technical analysis? Can we forget about looking for undervalued stocks and simply assume that today's price is our best estimate of a stock's value? Could we just throw darts at the stock list? Many intelligent, serious, informed, and reputable observers answer yes to all these questions. As we go on, we'll see why.

Part Two
The Efficient Market

5

The Great Debate:
Is the Market
Unbeatable?

Suppose the market were to function so that the price of each stock always equaled its intrinsic value. No stocks would be overvalued and none undervalued. Prices would change only in response to new financial and economic developments, and then they would change instantly. Unless you were holding a stock when the news broke, it would be too late for you to gain or lose from the development. No matter what stocks you selected, they would all have an equal likelihood of success, so there would be no need to do any research or analysis before investing.

This kind of market might reassure you. (It might bore you, too.) Many business and finance professors at leading universities would say that this is the kind of stock market we actually have. An economist would say that such a market is *efficient* and works the way a competitive market should. Your broker would find the idea preposterous.

The theory of an efficient market is simple, logical, powerful, and profound in its implications. It is also controversial, because it runs counter to our instincts and traditional ideas about investing. As investors, we can accept or reject the theory, but we can't afford to ignore it, for several reasons. First, the theory provides an excellent conceptual framework for organizing and evaluating our approaches to investing. Second, almost all modern research on the stock market is conducted in terms of this theory. Finally, this theory affects how professional managers are investing billions of dollars in the stock market, and their decisions shape the character and behavior of the market that the rest of us must deal in. It is almost impossible to make sense of the market without understanding the efficient market theory.

A COMPETITIVE SYSTEM

Let's imagine an investment market crowded with well-informed, skillful investors. They all have access to all current information relevant to stock values and prices, and they analyze it to determine values. They buy and sell stocks according to new information and changing market prices in an effort to maximize their returns.

In such a market, these alert investors try to acquire undervalued stocks and to avoid or dispose of stocks that are overvalued. They compete with one another, and that competition tends to drive up the prices of undervalued stocks and drive the prices of the overvalued stocks down. For example, if stock XYZ is undervalued, investors react by buying it, pushing its price up. If stock UVW is overvalued, they dump it, and the sell orders push its price down.

Figure 5.1 illustrates how this process operates. The figure shows supply and demand for a hypothetical stock, but it represents a situation somewhat different from the supply-and-demand concept you may have learned in economics courses. Instead of showing how many shares people want to buy or sell, the figure shows how many shares people want to *hold* at different prices, and how many shares are available for holding. The vertical axis shows the price per share, and the horizontal axis shows the number of shares.

Now suppose that line SS shows the outstanding supply of stock in a company at a given time. This line is drawn vertically, indicating that the supply of stock is fixed. The number of shares outstanding is not affected by the price per share.*

Line DD_1 shows the demand to hold shares. Its downward slope indicates that investors' willingness to own the stock depends on its price. The stock represents better value at lower prices. Also, a given amount of money will buy more shares at lower prices. The lower the price, the more shares investors want to hold. (All investors collectively must hold all the outstanding stock; there is no such thing as unowned stock.)

Let's imagine that at a certain moment the stock's price is A. At price A, investors evidently consider the stock undervalued, because they want to own more shares than actually exist. Since they cannot, the problem is

---

*If a company considers its stock to be priced extremely high, it may respond by issuing more stock to raise capital. Conversely, if it feels the stock is priced too low, it may institute a buyback plan. In the short run, however, the number of shares is constant.

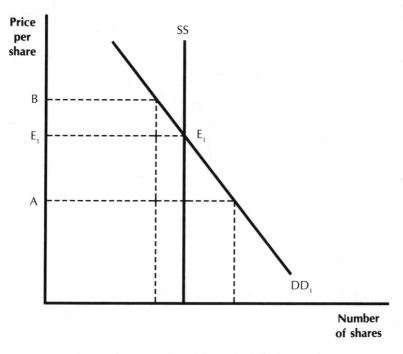

FIGURE 5.1. Supply and demand-to-hold for a stock

resolved in the only possible way: Investors trying to acquire the stock bid the price up. We see the opposite phenomenon when the stock is priced at B. In this case, the stock is apparently overvalued, because investors are unwilling to hold all the stock at that price. Again, the disparity is resolved through the market mechanism: To reduce their holdings, investors accept lower prices as they compete with each other to unload the stock.

There is only one price at which there is no pressure for change. That price is E_1. At E_1, investors collectively want to hold all the available stock, no more and no less. For obvious reasons, E_1 is called the *equilibrium price.*

Competition among investors keeps prices moving toward the equilibrium point. The overvalued securities are sold, and the undervalued ones are bought. In this process, disparities between prices and values are reduced or eliminated. If the competition is keen enough, prices never diverge significantly from values.

Such competition is effective both in static and dynamic situations. New information alters values, but if this information is widely available, market prices will quickly adjust to reflect it, as shown in Figure 5.2. With demand curve DD_1 and price E_1, the market is in equilibrium; there is no reason for the price to change. Now suppose that some new and very positive

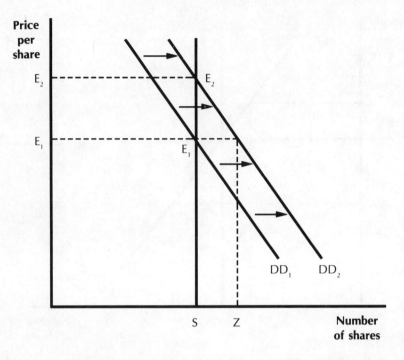

FIGURE 5.2 Supply and dynamic demand-to-hold for a stock

information becomes available (perhaps there has been a large new order for the company's products). This information shifts the entire demand curve for the stock to DD_2, reflecting the altered outlook; E_1 is no longer the equilibrium price. At E_1, investors want to hold amount Z, more shares than are available. Therefore the competitive forces begin the process of adjustment, leading to the new equilibrium price, E_2.

Watching the movement of prices, we may find it hard to believe that the stock market is an equilibrium system. We certainly don't always get the impression that prices are moving in an orderly, purposeful way. Still, this idea is easier to accept once we realize that the equilibrium is continually being disturbed by the arrival of new information. Consider the almost unlimited supply of news and reports on the national and international economy. Add all the developments in various industries, as well as new information that applies to particular companies, and you can see that an equilibrium price is a moving target. It's usually gone by the time we get there.

A Random Walk

If we expand a bit on this idea, we can see that there are only two sources of changes in stock prices: coincidence and new information. Some small, short-term changes result primarily from temporary imbalances between buyers and sellers. These changes are coincidental. Even when the market is in equilibrium, people are buying or selling stocks for various personal reasons, timing their actions independently of one another. This activity leads to short-term, random price changes. Each bit of new information, the second source of price changes, also alters equilibrium, if only by a small amount. New information, however, is unpredictable in its content, timing, and importance. In other words, it, too, is random.

Thus we have two essentially random sources of price changes. If so, then the price changes themselves must also be essentially random. This, very briefly, is the much-discussed *random walk* theory of the stock market. We should pay attention to what the random walk theory really says, because it is widely misunderstood. It does not say that stock prices meander aimlessly. Prices respond to new information; the new information is random (if it weren't, it wouldn't be news). Therefore, stock prices move *as if* they were random, too. Stock prices are considered random in that they are unpredictable, but not irrational.

THE EFFICIENT MARKET

Competition in the market works to keep stock prices moving toward their equilibrium values. The term *market efficiency* refers to how rapidly, accurately, and smoothly this process occurs. Efficiency is not something that the market either has or does not have; it's a matter of degree. For our purposes, here is a working definition: *An efficient market is one in which the price of any stock reflects everything known or knowable that is relevant to that stock's value.* Or, to put it another way, in an efficient market, all available information is reflected in current stock prices, and new information is very quickly translated into new prices. In other words, the process illustrated by Figure 5.2 works very rapidly; prices are never far from their equilibrium levels.

This kind of efficiency is very significant, because if a stock's current price always reflects all the available information about that stock, then its price at any given time equals its value at that time. Thus the stock is neither undervalued nor overvalued. (Actually, the current price will not always be perfectly correct, but it will be what mathematicians call an unbiased estimate of the true value: If the price is wrong, it is just as likely to be too high as too low.) Speaking a bit more conservatively, then, we can say that in an efficient market, the current price of a stock is the *best available estimate* of the stock's actual value.

This proposition has some startling implications. For example, if the market is efficient, so that today's price for any stock is the best available estimate of that stock's value, then stocks are neither undervalued nor over-valued (as far as we can tell, at least). Therefore, the collective judgment of a competitive, efficient market is accurate enough to make individual analysis pointless.

Again, consider that Wall Street's primary products are information and analysis. These have one primary purpose: to identify significantly undervalued or overvalued stocks and exploit the corresponding profit opportunities. Thousands of highly trained people, with large staffs, state-of-the-art communications and data-processing equipment, and enormous budgets, devote their professional lives to this exercise. If the stock market is efficient, however, it is an exercise in futility. Security analysis, in any of its forms, will not gain you an edge over other investors. You can't beat the market.

Here is a great paradox: Analysis makes the market efficient, but analysis is useless in an efficient market. If everyone recognized the market's efficiency and gave analysis up, the market would soon stop being efficient; thus analysis is necessary. But—and this is the crucial point—as long as plenty of other people are performing the necessary analysis, there's no need for *us* to do it. Investors, in effect, can take a free ride on the analytical efforts of others. The informed have no advantages over the ignorant.

What's true for stock selection also applies to market timing. In an efficient market, the current price of any stock is the best estimate of its true value. In the same way, the current level of the entire market is the best estimate of the market's true value. The market's future will be determined by new developments and new information. Because these are unpredictable, so is the market.

I said at the beginning of this chapter that the implications of the efficient market theory turn our traditional ideas about investing upside down, and we've seen examples of how this is true. The theory of an efficient market implies that all stocks are equally plausible investments and that all times are equally good times to buy, own, or sell stocks. Therefore, it seems that we can do no better than to buy and hold stocks, acquiring an essentially random portfolio and taking what comes.

A Little Clarification

If the stock market is efficient, then investment skill is inconsequential, because all stocks are fairly valued. Nevertheless, even if they are all fairly valued and equally viable investment candidates, they certainly will not all turn out equally well. Unpredictable future developments will affect the performance of each stock, and results will vary widely. In an efficient market, we may not be rewarded for our skill; we will be rewarded—or punished—for our luck.

There is more involved than skill and luck, however. There is a third factor: risk. The basic concept is simple. Not all stocks are equally risky, and riskier stocks generally have higher returns than safer ones. In fact, in a market where skill is irrelevant and luck balances out, risk taking is the only thing for which investors are compensated. If the market is efficient, investing is not a skill/reward game; it is a risk/reward game.

Thus, in an efficient market, all stocks may be equally promising, but they do not all promise the same returns. Their expected returns are in proportion to their riskiness. This idea gives us a new understanding of what it means to beat the market. Simply outperforming the S&P 500 or some other common index is not enough. Beating the market means achieving returns that are disproportionate to the amount of risk assumed. The efficient market theory holds that this cannot be done consistently.

The Source of Efficiency

Since the implications of this theory are so great, it's important to know what is required for the stock market to be efficient. We've already touched on the answers, but now let's clarify and expand on them.

We've seen that competition is the source of market efficiency, and effective competition requires a large number of able, well-informed people who are quick to act on new information. Information is at the heart of stock valuation. If competition is supposed to keep prices in line with values, then competitors must have access to the information necessary to determine values. Thus, availability of information is fundamental to an efficient market.

If we listed all the kinds of information that affect stock valuation, most of them would be facts of one sort or another. Not all the information that creates an efficient market is factual, however. We must include opinions, estimates, analyses, and projections, especially those that come from people or firms who have large followings of investors. This subjective information does double duty: It proceeds from the facts but in turn becomes part of the information base.

For example, let's look at analysts' earnings estimates. These estimates are an important factor in how the market values a stock. When actual earnings are announced, the stock market's reaction will probably not be based on how these earnings compare to previous earnings of the company, to the earnings of competitors, or to earnings in the general economy. Rather, the market's reaction is more likely to be based on how these earnings compare to analysts' forecasts, because those forecasts have been built into the valuation of the stock; they are embodied in the expectations of the market.

In an efficient market, as we have seen, current price is the best estimate of a security's actual value. Nevertheless, not every competitor agrees on that value. In the market we have consensus pricing. At any time, some investors think a stock is correctly priced, others think it is undervalued, and still others find it overpriced. Until new information comes along, or until the stock's price changes, the first group may well be content to hold the stock. The people who think it is overpriced will avoid the stock or dispose of what they hold, perhaps selling it to people who consider the stock a bargain. This process works itself out through the market mechanism, with investors adjusting their holdings according to their own views of the outlook.

For the market to be efficient, competing investors must be able to make effective use of the information at their disposal, but most investors cannot do this; they cannot even remotely be considered security analysts. Does this mean an efficient market is impossible? Not at all. First, many investors who are not security analysts are being directed or guided by professional analysts, brokerage-house research, subscription investment-advisory services, and private investment counselors. Second, it is not necessary for all participants to be good analysts; an efficient market needs only enough good analysts to keep prices from getting too far out of line with values.

Horse racing provides an analogy. Some people bet on hunches, choosing a horse because he has a name to which they attach superstitious value or because his jockey is wearing their favorite colors. This kind of behavior tends to make the betting odds diverge from the true odds on the horses running in the race. When such divergences appear, however, competent handicappers hurry to the parimutuel windows to take advantage of the anomaly. In doing so, they tend to correct it.

This is a tricky point. If, as we have already seen, even professional analysts are incapable of great accuracy in their estimates of value, why should their efforts create an efficient market?

First, inaccuracy means little in itself. The world is too complex and inherently too unpredictable for security analysis to be an exact science. Inaccuracy doesn't imply incompetence.

More important, analysts' individual errors tend to cancel each other out in consensus pricing. To put this proposition mathematically, if the forecasting errors of different analysts are independent, then the error of a consensus forecast declines with the square root of the number of forecasters. For example, if 25 people make forecasts, then the average errors in the consensus forecasts will be one-fifth the average errors in the individual forecasts (since the square root of 25 is 5). The Law of Large Numbers is very powerful. In a highly compettitive, highly informed market in which consensus pricing prevails, individual participants may be well off the mark in their appraisals, but the market synthesizes their errors into reasonably accurate valuations. The point of the efficient market theory is not that analysis is perfectly accurate, or that accurate analysis has no value.

Rather, the point is that the collective judgment of the market is superior to what any of us, amateurs or professionals, can achieve individually.

Investors raised on traditional Wall Street thinking find this idea very difficult to accept. In brokerage offices, at lunch, and at cocktail parties, they debate the investment merits of various stocks, but they invariably rely on second-hand analysis and on opinions that are widely known and already reflected in current stock prices. Where is their edge?

Consider IBM. Dozens of professional security analysts follow IBM stock. Their forecasts and judgments go out to millions of investors, whose collective judgments and actions determine the market price of the stock. These analysts do not hold identical opinions, nor do they offer identical earnings forecasts. Over any given period, some are very close to the mark in their analyses and some are very far off, but all that information and opinion is synthesized by the market.

What happens when IBM's quarterly earnings are reported? Suppose that our dozens of analysts projected earnings increases ranging from 0 to 12 percent, but that the actual earnings increase turns out to be 30 percent, and the stock immediately jumps six points. Was the market inefficient? No. The analysts were just wrong. In fact, the immediate rise in the stock demonstrates efficiency: a rapid response to new information.

Faced with this situation, how can investors beat the market in IBM? There are three possible ways. First, they can use available information and outperform the professional analysts. Second, they can successfully predict which analyst out of dozens will be the most accurate (or, again, outperform the analysts). Third, they can obtain important information that the professional analysts don't have. The chance of anyone's doing any of these things on a consistent basis is practically nil.

IS THIS THEORY PLAUSIBLE?

It's not surprising that the efficient market theory did not originate on Wall Street, where there is a vested interest in the belief that the market is not efficient. Brokers and advisory services compete for our business. They attempt to convince us that their research departments can distinguish undervalued from overvalued stocks, that they can do it more successfully than their competitors, and that following their advice will bring us extraordinary profits. (I particularly enjoyed one TV commercial that featured a well-known bull pawing his way through a haystack and finding, naturally, a needle.)

Of course, our brokers also want us to be active traders and generate commission revenue for them. They need to have us believe that they can distinguish value independent of the market's judgment. It is very common for a broker to tell a client to sell stock A, ''which our research department feels is fully priced," and buy stock B, "which is undervalued." Sometime later, depending on how stock B has fared, the client will be advised to sell it because "it has met our objectives," because "the outlook has changed," and so on. The client will be offered stock C, which is, of course, "undervalued."

If the stock market is efficient, then none of this makes any sense, and if belief in the market's efficiency became widespread, the implications for the investment community, the purveyors of investment advice and services, would be ominous. Most investment advisory letters would be superfluous, and brokerage houses would have to compete in such mundane areas as commission costs and accuracy of record keeping. Most important, trading volume would decrease significantly. Since volume creates the commissions on which the entire investment community survives and prospers, it is not surprising that the efficient market theory is anathema on Wall Street.

Just as Wall Street has a vested interest in market inefficiency, so does the academic community have a vested interest in the efficient market theory. Here, the interest is not financial, but intellectual. Scientists are strong respecters of theory, and in this case we are dealing with the simplest and most fundamental economic concepts: supply and demand, and competition.

The theory of economic competition has been with us at least since Adam Smith published *The Wealth of Nations* in 1776. Our entire economic system is derived from the principles expressed there. An efficient market is nothing more than a manifestation of intense competition: The stock market, with its huge number of participants and its open format, is highly competitive; hence, it ought to be highly efficient, too. Anything less would be highly distasteful to one who respects economic theory. The academic viewpoint is expressed by the well-known finance professor William Sharpe, who wrote in 1981, "Any substantial disparity between price and value would reflect market inefficiency. In a well-developed and free market, such inefficiencies are rare" (p. 72).

The battle lines are clearly drawn. Wall Street accuses the efficient market theorists of trying to impose idealized and unrealistic concepts on real-world markets they have never dealt in and do not understand. Meanwhile, back in the Ivory Tower, academics reply that investment professionals practice deception on customers (and perhaps on themselves), and that competition in the investment business is so great that arguments for anything other than a highly efficient market are patently absurd.

Fortunately, we're not restricted to making judgments solely on the basis of persuasive arguments. Factual research has already been brought to bear on the controversy. As we'll soon see, academics scored an early victory.

6

Testing the Theory

With all due respect for theory and logic, if the hypothesis of an efficient stock market is ultimately going to stand, it must do so on the basis of evidence.

Can market efficiency be measured or tested directly? To do this, we would need to compare market prices with intrinsic values. If intrinsic values were known, however, the market would automatically be efficient, because there would be no reason for stocks ever to be priced at anything but intrinsic value. No one would be willing to pay more; no one would sell for less.

The theory can be measured and tested indirectly, though, because it makes three statements about the process and the results of efficiency. First, an efficient market should respond very rapidly to new information that is relevant to stock values. Second, since stock prices are presumed to reflect all available information, it should be impossible for investors to use that information for beating the market. Third, investors should not be able to beat the market except by chance. We can test these three statements.

Testing the theory of market efficiency hinges on the concept of beating the market, and so we must reconsider what both *beating* and *the market* mean. *The market* refers to a broad collection of stocks. The S&P 500 is typically used for research because of its broad, value-weighted coverage. The idea is to compare a proposed investment strategy to a naive strategy of simply buying the S&P 500 and holding it. This strategy is considered naive because it requires no judgments, decisions, or skills. *Beating the market* means more than achieving higher returns than the S&P 500; it means achieving returns greater than can be explained by the risks incurred. (We will see this in detail in Part Three.)

TAKING ON THE TECHNICIANS

Essentially two types of information are available to investors. The first is what we can call fundamental information, such as sales, earnings, and dividends. The second is market information, which comes from stock trading itself. This is the realm of technical analysts, who believe that past trading patterns hold the key to future prices.

The first form* of the efficient market hypothesis, known in the trade as the *weak form*, states that market information is useless for predicting future market action. In other words, no useful information is contained in the history of stock prices and volume patterns; technical analysis doesn't work.

The first tests of technical analysis were the most devastating. They showed that stock price charts were not significantly different from charts produced by random processes: Stocks' movements could not be distinguished from a random walk.

This was demonstrated both by some fancy mathematics and by some down-to-earth simulations.** Malkiel, for example, reports on classroom experiments in which coin tosses were used to simulate stock price movements. A hypothetical stock was started at an assumed price of 50. Every time heads came up, the price rose half a point; every time tails came up, the price fell half a point. This experiment produced the full spectrum of technical chart patterns: uptrends and downtrends, trading ranges, support and resistance, reversals, momentum, cycles, and so on, all generated by a purely random process. In one instance, Malkiel took a chart created in this way and showed it to a technician friend, who instantly recognized the pattern of "upward breakout from an inverted head and shoulders." The man excitedly demanded to know the name of the company, realizing that immediate purchase was called for. Needless to say, he was not amused when he discovered the truth behind the chart.

But the researchers weren't done with the chartists yet. Computers were programmed to recognize leading chart patterns. Sifting through actual stock charts, researchers pulled these patterns out to see if they actually portended anything about future price action. No luck, and so they tried the experiment the other way around. This time the computer pulled out the stocks that had performed best and worst, and researchers went through actual

*Two other forms of the hypothesis will be discussed later in this chapter.
**This idea was first established in 1900 by a French mathematician, Louis Bachelier. His work was promptly forgotten, not to be seriously revived for more than half a century.

charts of prior price action to find predictive patterns—again, with no success. No matter what they tried, researchers could find nothing in previous price behavior to successfully predict future action.

Other tests of technical analysis were equally discouraging. *Filter rules* of all sorts were tested. These are trading rules based on the principle of trend following. For example, with a 5 percent filter, a stock is bought after it rises 5 percent from a low (an uptrend is presumably established), and it is sold when it declines 5 percent from a high (a downtrend now takes over). Again, no matter what the filter, the results were negative. No strategies were found superior to the naïve buy-and-hold approach to the market.*

The Dow Theory was also tested, along with trading rules that use advance-decline lines and measures of momentum. Tests of other rules, based on particular categories of traders (the odd-lot ratio; the short interest ratio), were conducted as well. The technical methods failed to produce accurate results, and the random walk theory was vindicated.

Were no successful technical methods discovered by these tests? Some were, but they were useful only in a sense. Some filter rules proved successful when the filters were extremely small, and there were some other indications of imperfect market efficiency. These results all had a severe drawback, however: They could not be used to outperform the market when transaction costs (commissions and spreads) were also taken into account. Any active market strategy entails more costs than simply buying and holding. If the added returns don't exceed those extra costs, the strategy can hardly be called successful, even if it demonstrates that the market isn't perfectly efficient.

In yet another sense, many technical methods were successful: They were profitable. This finding is not as exciting as it may seem. Most strategies for stock selection are profitable, even in an efficient market, because the market rewards stockholders (if it didn't, there would be none). Research has shown that, historically, approximately three-fourths of randomly selected stock investments, held for randomly chosen periods, have been profitable. Therefore, simply making money neither proves the success of a strategy nor disproves the theory of market efficiency. The test of a strategy is its ability to beat the market, to outperform a buy-and-hold strategy and not simply earn returns. Market-beating strategies did not emerge from the methods of technical analysis.

---

*Stop-loss orders, so commonly recommended and used, are nothing more than filter rules. Wherever a particular stop may be, its placement is based on the assumption that if the stock's price descends to that level, a downtrend is established and lower prices are probable. Thus stop-loss orders are technical tactics, even though they are often used by investors who do not consider themselves technically oriented. (A stop-loss order that is entered only because the investor cannot afford or does not want to lose more than a certain amount of money is not an example of investment analysis or judgment; it is just a form of money management.)

Of course, not every technical scheme for beating the market has been or can be tested. New methods and models are conceived faster than independent researchers can test them. Moreover, as we saw in Chapter 3, these new models always come from back-testing: They would have worked in the past, but we don't know how or if they will work in the future. To say that research has proved the inadequacy of technical analysis would be an exaggeration, but the burden of proof clearly has passed from the professors to the practitioners.

Research on the value of technical analysis encompasses scores of studies conducted over a couple of decades. This has been only a brief review of it, but rest assured that the research conclusions have been overwhelmingly unanimous—and the proponents of the efficient market theory have made no secret of their pleasure. Malkiel wrote, ''Our bullying tactics are prompted by two considerations: (1) the method is patently false; and (2) it's easy to pick on'' (p. 127). Another leading exponent of the efficient market theory has suggested that technical analysis is not only useless but, under ERISA (the federal pension law), might also be considered criminal. Theoreticians can be a rough bunch!

ANOTHER OX TO GORE

As the academics piled up evidence debunking technical analysis, few tears were shed. The technicians themselves howled, of course, complaining that the research was simplistic and unfair, but few others seemed to mind. After all, technicians had always been considered the lunatic fringe of the investment world, akin to crystal-ball gazers and readers of tea leaves. Fundamentalists, with their professional dominance and their air of respectability, were only too pleased to see the chartists unmasked. Little did they know that they were next.

As we have learned, the proposition that items of trading information (i.e., price and volume data) are useless for predicting future price changes is called the *weak form* of the efficient market hypothesis. Is there a stronger form? Indeed there is, and it is called (I swear it) the *semi-strong form*. This proposition is much more encompassing, and we've seen it before: No public information whatsoever is useful to investors; all available information is fully reflected in the prices of stocks. In other words, not only is technical information worthless, so are fundamental information and analysis. This proposition says just what we suggested earlier: Once new information is available (say, the latest GNP figures), it is too late for investors to profit from it, because the market already reflects it.

How can we test this idea straightforwardly? We can look at how the market responds to new information. If the market is efficient, the information should be absorbed rapidly.

Let's say we start by choosing some news or event commonly thought important in determining stock values—say, a stock split. Next, we find stocks that have this characteristic and track their performance (relative to the market) both before and after the splits. If the splits are good news, these stocks probably will either match the general market or outperform it in the period leading up to the announcement of the news.*

The crucial test for market efficiency is what happens once the news is released. In an efficient market, reaction will be instantaneous and accurate, so that it will be impossible for investors to profit later from the news. That is, the stocks that have shown the particular development will have no general tendency either to outperform or underperform the market once the news is out.

A study famous in academic circles looked at stock splits in exactly this way. In Wall Street folklore, a stock split is considered a bullish omen, though it is not clear why: A stock split does not change the financial structure of a corporation, nor does it alter the positions of stockholders, and 100 shares at $100 are certainly equal to 200 shares at $50. One explanation is that lower prices increase liquidity and stimulate wider interest. Another is that splits are an expression of confidence in the future by corporate officers and directors. By whatever logic, corporations traditionally have acted as if they were giving shareholders benefits by splitting stocks (or declaring stock dividends), and investors traditionally have believed that stock splits are good news, portending extraordinary returns in the future. But do stock splits really convey any valuable information to investors?

The study in question examined 622 NYSE stocks that had split between 1926 and 1960. It chronicled their price behavior immediately before and after the splits. The overall results are shown in Figure 6.1. The figure shows how the stocks as a group performed, relative to the market, during the 30 months preceding and following the splits. The chart shows excess returns (returns above those of the market), and it is cumulative. When the chart pattern was rising, the splitting stocks outperformed the market; when it was falling, they underperformed. The implication of the figure is clear: Stocks that split were superior performers before the splits, but once the splits occurred, that difference ceased. Therefore, either investors anticipated the splits, or the splits occurred simply because the stocks had risen greatly in price. In either case, any useful information conveyed by the splits was fully absorbed into market prices quite rapidly, just as we would expect in an efficient market.

---

*Outperformance of the market before such an announcement does not imply market inefficiency; outperformance can result from ongoing analysis. For example, a dividend increase normally follows a strong earnings performance. Security analysts and investors are likely to be aware of a positive trend before an actual announcement of a higher dividend.

Cumulative Excess
Risk–Adjusted
Returns Relative
to Market

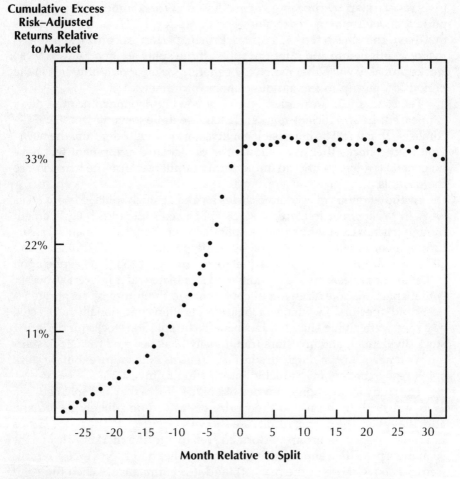

FIGURE 6.1. Performance of splitting stocks relative to market (622 NYSE splits, 1926–1960). *SOURCE:* Fama, Fisher, Jensen, and Roll, 1969.

Similar studies were conducted on various other kinds of information considered important to stock values and prices. For example, the market's reactions to earnings and dividend announcements and to changes in the Federal Reserve's discount rate have also been examined, with results similar to those for stock splits: Because of ongoing analysis, the bulk of the reaction occurs before the news. The remaining reaction doesn't always occur instantly (the market is not perfectly efficient), but it comes quickly. There were a few exceptions, which we will discuss later, but the general conclusion was widely accepted: Once the costs of implementing particular investment strategies were accounted for, there were few if any opportunities for consistently achieving extraordinary returns on the basis of publicly available information.

The ability of the competitive market to arrive quickly at unbiased estimates of value is further demonstrated by a recent study that examined the valuation of new issues (initial public offerings). It has been widely established that new issues as a group are bargains at their offering prices. They tend to go to significant premiums on the day trading in them begins.* Chalk and Peavy studied 400 initial offerings from 1975 through 1982. They confirmed that the new issues were bargains: They had an average first-day return of more than 21 percent. But Chalk and Peavy also tracked these stocks for the nine months afterward and found that the new issues' returns were not significantly different from those of non-new issues of similar riskiness. In other words, even though new issues are mispriced when first offered, the market is so efficient that it accurately prices the new stocks in one trading session.

THE FINAL NAIL

A great deal of research has been conducted on both the usefulness of information and the market's response to the arrival of new information. The results have corresponded to what is implied by the efficient market and random walk theories. Skeptics are not easily convinced, however, and it is possible to find fault with the research. Not every conceivable approach to analyzing and valuing stocks has been studied (or ever will be, as a practical matter), and the kinds of information that have been evaluated are perhaps too basic and unsophisticated. After all, serious analysts and investors don't base their decisions on single indicators or measures; they consider many factors simultaneously, combining them in an exercise in judgment.

For example, even though new issues as a group may be fairly priced after one day, some will be overpriced and others underpriced; a good analyst may be able to tell which are which. Therefore, the objection goes, academic researchers have used simplistic and unrealistic examples to evaluate their theories, creating straw men easily knocked down. While no single piece of information may be of statistically significant value in selecting stocks, the argument continues, astute investors may still be able to use the wealth of available information to create market-beating strategies. (One institutional investment manager has described this approach as using proprietary methods to create private knowledge out of public information.)

---

*It is impossible for investors to get significant amounts of good new issues at the offering prices unless they are very big customers for the regular services of underwriting brokers. The cost of these services is so high that there is no such thing as a practical new-issue strategy.

This argument has intuitive appeal. It even sounds sensible. It amounts to saying, "Don't judge the information; judge the investors" Very well—if astute, well-informed investors can take available information and use it to beat the market consistently, then it should be possible to find those investors.

Those in the best position to realize maximum returns are professional investment managers. They have training, information, analyses, models, and communications and data-processing capabilities superior to those of other investors. Given the stakes and the competitiveness of their game, they are also among the most highly motivated investors. If the market really can be beaten, and if the efficient market theory can be refuted, then professional investors are the ones most likely to do so.

Because the portfolio compositions and the financial results of many professionally managed funds (especially mutual funds) are public information, this issue can be studied scientifically. Numerous researchers, using various samples and various time periods, have done just that, and the conclusion is inescapable: *Professionals do not beat the market.* This is true in two senses. First, professionals as a group do not outperform the market, except for occasional very short periods. Second, while individual professionally managed funds do sometimes beat the market, they don't do it with any consistency. Different funds do well at different times, and the pattern is like one governed purely by chance—random.

The simplest way to illustrate the performance of professionals is just to tabulate fund returns, something that researchers do frequently. Typical is a survey commissioned by *Consumer Reports* in 1985. This survey studied 289 stock mutual funds over five years, from 1980 through 1984. Of those funds, only 63 outperformed the S&P 500 over that period.

Other studies, made over reasonably long periods, have shown similar results, not only for mutual funds but also for pension funds, college endowment funds, and the like. A monotonous patterns exists: Year after year, about 70 to 80 percent of professionally managed funds fail to equal the performance of the S&P 500.

Returns are related to risk, however, and so a simple tabulation of returns is not adequate for evaluating fund performance. Even so, other research demonstrates that fund performance on a risk-adjusted basis is not much better. The most extensive study was conducted by Michael Jensen in the late 1960s. He tracked the performance of 115 mutual funds from 1955 through 1964, as well as the performance of 56 of these funds for which data was available from 1945 through 1954. Jensen adjusted the funds' returns to account for differing risk levels, using a measure called *beta*, which we will explore in detail later.

Jensen found that the funds' performance was clearly related to the riskiness of their portfolios, but that, on a risk-adjusted basis, the funds as a group underperformed the market by just under 1 percent per year. Their expenses aside, they almost exactly matched the market. The funds did not all perform equally, of course, but there was no statistical evidence that any of the funds had achieved superior performance not attributable to chance.

Jensen also confirmed the inconsistency of fund results by investigating how funds that had outperformed the market in one or more periods fared later (see Table 6.1). He found that past successful performance had no predictive value. No matter how many consecutive years a fund had outperformed the market, its chances of doing so for another year were roughly 50-50.

These odds are similar to those involved in tossing coins or rolling dice. A large number of people, playing for a long time, will inevitably produce some long runs. Thus, in Las Vegas, a player may make 12 straight passes at the craps table. To the other players, this is a miracle, because they know that the odds against any one player doing this are astronomical. The casino operator, however, who watches millions of players and billions of throws of the dice, merely sees the laws of chance and probability in action.

In various forms, Jensen's research has been duplicated by others, who have covered different portfolios and different periods, long and short, recent and distant. The results are always similar: Adjusted for risk, and before their costs are deducted, professionally managed portfolios as a group roughly match the market, at best. Moreover, individual portfolio managers achieve results that can be explained almost entirely by the laws of chance.

STILL MORE?

Having discussed the weak and semi-strong forms of the efficient market hypothesis, let's consider the *strong form.* It states that no information of

TABLE 6.1 Conditional Probability of Superior Performance 115 Mutual Funds, 1955–1964 Risk-Adjusted Returns

Number of Consecutive Years Outperforming S&P 500 Prior to Year t	Number of Occurrences	Probability (in Percentages) of Outperforming S&P 500 in Year t
1	574	50.4
2	312	52.0
3	161	53.4
4	79	55.8
5	41	46.4
6	17	35.3
7	4	25.0

SOURCE: Michael C. Jensen, "Risk, the Pricing of Capital Assets, and the Evaluation of Investment Portfolios," *The Journal of Business,* April 1969.

any kind, public or private, will help investors achieve superior returns. Will this extension of the theory hold up under scrutiny? Hardly. A great deal of evidence suggests that corporate insiders (officers, directors) achieve excess returns. Therefore, nonpublic information is valuable. Unfortunately, it is difficult to become an insider.

THE VALUE OF ANALYSIS

In Chapter 5, we faced a difficult proposition: Market efficiency is assumed to result from the analytical efforts of competing investors, but analysts are not very accurate forecasters. We can reconcile this apparent contradiction if we know that accuracy is not the prerequisite of efficiency. What matters is that investors respond to new information in an unbiased way. The real issue is not whether analysts make errors, but whether their errors are systematically one-sided. Let's return to an earlier example, the stock-split study, to understand this point.

That study had an additional hypothesis: that investors interpreted a stock split as a sign that a dividend increase was coming (splits are, in fact, leading indicators of dividend increases, which are often announced simultaneously with announcements of splits). The research showed that stocks with dividend increases did have a very slight tendency to outperform the market during the first year after splitting. Stocks in which the expectation of increases went unfulfilled had a more pronounced tendency to underperform in the year following a split.

This pattern makes sense. Investors apparently know that the odds favor dividend increases, and confirmation causes only marginal upward revaluation. But the failure to raise dividends means that expectations were wrong, and investors become disenchanted as the months go by. What is most important is that expectations be unbiased, even though they are wrong. As we have seen, for all splitting stocks *taken together*, there is no tendency for either superior or inferior performance afterward. Apparently, the market correctly estimates the probability of dividend increases. It is true that for some stocks, the expectation of such increases will prove wrong, and in that sense the analysis can be thought to be inaccurate. The market can be efficient, however, even when analysis is inaccurate, if the inaccuracies are not consistently one-sided.

WHERE ARE WE NOW?

The test of any theory is its ability to describe, explain, and make sense of reality. The efficient market hypothesis tells us that the stock market is so competitive and its participants so well informed that there are no consistent opportunities to reap excess returns by using publicly available information. Returns in excess of the market return result only from assuming higher risks or from good luck.

There is strong evidence to support this idea. Stock prices seem to follow a random walk over time, and studies have shown that the market responds very rapidly to new information. Indeed, most news actually seems to be anticipated, whether by ongoing analysis or by insider trading. Researchers looked high and low for market-beating strategies that used publicly available information. This search was notably fruitless, especially when the costs of implementing the strategies were considered.

Most important, we have seen that the efficient market theory explains the most vexing and perplexing truth in the market: The professionals don't win. For all their advantages, they can't beat the market.

The logical explanation for all these phenomena is that the market can't be beaten. It is too efficient.

THE REVOLUTION

Both the theory and the evidence of stock market efficiency have convinced a lot of sophisticated people. Many institutional fund sponsors and executives—not the people who manage the portfolios and select the stocks, but the people who hire the managers—saw the light. Something finally explained the managers' generally mediocre returns, as well as why a particular portfolio manager or strategist can be so hot one period and cold the next. Sponsors and executives realized that they didn't need to switch investment advisors; they needed to change strategies. If the market cannot be beaten, then why pay hefty management fees and trading commissions for a doomed effort? If active investment strategies don't and can't work, adopt passive ones. If you can't beat the market, why not join it?

Thus were the famous (or infamous) index funds created. Mutual funds and institutional portfolios were set up to match the S&P 500 index exactly—an easy task, with the aid of a computer. The 500 stocks are held in proportion to their individual market values, and dividends are reinvested the same way. The only trading required is to invest newly arrived money or liquidate to meet redemptions. Otherwise, the only activity comes when Standard and Poor's occasionally replaces a stock in the index.

Professional investing was revolutionized. At the end of 1986, the largest institutional equity-fund manager was Wells Fargo Investment Advisors, managing a total of more than $60 billion. Next came Bankers Trust and the College Retirement Equities Fund. These are all index fund specialists, and they consistently outperform most traditional, actively managed portfolios. Wells Fargo's president, Fred Grauer, puts the case for indexing succinctly: "There aren't that many mispriced securities anymore" (Anders, 1987, p. 1). Standard & Poor's estimated that at the end of 1986, $150 billion was invested in index funds based on the S&P 500.

Not everyone has converted to index investing, of course, not even everyone who subscribes to the efficient market theory, but there is a second, broader part of the revolution. In an efficient market, the primary factor in determining investment results is not stock selection but risk management. Today, institutional investing and its evaluation are both based on an explicit recognition of the relationship between risk and return. As a result, an entire industry has sprung up to measure and evaluate the risk-and-return characteristics of professionally managed institutional funds. The principles derived from the efficient market hypothesis have become the cornerstone of modern investing.

THE CONVERSION

The theory that the market is efficient (and thus unbeatable) is not universally accepted, of course. Millions of amateur investors, as well as a good many professionals, continue to believe they can consistently beat the market, even on a risk-adjusted basis. All the major brokerage houses still employ technical analysts and publish their opinions. Fundamental analysis is still alive and well, too, and professional security analysts number in the thousands. Subscription advisory services, both technical and fundamental, seem to steadily proliferate. This is all to the good, in a way: The market could not be efficient without it.

No market is perfectly competitive, and no one seriously proposes that the stock market is perfectly efficient. Moreover, research has demonstrated some actual areas of inefficiency. The real question is whether the market is *efficient enough* to make traditional investment approaches pointless.

The answer may be a matter of opinion, but, as always, some people's opinions deservedly carry more weight than others. Paul Samuelson, Nobel Prize-winning economist, has expressed his conclusions succinctly: "A respect for evidence compels me to incline toward the hypothesis that most portfolio decision makers should go out of business" (p. 18). He was merciless in his appraisal of skeptics: "The sad truth is that it is precisely those who disagree most with the hypothesis of efficient market pricing of stocks...who *are least able to understand the analysis needed to test that hypothesis*" (p. 18). Putting his money where his mouth was, Samuelson announced that he was investing in index funds and suggested that others do the same.

Ivory-tower types are not the only ones who have come to accept the theory of an efficient market. Benjamin Graham is considered the father of security analysis. In a long, illustrious, and highly profitable investing career, he set out the basic principles of stock valuation in a detailed and rigorous fashion. With David Dodd, he wrote the classic text *Security Analysis* in 1934. New editions of this work appeared regularly for three decades and had enormous impact on the professional investment community. Using Graham's methods, many of his students and protégés went on to great success. In short, Graham was the very model of a successful, value-oriented investor—a Wall Street legend. Yet Graham was also well aware of the profound changes taking place on Wall Street in the availability of both information and analysis, and he recognized the implications of those changes. He understood that the market was becoming more open and more competitive. Thus Graham, the father of analysis, was moved to state in 1976:

> I am no longer an advocate of elaborate techniques of security analysis in order to find superior value opportunities. This was a rewarding activity, say, 40 years ago, when "Graham and Dodd" was first published; but the situation has changed . . . [today] I doubt whether such extensive efforts will generate sufficiently superior selections to justify their costs. . .I'm on the side of the "efficient market" school of thought [quoted in Ellis, 1976].

It is difficult to imagine a more significant conversion or endorsement than this one.

Part Three
Risk, Reward, and You

7

Risk: The Price of
Market Success

Investing in stocks is risky; experience, if nothing else, has convinced investors of that. Risk is simply the price you must pay to seek the exceptional rewards that are at least potentially available in the market. Risk is the entry fee for the Wall Street tournament.

All investors pay lip service to the idea of risk, but few understand what risk really is, where it comes from, how it relates to returns, and how it can be controlled and managed. The typical investor says, "Yes, I know that stocks are risky. Big deal! What should I buy Monday morning?"

Well, it turns out that risk *is* a very big deal. It's the most important factor in investment management and success. If the market is efficient, risk is all that matters. It's the only thing investors need to consider and make decisions about. Understanding risk is essential. Fortunately, it is also easy.

THE CONCEPT OF RISK

The essential characteristic of a risky endeavor or situation is not the possibility of loss; it is that the result—the outcome—is uncertain. A situation can be risky even if there is no possibility of loss. For example, suppose you were offered an investment that had only two possible outcomes: a 10 percent gain or a 20 percent gain. This would be a risky investment because the outcome is uncertain even though you couldn't suffer a loss.

We deal constantly with uncertainty in our day-to-day lives. Almost nothing we do has a totally predictable result; we are continually taking risks, because we are always dealing with uncertain outcomes. What are my chances of winning, and what will be the reward? What are my chances of losing, and what will be the penalty?

Let's consider how we make decisions. In most situations, we face one or more possible positive outcomes and one or more negative ones. We may not normally see decisions this way, but what we actually do is determine the possible outcomes and estimate their likelihood: We calculate both the risk and the expected return from a situation or an activity. In most daily situations, our calculations are instinctive and intuitive, but make them we do, because they are implicit in decision making whenever there is uncertainty. Risk is simply the manifestation of uncertainty in real-life situations.

MEASURING RISK

When most of us think of risky situations, we think in terms of only two possible results. A coin comes up heads or tails. If I exceed the speed limit, I'll either get caught or I won't. In such situations, thinking about risk is simple, even if calculating it may not be.

In investing, however, the situation is different. The range of possible outcomes is unlimited. You may lose your entire investment or gain an unlimited amount. In the market, calculating your chances of simply losing money is an inadequate approach to risk. After all, a 50 percent chance of losing 10 percent of your investment is far different from a 50 percent chance of losing half of it. We need a definition and a measure of risk that will encompass the full spectrum of possible outcomes. We must understand the concept of *expected return.*

Expected return is not the return we are hoping for, nor is it even the most likely return. Expected return is more like the average return. More precisely, it is the weighted average return—all possible returns (positive or negative) weighted by the probabilities that they will occur. In determining expected return, we give a return that is highly unlikely less weight than one that is more likely.

For example, suppose that an investment has three possible outcomes: returns of 30 percent, 20 percent, and 10 percent. The respective probabilities of these outcomes are 20 percent, 30 percent, and 50 percent. The most likely return is 10 percent. The simple average return is 20 percent, but the expected return is 17 percent. The calculation is as follows:

$$\text{expected return} = .30(.20) + .20(.30) + .10(.50)$$
$$= .06 + .06 + .05$$
$$= .17$$

Each possible return has simply been weighted by its likelihood of occurring.

In this example, the expected return does not match any of the possible returns, and this outcome is quite common when there is a limited number of possible outcomes. In real-life investing, of course, the range of possible outcomes is continuous.

Risk is uncertainty, but what is uncertainty? Simple: It is the variability of possible or actual returns. Suppose I offered you two possible investments, A and B. Each investment has only two possible outcomes, both of which are equally likely (each has a 50-50 chance). In A, you will have either a 40 percent gain or a 10 percent loss. In B, you will have either a 60 percent gain or a 30 percent loss. Both investments have the same expected return, 15 percent:

$$A = .40(.50) - .10(.50) = .15$$
$$B = .60(.50) - .30(.50) = .15$$

B is riskier because the dispersion of possible returns (the variability) is greater for B than for A.

When there are only a few possible returns, uncertainty (risk) can be described in this simple way, just by listing the outcomes and their likelihood. With a large number of possible returns, however, this process gets a bit unwieldy. With an infinite number of potential outcomes, as in the stock market, it is impossible. Fortunately, a common statistical measure covers the situation: the *standard deviation*, simply a mathematical description of how much variability there is in a group of figures.

Figure 7.1 illustrates the idea. It shows a series of monthly returns for two different investments. The average return is the same for each, but #2 is clearly much more consistent than #1; that is, the returns do not vary as much. The standard deviation of the returns would give us a specific measure of the variability of each investment's performance, as well as an expression of the degree of uncertainty about each one's expected results. To put it another way, the standard deviation provides an estimate of how much divergence there is likely to be between actual return and expected return. It is not only a useful measure of investment risk; for most purposes, it is *the* measure of investment risk.

Figure 7.2 shows this concept in a different way. Suppose we tracked the returns on an investment over many periods and plotted the frequency of returns in different ranges. For example, we might record monthly returns for five years and plot how many of the 60 results were between 0 and 1 percent, how many between 1 percent and 2 percent, how many between 0 and − 1 percent, and so on. The result would probably have a pattern similar to that in Figure 7.2.

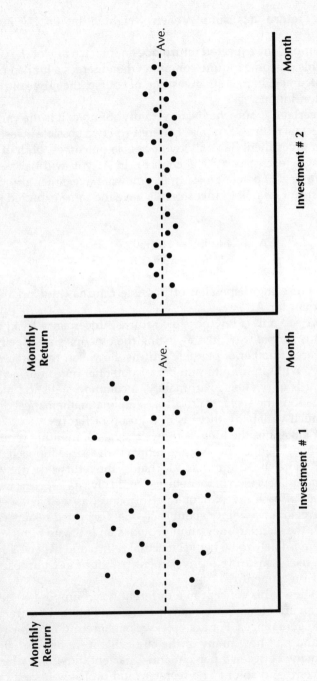

FIGURE 7.1 Hypothetical monthly investment returns

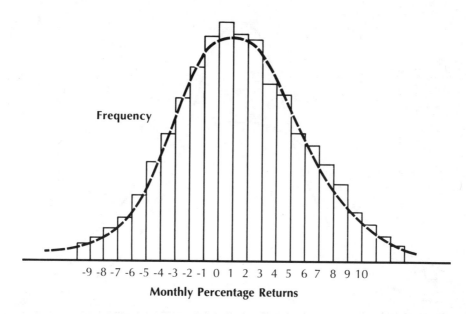

Frequency

Monthly Percentage Returns

-9 -8 -7 -6 -5 -4 -3 -2 -1 0 1 2 3 4 5 6 7 8 9 10

FIGURE 7.2 Hypothetical monthly investment returns

Two things are apparent. First, the figure shows the dispersion of returns from the investment. For a different investment, the general pattern might look similar, but the degree of dispersion would be different. Second, the pattern probably looks familiar: It is the bell curve that you may have learned in school. I have actually superimposed an idealized curve on the figure. This curve is what would result if we had an infinite number of observations and infinitely small return intervals.

Let's see how standard deviation relates to this pattern. If we assume that returns follow this bell curve, then the standard deviation is a single number that describes the variability of returns (riskiness) for the particular investment. In Figure 7.3, two bell curves are shown, representing two different investments. Both curves have the same center, indicating that the expected returns are equal. Investment #2, however, has much greater dispersion; that is, the returns are more variable, less certain, riskier. How much riskier? The respective standard deviations would give us a mathematical measure of each investment's riskiness.

You will seldom need to calculate a standard deviation, but the concept is so important in statistical research of all kinds that we should explore it a bit.

The standard deviation of a group of observations is calculated as follows: (1) Calculate the mean (average) of the observations; (2) calculate

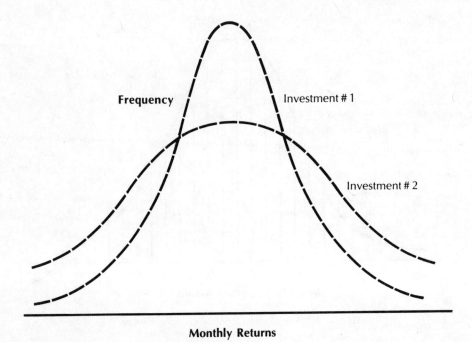

FIGURE 7.3 Hypothetical monthly returns—Two alternative investments

the difference between each individual observation and the mean; (3) square each deviation; (4) take the mean of the squared deviations; and (5) calculate the square root of this mean. We average the squared deviations, and then we take the square root of the result.*

Standard deviation has three important uses for investors. First, we can use it to compare the riskiness of alternative investments—for example, the different investments we looked at in Chapter 2 (Treasury Bills, long-term government and corporate bonds, and common stocks, as represented by the S&P 500).** Second, standard deviation lets us measure risk in relation to average or expected return. Third, and most important, we can use

---

*It might seem easier just to average the deviations themselves, rather than get involved in taking squares and square roots. The reason why the calculation is done as described is very complicated mathematically, but it comes down to this: Standard deviation has mathematical properties that are indespensable to statistical research, properties that would not exist for simpler measures.

**Standard deviation figures for T-Bills are somewhat misleading. That the annual returns vary does imply risk, but T-Bills mature in a year or less. Therefore, if held to maturity, T-Bills are riskless on an *annual* basis. They are risky in that we don't know what *future* annual returns will be.

standard deviation to determine the probability of a particular range of results occurring, at least if we assume that investment returns are normally distributed along the bell curve. Approximately 67 percent of all outcomes (returns) will fall within one standard deviation of the average, and 95 percent will fall within two standard deviations.

Thus, once we know the mean and the standard deviation, we have an important insight into the market's behavior. For example, we saw in Table 2.1 that, over a 61-year period, the mean annual return for the S&P 500 was 12.1 percent. The standard deviation was not shown, but it can be calculated as 21.2 percent. This figure implies that two-thirds of the annual returns should fall between 33.3 percent (the mean plus one standard deviation) and −9.1 percent (the mean less one standard deviation). In other words, about one-sixth of the annual returns can be expected to exceed 33.3 percent, and one-sixth will be less than −9.1 percent. This pattern is illustrated in Figure 7.4.

Not surprisingly, research shows that stock returns do not follow perfectly symmetrical distribution patterns, but the actual patterns are symmetrical enough for the standard deviation to be a very useful statistic, providing us with real insights into the behavior we can expect from various investments. It particularly enables us to study the performance of different investors and strategies. I have said before that a pattern of the results of

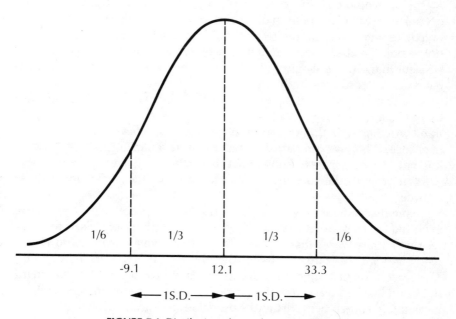

FIGURE 7.4 Distribution of annual returns—S&P 500

professional investors would be essentially indistinguishable from a pattern governed by chance. Standard deviation makes such an analysis possible.

John G. McDonald's study of the 1972 market illustrates the method. McDonald created 100 equally weighted portfolios of 20 stocks each. The stocks in each portfolio were chosen at random from a sample of 912 stocks. For the year, the mean return for these 912 stocks was 10.5 percent. The 20-stock portfolios had various returns, of course, and the standard deviation of portfolio returns was 7.6 percent. Thus, about 33 of the portfolios could be expected to have returns either of more than 18.1 percent or of less than 2.9 percent (the mean plus or minus one standard deviation), and 4 or 5 would show returns either above 25.7 percent or below − 4.7 percent (the mean plus or minus two standard deviations). These results, by the nature of how the portfolios were constructed, would be due entirely to luck.

Suppose now that we were examining actual 20-stock portfolios assembled by 100 actual professional portfolio managers, who were using all their skills and analytical tools. Suppose further that the results looked just like those described above. One or two managers would achieve returns of 25 percent or more, while the market was returning only 10 percent. We can be sure that these managers would trumpet their success far and wide (probably abetted by an unwitting press). Thousands of investors would be convinced that the superior results stemmed from superior skill. Meanwhile, the poor souls whose portfolios underperformed the market by 15 percentage points would be losing clients right and left. We know this is nonsense, of course, because the pattern of results would be exactly the same as if the outcomes were random; the results could reasonably be attributed to luck, not to skill. Further, they would be exactly what we would expect from an efficient market. We would not know this, however, without using standard deviation to analyze them.

Standard deviation as a measure of risk and variability is indispensable to understanding what is really going on in the market. We need it to determine whether something we have observed is significant or just a matter of chance. When we compare different investments, investors, or strategies, it is not enough for us to know what their respective average returns are. We can draw useful conclusions only if we know the variability of those returns.

Note that standard deviation measures deviations both below and above expected or average returns. Most of us tend to think of risk in terms of results that are worse than those we expect. We've all heard of downside risk, but what about upside risk? (Now, there's a risk we can all live with!) The reason for including both deviations is simple practicality. Standard deviation takes into account all variations, by the pure mathematics of the measure. No other measure has the desirable statistical and analytical properties of this one, and that's why we use it. Besides, if the distribution of returns is reasonably symmetrical, the positive surprises will simply mirror the negative ones.

RISK AVERSION

Suppose I offered you the choice of two $100 investments, A and B. With A, there are two possible outcomes: no return on your investment (it will still be worth $100 at the end of the period), or a $100 return (you will double your money). There is an 85 percent chance of the $100 gain and a 15 percent chance of no gain. The alternative investment, B, has only one possible outcome: an $80 gain. Which do you choose?

I have presented this hypothetical choice to groups of investors, and the overwhelming majority opts for investment B, despite the fact that the expected return from A, $85, is greater than the expected return of $80 from B. Why do investors make this choice? The return from B is certain, and the return from A is uncertain. In other words, A is risky. Investors are unwilling to assume the risks associated with A, even to gain the higher expected return.*

In choosing investment B, investors are demonstrating *risk aversion*, a central concept in investment analysis and management. This is really an assumption, but it corresponds to most investors' behavior. The concept is simple enough: Investors prefer certainty to uncertainty; they dislike risk; and, faced with two investments that have the same expected returns, they will choose the one with lower risk. This doesn't mean they will not take risks, but they will expect to be compensated for risk by higher expected returns. In the example we have just considered, the expected returns from A apparently are not high enough to compensate for the risk involved, at least not for most people. Suppose that instead of an 85 percent chance of a $100 gain, investment A offered an 85 percent chance of a $150 gain, a $200 gain, and so on. As expected returns rise, more and more people will choose A; they will decide that the higher expected returns justify the risk. The crossover point, of course, will be different for different people, depending on their individual ideas about risk and reward.

It is easy to find examples, both hypothetical and real, in which investors make risk-seeking rather than risk-avoiding choices. Risk seeking commonly occurs when small amounts of money are ventured, with a very small chance of a very large return and a very high probability of losing the whole investment. Consider a state lottery. Not only is the risk high; the expected

*Remember that expected return is simply all possible returns weighted by their likelihood; in this case, expected return A = $100(.85) + $0(.15) = $85.

return is also negative.* Yet millions of people buy tickets. This risk-seeking behavior has to do with what economists call the utility of wealth: The perceived value of a large windfall, no matter how unlikely, overwhelms the cost of a losing ticket. Buying lottery tickets may not be smart, but it is not necessarily irrational.

Despite investors' occasional risk-seeking behavior, research and experience suggest that most investors are risk-averse most of the time. They will not take on additional risk without the prospect of higher rewards (in the form of higher expected returns). This behavior is clearly shown in the figures from Table 2.1. Stocks are riskier than bonds, which in turn are riskier than T-Bills. The average returns (as good a proxy as we have for expected returns) correspond to this risk distribution, compensating investors who are willing to accept more risk. If investors were not risk-averse, no one would buy T-Bills.

RISK AND REWARD: TAKING IT PERSONALLY

If people tend to be risk-averse, they are certainly not equally risk-averse. Some will keep their money nowhere but in insured savings accounts or T-Bills, and others seem almost reckless in their investments. No attitude toward risk is superior to another. Risk tolerance is just a reflection of personality, circumstances, and experience. This is hardly news, but some of the implications are important.

It is clear that risk taking is rewarded, at least over reasonably long periods of time. Joe, who is willing to accept the risks of stock ownership, will generally have higher returns than Sam, who demands the safety of T-Bills. Joe will make more money. Since money is so highly valued in our society, it is easy to fall into the trap of saying that Joe is a superior investor. Not so: Joe is simply a different investor. Sam has the security of never seeing the value of his investments decline; Joe trades that security for the probability of higher average returns. He reaps higher returns because he accepts higher risks—greater uncertainty.

To judge the relative performances of different investors or the relative merits of different investments, we have to look at more than how much money they make. We must consider what it took to make that money— how much risk was assumed. The general principle works like this: Suppose we are comparing two alternative investments (or investors). If A has higher returns than B, as well as equal or lower risk, then A is said to dominate B. Similarly, if the two investments have equal returns, but A has

*Expected return is negative because only about half the ticket revenues are paid out as prizes.

lower risk, then, again, A dominates B. If A has both higher returns and higher risk, then the situation is inconclusive. The decision depends largely on personal judgment of the trade-off between risk and return.

Any venture in which the expected returns are positive can be considered a good bet (at least if we ignore the time value of money), but that doesn't mean that every good bet is a good investment. First, a good bet may not be a good investment if the size of the investment is excessive. Getting slightly better than even odds on the toss of a coin would make for a good bet, but wagering your entire net worth on one toss would be a foolish investment. Second, a good bet may not be a good investment if it involves unnecessary risk, more than must be taken to achieve the expected return. You can eliminate much risk without reducing your expected returns. Also, while some stock market risks are rewarded, others are not; we need to know which are which. The key to success in the risk/return game is not to minimize or maximize risk, but to manage it. In the next two chapters, we will see how.

(On the off chance that you may actually want to calculate standard deviations—perhaps to analyze your golf scores—formulas and examples are on the two following pages.)

CALCULATING STANDARD DEVIATION

The formula for calculating the standard deviation of a group of n observations is

$$s = \sqrt{\frac{\sum_{i=1}^{n}(x_i - \bar{x})^2}{n}}$$

where $\bar{x}$ is the mean.

This formula corresponds to the verbal description given earlier: averaging the squared deviations and taking the square root of the result.

To illustrate, suppose we have the following 12 observations:

$$15, 10, 12, 8, 7, 11, 20, 5, 14, 17, 16, 12$$

$$\bar{x} = 12.25$$

Using the formula, we get

x_i	$x_i - \bar{x}$	$(x_i - \bar{x})^2$
15	2.75	7.5625
10	-2.25	5.0625
12	-.25	.0625
8	-4.25	18.0625
7	-5.25	27.5625
11	-1.25	1.5625
20	7.75	60.0625
5	-7.25	52.5625
14	1.75	3.0625
17	4.75	22.5625
16	3.75	14.0625
12	-.25	.0625
		212.2500

$$\bar{x} = \frac{147}{12} = 12.25$$

$$s = \sqrt{\frac{212.25}{12}}$$

$$= 4.2 \text{ (approx.)}$$

Actually calculating standard deviation from this formula is a time-consuming process, because you must calculate each of the deviations. Fortunately, there is an equivalent formula that is simpler to compute:

$$s = \frac{1}{n}\sqrt{n \cdot \sum_{i=1}^{n} x_i^2 - \left(\sum_{i=1}^{n} x_i\right)^2}$$

Using the second formula, we get

x_i	x_i^2
15	225
10	100
12	144
8	64
7	49
11	121
20	400
5	25
14	196
17	289
16	256
12	144
147	2013

$$s = \frac{1}{12}\sqrt{12(2013) - (147)^2}$$

$$= \frac{1}{12}\sqrt{2547}$$

$$= 4.2 \text{ (approx.)}$$

The second set of calculations is much simpler, but there is still an easier way. Many personal computer spreadsheet programs have a standard deviation function built in. Essentially all you have to do is enter the raw data. Other programs at least have a square-root function, and so it is easy to set up these programs to calculate standard deviation.

8

Diversification:
Safety in Numbers

DOUBLE JEOPARDY

There are two basic types of risk in the stock market, because how a stock performs depends on two basic types of influences. The first is the particular news, events, and analyses relevant to the stock. These will affect how investors perceive the stock's outlook and thus its value.

The second influence is the effect of the overall market trend. Some developments (e.g., changing interest rates and levels of economic activity) affect the whole market, increasing or decreasing the general value of stocks. If you own a stock, risk and return are associated with holding it, but risk and return are also just part of being in the market, regardless of which stocks you hold.

These two basic elements of risk go by several different names. Here, we will use *market risk* to mean the risk associated with the market as a whole and *specific risk* to mean the risk associated with particular stocks.*

Diversification of Specific Risk

In Chapter 7, we looked at a hypothetical investment that had only two possible outcomes: a 40 percent gain or a 10 percent loss. Both results were

*Many academics and investment professionals use the terms *market* and *nonmarket risk*; others use *systematic* and *unsystematic risk*. These terms are exactly parallel to ours. *Specific risk* can also apply to stock groups, as well as to individual stocks. For example, oil stocks tend to move together because they are subject to many of the same influences.

equally likely, and the expected return was 15 percent. Now let's consider a portfolio of two stocks, each having these same characteristics (the 50 percent chance of a 40 percent gain, etc.). Let's assume that an equal amount of money is invested in each one. There are four possible outcomes:

1. Both stocks lose 10 percent (portfolio loses 10 percent)
2. Both stocks gain 40 percent (portfolio gains 40 percent)
3. Stock A gains 40 percent, stock B loses 10 percent (portfolio gains 15 percent)
4. Stock A loses 10 percent, stock B gains 40 percent (portfolio gains 15 percent)

Each of these results is equally likely (each has a 25 percent chance), but outcomes 3 and 4 are identical. The expected return is 15 percent, the same as in our example with one stock.* Now, though, the chances of losing 10 percent or gaining 40 percent are only 25 percent each, instead of 50 percent. We have reduced risk *without reducing our expected return*.

If we expand this example to include three stocks, the probabilities of an overall return at the extremes of 40 percent and −10 percent are further reduced to 12.5 percent each. This time, eight possible results are equally probable:

1. All three stocks lose 10 percent (portfolio loses 10 percent)
2. All three stocks gain 40 percent (portfolio gains 40 percent)
3. A gains 40 percent, B gains 40 percent, C loses 10 percent (portfolio gains 23.3 percent)
4. A gains 40 percent, B loses 10 percent, C loses 10 percent (portfolio gains 6.7 percent)
5. A gains 40 percent, B loses 10 percent, C gains 40 percent (portfolio gains 23.3 percent)
6. A loses 10 percent, B gains 40 percent, C gains 40 percent (portfolio gains 23.3 percent)
7. A loses 10 percent, B loses 10 percent, C gains 40 percent (portfolio gains 6.7 percent)
8. A loses 10 percent, B gains 40 percent, C loses 10 percent (portfolio gains 6.7 percent)

*Expected return = − .10(.25) + .40(.25) + .15(.50)
                 = − .025 + .10 + .075
                 = .15

We have reduced risk, again without reducing our expected return. The risk reduction is obvious, but it is also reflected in standard deviation (SD) figures. The SD for the one-stock portfolio is .25; for the two-stock portfolio, .177; and for the three-stock portfolio, .144.

This is a simple, pure example of the effects of *diversification*, our primary tool for reducing and managing risk. An unstated assumption made these results possible: We assumed that the stocks moved independently of each other and that whether one stock goes up or down does not affect the outcome probabilities of any other stock.

Let's suppose now that the stocks do not move independently. Whatever determines whether stock A rises 40 percent or falls 10 percent will also determine the same behavior for B and C. In this situation, diversification will not reduce risk at all, because the stocks are perfectly dependent: All three stocks will go up 40 percent or all three will decline 10 percent, and so a portfolio composed of these three is really no different from a one-stock portfolio. Diversification in this case has no impact on either risk or return.*

We can diversify to reduce risk only when our stocks' movements do not display perfect positive correlation. If all stocks were completely independent or negatively correlated, we could use enough diversification to reduce our risk (variability of returns) to essentially zero. The fact is, though, stocks are neither completely dependent nor completely independent.

Diversifiable Risk

Diversification is only a tool for reducing the specific risk associated with holding individual stocks or stock groups. Specific risk is also called *diversifiable risk*, because diversification can reduce or eliminate it.

Figure 8.1 illustrates this idea. Portfolio size (number of stocks) is shown on the horizontal axis, and total portfolio riskiness (standard deviation of returns) is on the vertical axis. The curved line shows the amount of risk for different sizes of portfolios. Risk declines as the number of stocks in the portfolio increases (this is diversification at work), but what is reduced is only specific risk. No matter how many stocks you include, your total portfolio risk will never drop below the dotted line, which represents market risk. You can eliminate market risk only by getting out of the market altogether.

---

*The relevant mathematical term is *correlation coefficient*, a measure that ranges from -1.0 to 1.0. If two variables are completely independent, the correlation coefficient will be 0.0. If they are perfectly correlated, it will be 1.0 or -1.0, depending on whether they move in the same or opposite directions. Our example is based on positive correlation.

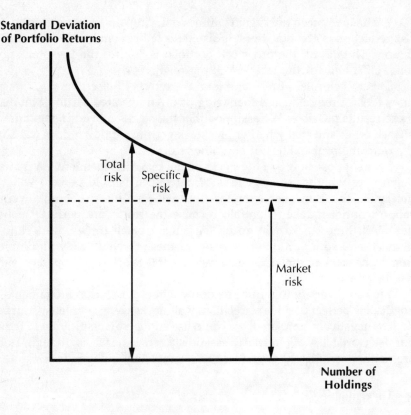

FIGURE 8.1 Specific and market risk

HOW MUCH DIVERSIFICATION?

Diversification is a wonderful tool for risk-averse investors, because it can reduce risk without reducing expected returns. Like most good things, however, it isn't free. Diversified portfolios cost more in commissions. The total commission on 100 shares each of two stocks will be more than the commission on 200 shares of one of them (and if we buy odd lots of fewer than 100 shares, commission costs soar). The more stocks we have, the more records we have to keep, and the more research we may have to conduct. Diversification costs money, time, and effort. That's why it's important to know how much is necessary. Happily, research shows that a small amount goes a very long way.

To understand the impact of diversification, look at Figure 8.2. It is identical to Figure 8.1, except that it isn't hypothetical. It is based on actual research and covers the monthly returns of 200 New York Stock Exchange

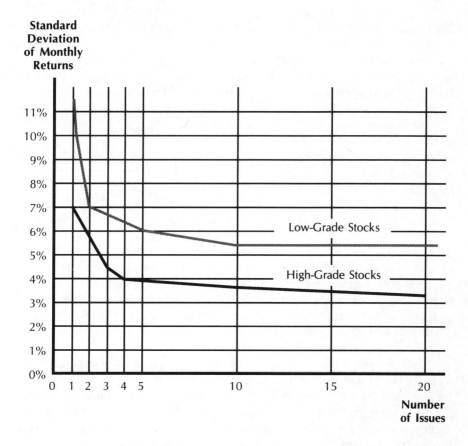

FIGURE 8.2 Risk and portfolio size
SOURCE: Adapted from Wagner and Lau, 1971.

issues over ten years. As in Figure 8.1, total portfolio risk is shown on the vertical axis, with portfolio size on the horizontal axis.

The effect of diversification is obvious and dramatic. We reduce risk very rapidly as we increase the number of stocks in a portfolio, but the benefits of diversification come largely as we move from 1 stock to about 10. Beyond 15, further diversification brings only small gains. As you can see, you don't need a very large portfolio to reduce risk dramatically.

Figure 8.2 shows risk for *low-grade* and *high-grade* stocks. The distinction is based on Standard and Poor's quality ratings, an assessment of stocks similar to S&P's bond ratings. A high-grade stock tends to be associated with a large, well-established company that has a history of profitability, strong balance sheets, consistent payment of dividends, and so on. In this figure, high-grade stocks have quality ratings of B+ or higher, while low-grade stocks are rated B or lower.

At any level of diversification, the low-grade group is riskier, but this does not mean that diversification is less effective for this group. On the contrary, the shapes of the two curves are almost identical, because the gains from diversification are similar. The reason for the difference in risk levels is simply that lower-grade stocks generally have greater variability of returns—they are more volatile. We saw in Figure 8.1 that the risk line approaches but will not cross the dotted line representing market risk. What we see in Figure 8.2 is that low-grade stocks have more market risk than high-grade stocks. This kind of risk cannot be diversified away.

Still another view of diversification effects is presented in Figure 8.3, based on the same data used in the previous figure. Here, portfolio size is related to R-squared (R^2). As we have already noted, the statistical measure that indicates how reliably two variables tend to move together is the correlation coefficient, which has the symbol R in mathematics. R^2 shows what proportion of the movement of one of the variables is explained by the other. In this case, R^2 measures how closely the portfolios track the market—what proportion of a portfolio's total risk is market risk. For example, an R^2 of .70 means that 70 percent of the portfolio's total risk is market risk, and the remaining 30 percent is specific risk.

Since the result (and the goal) of diversification is to reduce specific risk, R^2 is a good measure of how effective diversification is. Figure 8.3 confirms what we saw earlier: For individual stocks (one-stock portfolios), R^2 is about .30, indicating that market risk (the risk associated with the overall market) is only about 30 percent of total portfolio risk. The rest is associated with the particular stock.

As we increase the size of the portfolio, R^2 also increases rapidly. In portfolios of 15 stocks, it is around .85, and specific risk has been reduced to about 15 percent of total risk. (Again, beyond about 15 stocks, gains from further diversification come very slowly.)

R^2 shows proportions, not amounts. The *proportion* of market risk goes up as we diversify, because the *amount* of specific risk goes down. (The *amount* of market risk remains constant because it is not affected by diversification.)

IN A NUTSHELL

Understanding and appreciating what diversification can and cannot achieve is essential to successful risk management. Perhaps you saw the episode of the TV sitcom "Taxi" in which the cab company shuts down and the staff has to find other work. The dispatcher, the scurrilous Louie DePalma,

R-Squared

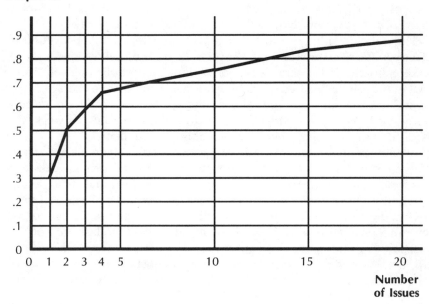

FIGURE 8.3. Correlation and portfolio size
SOURCE: Ibid.

becomes a stockbroker. In one scene, he calls one of his firm's clients and says, "I've been looking over your account, and I see you have all your money in one stock. You need diversification." The client resists, and Louie sneers, "Well, if you want to bounce around the board with AT&T...." This line got big laughs, but Louie was right. A portfolio consisting of one conservative, blue-chip stock—even AT&T—is usually riskier than one containing a number of so-called risky stocks.

In summary, diversification is an extremely powerful tool for risk reduction, with the early stages of diversification providing the greatest benefits. Increasing a portfolio from 1 to 5 stocks reduces risk enormously. After 15 or so, the benefits of diversification come very slowly and need to be weighed against the costs.*

---

*If this is true, you may wonder why the portfolios of pension funds and mutual funds often contain scores or even hundreds of stocks. In the first place, marginal gains in risk reduction

EFFECTIVE DIVERSIFICATION

In discussing diversification, we have been talking only about the number of stocks in a portfolio. Now let's talk about *effective* diversification.

This concept simply means that if you want to use diversification to reduce specific risk, the stocks in your portfolio must not all respond to every market influence in the same way. For example, a portfolio of 10 oil stocks is not effectively diversified. Each oil stock has some unique characteristics and influences, but there are very strong influences on oil stocks as a group—they tend to move together. For diversification to do its work, the stocks in your portfolio must be reasonably independent.

A fully scientific approach to diversification would require us to do enormous statistical analyses of the relationships among individual stocks and stock groups. There are institutional investment professionals who do just that, statistically determining what are known as *covariances of price movements* between the millions of possible pairs of thousands of stocks, and all so that they can figure out how to make diversification yield the last drop of risk reduction. For most of the rest of us, the seat-of-the-pants approach is quite sufficient. We don't need mainframe computers, just a little common sense, to decide on an appropriate number of stocks and spread them over a broad spectrum of dissimilar industries.

THE OTHER SIDE OF THE COIN

Almost every serious investment professional stresses diversification. After all, if you choose a stock that turns out to be a lemon, it won't ruin your overall investment results. There is safety in numbers.

While it's true that diversification reduces risk, let's remember that risk is the variability of returns, both below and *above* average or expected returns. Diversification increases the likelihood that actual returns will be near expected returns. It reduces the chances of an extremely negative outcome, but it also reduces the chances of an extremely positive one. In risk reduction, we give up big killings to avoid big disasters.

Diversification reduces risk without reducing expected returns. The corollary is that *failure* to diversify will not lead to *higher* expected returns.

can be made from additional diversification. More important, most of these funds are so large that it is impossible to hold, say, two dozen stocks; the funds would have to take impractically large positions in the companies, perhaps large enough to be prohibited by the funds' charters or by law. Finally (to speak more cynically), long lists of stocks may help convince clients that investment managers are working hard and justifying their fees.

The market does not reward diversifiable risk. What kind of risk is rewarded? The only kind left—market risk, the risk in owning stocks generally. Short of abandoning the stock market, this risk cannot be eliminated, but it can be managed and controlled, as we will see in the next chapter.

9

Market Risk

We may doubt Wall Street's ability to produce exceptional profits for investors, but we can't deny its success in producing colorful adages. Here are two of the best: "Don't confuse brains with a bull market" and "When the paddy wagon comes, they take the good girls along with the bad."

LEVELS OF MARKET RISK

When the market moves up, most of the individual stocks move up, and when it falls, most of the stocks fall, too, but they don't all rise and fall at the same rate. Some stocks tend to rise and fall more rapidly than the market, others less.

We have all observed that different stocks seem to have different personalities and behavior patterns in the market. There are glamour stocks that alternately soar and swoon, and conservative issues that seldom seem to budge. The volatile "high fliers" are riskier, in both the intuitive and the technical sense, than their staid blue-chip brothers. What we may not see is that the high fliers have not only higher specific (individual) risk but also higher market risk.

Consider brokerage-house stocks, such as Merrill Lynch. A soaring market raises the valuation of stocks generally, including Merrill Lynch. Rising markets are usually also accompanied by rising volume (more profit for brokers) and by surges in underwriting activity (ditto). In addition, the value of the firm's own investment portfolio is rising (yes, your full-service broker is often your full-fledged competitor). It is not surprising, then, that brokerage-house stocks tend to outperform the market on the upside. In effect, they are leveraged on the market's performance. Since all these things are true in reverse during bear markets, these stocks also tend to perform worse than the market when it is headed south.

Similarly, some stocks tend to move less rapidly than the market (e.g., food, tobacco, and utility stocks). Demand for these products is not very sensitive to the overall economy, and so these stocks are not generally subject to the boom-or-bust syndrome. They tend to fall less than the overall market during bearish periods. As a result, the stocks are often described as *defensive*. Conversely, they tend to underperform the market on the upside.

If individual stocks tend either to exaggerate or to underreflect the market's moves, then they have varying degrees of market risk. Thus, how much market risk you take on is not just a matter of how much money you have in the market; it also depends on what stocks you own. Market risk varies from stock to stock and from industry to industry. It also varies according to the stature of the companies: As we saw in Chapter 8, high-grade stocks carry less market risk than low-grade ones. This phenomenon is logical; in times of pessimism (during a falling market), investors retreat to quality, and in times of optimism they are more adventurous.

BETA

Different stocks respond differently to movements of the market and have different levels of market risk. How can we measure this factor? Fortunately, there is a simple and convenient way: *beta*.

Beta is one of those wonderful mathematical things that start out being esoteric and mysterious (anything with a mathematical formula and Greek letters would be considered mysterious on Wall Street), then become fads, and wind up being misunderstood, oversimplified, and often oversold. Beta is simply a statistical measure for describing a stock's movement in relation to that of the entire market. It is a multiplier that relates return on a stock to return on the market. In other words, it measures a stock's sensitivity to the moves of the market, the amount of market risk in a stock.

Just as stocks have betas, so do portfolios. The beta of a portfolio is simply the betas of the individual stocks, weighted by their importance in the portfolio (i.e., the amount of money invested in each of them; for an illustration of how to calculate portfolio beta, see Chapter 18).

The beta of the market is 1.0, by definition, because the market (which usually means the S&P 500) is the benchmark against which individual stocks are measured. A single stock with a beta of 1.0 moves, on average, at the same percentage rate as the market. A defensive stock moves at a rate slower than the market's. A stock with a beta of 0.8, for example, generally lags market moves by about 20 percent. If the market rises 10 percent, this stock can be expected to rise only 8 percent. An *aggressive* stock—one with a beta of, say, 1.4—tends to exaggerate the market's fluctuations by about 40 percent.*

Where Does Beta Come From?

A stock's beta seems intrinsic, part of the stock's basic personality. But a stock does not come with a label stating its beta; it has to be determined (estimated) by statistical methods. What we have to do is compare the price behavior of the stock with the behavior of the market over many time periods. Then we are able to determine the average relationship.

The key word here is *average*. No stock tracks the market perfectly all the time. For an individual stock, specific (individual) forces are much more significant than market forces. A stock rises and falls for its own reasons, quite apart from the action of the entire market. In calculating beta, we are only getting an average relationship between the stock and the market—a tendency, not a rule. Even if we could predict the action of the market, beta would not be a reliable or accurate predictor of an individual stock's action, because market risk is simply too small a part of the total variability in the returns of individual stocks.

Therefore, beta is not a very complete or reliable measure of a stock's total riskiness or its price behavior. For individual stocks, these are best described by the standard deviation of returns. We must also remember that the calculated beta is only an estimate of the stock's true beta. We calculate beta by observing the past and extrapolating into the future. This is an uncertain proposition; research shows that calculated (i.e., past) beta is not a highly accurate predictor of future beta. Besides, different organizations use different methods for calculating beta. For example, Value Line uses weekly observations covering the previous five years; Merrill Lynch also uses five years of data, but at monthly intervals. The betas that these two organizations (and others) report can differ, often by wide margins.

What Good Is Beta?

Since beta is only marginally accurate, an incomplete and inadequate risk measure for individual stocks, we might be tempted to conclude that it is not very useful or important. That would be a mistake. Beta is a very important risk-management tool if we understand it and use it properly.

---

*Technically, beta relates the excess returns on a stock to the excess returns on the market. Excess returns are actual returns, less the risk-free rate of return—the T-Bill rate. This concept results from the attempt to measure the risk premium in stock returns.

We have already mentioned the Law of Large Numbers. This law simply states that when we have large numbers of observations, errors in individual observations tend to offset each other, so that the accuracy of the average will be a lot greater than the accuracy of individual observations. This is the point with beta, too: Errors in individual beta measurements (both too high and too low) are cancelled out in a *portfolio* of stocks. Moreover, in a well-diversified portfolio, beta's limitations as a risk measure are overcome. Beta measures only market risk, a small part of the total risk of one stock, but market risk is essentially the *only* risk in a diversified portfolio.

Let's clear up what beta is and what it measures. The beta of an individual stock is not its riskiness; it is the amount of risk that the stock *contributes to a diversified portfolio*. The beta of a stock portfolio is the riskiness of the total portfolio in relation to the market.

Once we understand beta, its usefulness becomes apparent. Beta defines the character, the riskiness, of *your* portfolio—the riskiness that you expect or at least hope to be rewarded for.

Just as important, beta provides a basis for comparing the performances of different investors. We noted earlier that one investor can achieve higher returns (and incur higher risk), than another, but that doesn't mean he is a superior or smarter investor. Beta lets us adjust returns for the amount of risk involved, making comparisons possible. This capability is of particular interest to pension fund administrators, who must evaluate prospective investment managers on the basis of past performance. It is also important to researchers studying the stock market.

Our discussion of mutual fund returns in Chapter 6 was based on relating returns to beta. This helped make the academic case for market efficiency, but beta is also useful for individuals who are choosing and using mutual funds. Mutual funds vary enormously in the character and riskiness of their portfolios. *The Individual Investor's Guide to No-Load Mutual Funds*, published annually by the American Association of Individual Investors, lists about 100 common-stock funds. Their 1985 betas ranged from 0.55 to 2.03 (i.e., from about half the risk of the general market to more than twice the risk). When the spread is this great, it is essential for us to judge performance in terms of the amount of risk assumed. Calculating risk-adjusted returns is complicated, tedious, and of doubtful value for most of us. Nevertheless, you should understand the general risk character of any fund or portfolio that you own or think about buying.

What About Alpha?

Beta is the second letter of the Greek alphabet; alpha is the first. Now, what self-respecting academic is going to use beta as the first parameter in a model? Alpha must come first. So what happened to alpha?

We are dealing with a mathematical model that sees stock returns as having two parts. The first is the influence that the general market has on individual stocks. This part is represented by beta. The second part is the return attributable to the individual stock—the nonmarket (specific) return. This part will vary—up and down, positive and negative—over the weeks, months, and years. The model is as follows:

$$Y = a + bX + e$$

where Y equals the net return on a stock for some period (the net return is the actual return, less the risk-free return available during the period); X equals the net return on the market portfolio for the same period; e is a random "error variable," representing random fluctuations in returns (for multiple periods or multiple stocks, errors cancel out, and the average value of e equals 0); and b, or beta, as we've noted, is a multiplier that relates individual stock returns to the returns on the market. Alpha (in this equation, a) measures a stock's *general tendency* to perform better or worse than the market. That is, if a stock outperforms the market, *apart* from the returns attributable to market risk, then it will have a positive alpha. If it underperforms the market, it will have a negative alpha.

An estimate of alpha comes automatically from the process of estimating beta (it all comes from a statistical technique called *linear regression*). Now, we investors should immediately get a bright idea: Since we are always looking for stocks that outperform the market, it seems obvious that a prime investment strategy would be to buy or hold stocks with positive alphas and avoid stocks with negative alphas. Alas, life for investors is not that simple. Remember, the estimate of alpha comes from *past* data; it measures how the stock *has done*. Unfortunately, evidence also shows that alpha is very unstable. Today's estimate of alpha, based on past performance, is not a reliable predictor of future alpha. Calculated alphas are considered so unreliable that most publishers of beta do not even report them. In other words, as a prospectus will always say, "Past results do not guarantee future performance." And it's future performance that we're looking for.

The Efficient Market Revisited

The term *efficient market* has scarcely turned up in this discussion of risk, return, and risk management, because the ideas and propositions we've examined are valid regardless of whether the market is efficient. Still, a few things should be mentioned about the relationship between market efficiency and the present discussion.

Alpha measures a stock's general tendency to outperform or underperform the market. The simple proposition of the efficient market is that all alphas are zero! This does not mean that all stocks perform equally well or that *measured* alphas are zero. It's obvious that different stocks have performed very differently (the past is the source of calculated alphas) and, of course, stocks will perform very differently in the future. If the market is efficient, however, all of what we might call the *expected* alphas are zero. This is just a slightly more formal way of stating the basic conclusion of the efficient market hypothesis: All stocks are equally promising investment candidates at the outset.

Effective diversification can be achieved through random stock selection. If the market is efficient, beta will measure the riskiness of the resulting portfolio. If the market is not efficient, however, or if you select stocks *as if* the market were not efficient, then the picture changes slightly. If you select stocks according to some particular characteristic (for example, you buy only stocks that are selling at a discount to book value), then beta will understate the riskiness of your portfolio, no matter how much you diversify. Why? Because you will not have eliminated one form of specific risk—the risk associated with that particular characteristic. You probably wouldn't use that characteristic (often called a *screen*) to select stocks unless you believed that using it was better than making random selections; but you should be warned that it adds risk.

A classic example of this kind of situation was documented by James Farrell. For the period of December 31, 1972, to July 31, 1974, he compared the performance of the S&P 500 and two mutual funds. The dramatic results are shown in Table 9.1.

The period was a very bad one for stocks, with the S&P 500 declining 29 percent. When we look at the performance of the two funds, we see a

TABLE 9.1 Performance of S&P 500 and Two Stock Mutual Funds Dec. 31, 1972–July 31, 1974

Market Sector	S&P 500	Affiliated Fund	T. Rowe Price Fund
		Portfolio Percentages	
Growth	39.8%	10.5%	80.2%
Cyclical	24.0	57.5	8.7
Stable	20.0	18.0	4.1
Oil	16.2	14.0	7.0
Estimated Betas	1.00	1.09	1.11
Performance for Period	−29%	−16%	−42%

SOURCE: Farrell, 1975.

striking pattern: One outperformed the market by 13 points, and the other underperformed it by 13. This happened even though the two funds had almost the same beta. Obviously, something more than market risk was operating on the returns. Table 9.1 clearly shows what that something was. Both funds had portfolios heavily weighted toward particular market sectors, relative to the composition of the S&P 500. The Affiliated Fund had overweighted cyclical stocks, largely by avoiding growth stocks. Conversely, the T. Rowe Price Fund was highly weighted toward growth stocks.

During this period, the cyclical stock strategy was rewarded, and the growth strategy was punished. (In another period, of course, things have been different; neither strategy is necessarily better than the other.) Both funds took on a great deal of specific risk by creating highly weighted portfolios. Both contained a very large number of issues, giving the impression of great diversification. In fact, though, neither fund was as diversified as it seemed. As a result, beta was not an adequate or accurate predictor of performance.

More Risk or More Money?

Suppose you have decided that you wish to take on $100,000 of market risk. There is more than one way to do this, because you can choose both the amount of money you invest and the beta (the riskiness) of the portfolio. You can invest $100,000 in a portfolio with a beta of 1.0, but you can also invest $80,000 in a portfolio with a beta of 1.25, $133,000 with a beta of 0.67, and so on. How to decide?

If the market is perfectly efficient, the optimal strategy is to hold the market portfolio, whose beta is 1.0, by definition. Unfortunately, this mathematical truth is completely irrelevant to anyone but a theoretician. It projects precision onto a situation that simply is not precise. We know that the market is not perfectly efficient. We also know that, unless they hold index funds, investors cannot in practicality hold the market portfolio. Any other portfolio relies on measured betas, which we know are not perfectly accurate. There just isn't a ready answer to the question "More risk or more money?" It will have to depend on your own feelings and circumstances.

A SIMPLE MODEL

Everything we have said about risk and return fits together in a simple model with a fancy name: the Capital Assets Pricing Model (CAPM). Arising from the random walk and efficient market concepts, CAPM *replaces* both fundamental and technical analysis. Not surprisingly, it has generated an enormous amount of professional and academic discussion, as well as the usual highly technical debates about definitions and measurements.

CAPM has basically attained state-of-the-art status among finance professors and institutional investment professionals. Since that's so, we should review what we've already covered and put it into a tidier package. Here are the essential propositions.

1. Investors are risk-averse and will take on additional risk only if offered higher expected returns.

2. Higher expected returns do not result from unnecessary, avoidable risk.

3. Stocks carry two kinds of risk: specific risk (associated with a particular stock or stock group) and market risk (associated with the stock market in general).

4. Specific risk can be eliminated through diversification, but market risk cannot.

5. Since specific risk is avoidable, there is no risk premium associated with it. Expected returns are not higher for undiversified portfolios. Market risk is the only type of risk to be compensated. Investors who accept higher levels of market risk have higher expected returns.

6. Stocks differ in their responsiveness to moves in the overall market; that is, they have differing amounts of market risk. This difference is measured by beta. Since market risk is the only risk in well-diversified portfolios, portfolio beta is the measure of risk in diversified portfolios.

7. Risk management in diversified portfolios consists of managing market risk by determining the amount of money invested in stocks and controlling the portfolio beta.

That's it. For the dozens of books, hundreds of articles, and thousands of equations that have been published, for all the arcane debates that have been waged, this is all you really need to know about CAPM, the modern science of investing. We can make CAPM even simpler, for it can all be boiled down to two basic instructions:

1. Control the amount of market risk assumed.

2. Diversify.

Not very mysterious or revolutionary, is it?

THREE WARNINGS

Beta measures the riskiness of a well-diversified portfolio, riskiness for which you expect to be rewarded. Historical evidence confirms that high-beta stocks (hence high-beta portfolios) do yield higher returns, but there are some caveats.

First, actual returns don't seem proportional to beta; high-beta stocks don't achieve returns as high as we might expect. In other words, the additional risk is only partially rewarded. The discrepancy is not large, but this factor may help us answer a question we asked earlier: Should a given level of market risk be achieved by our investing more money in low-beta stocks or less money in high-beta stocks?

Second, we must always remember that risk cuts both ways. High-beta portfolios achieve high returns *in the long run,* but in the short run they simply exaggerate the market trend. When the trend is positive, high-risk investors are richly rewarded, but when the market turns bearish, they are correspondingly punished.

Finally, beta sometimes simply fails to work. Sometimes low-beta stocks have been leaders in bull markets, and sometimes high-beta stocks have performed best in bear markets. These phenomena can occur when there are major shifts in investors' perceptions of different types of stocks. Growth may be in vogue during one period, stability and strong balance sheets during another. Beta may be the best or even the only measure we have for the kind of risk rewarded by the market, but beta isn't perfect.

Part Four
The Inefficient Market

10

Out-of-Favor Stocks: The Last Shall Be First

In academia, the pursuit of truth seems to flow inevitably. A long-standing theory is challenged by an upstart with a new idea. Immediately, a profusion of research corroborates the new theory, which itself then becomes the established wisdom. After a time, another challenge arises, and the research focus changes. As if by magic, the studies stop corroborating the established theory and start poking holes in it.

At best, this process increases our knowledge of the world and ourselves; at the very least, it provides plenty of material for graduate students who must write Ph.D. dissertations and for junior faculty members who must publish or perish. This inevitable flow seems to exist in every field, and the investment field is no exception.

From about 1960 to the mid-1970s, random walk/efficient market ideas were a building wave. Eventually they swept away everything in their path. Hundreds of articles and dissertations formalized the theories and proved the propositions. The culmination of this process was the neat, formal Capital Assets Pricing Model.

Life for the sophisticated investor became tidy and simple, and correspondingly dull. In an efficient market, there was really nothing to do but decide on a desired level of market risk, create widely diversified, essentially random portfolios, and then sit back and take whatever came. Indeed, a common expression to describe the optimal investment approach was *passive strategy*.

Well, take heart. Dull simplicity didn't hold sway for long. For years it seemed that every study confirmed the efficient market. Recently the picture has changed. The market may not be so efficient or tidy after all.

PSYCHOLOGY AGAIN

We have already examined the traditional approaches to analyzing stock values. We saw that fundamental and technical analysis are both based on the proposition that stock prices range far above and below their intrinsic values. The explanation was that investors' fear, greed, optimism, and pessimism do not change at the same rate as value; in the short run, at least, psychology will tend to overwhelm reality. The goal of analysis is either to capture the psychology itself (technical analysis) or to determine how far it has taken prices away from true values (fundamental analysis).

To a disciple of the efficient market theory, these beliefs are nonsense. In an efficient market, current prices are unbiased estimates of intrinsic values. Prices don't move significantly away from values, because there are alert, rational, value-oriented investors ready to buy or sell stocks when prices get out of line. The efficient market is thus a self-correcting equilibrium system. Psychology may play a role, but a very limited one, because the proverbial smart money never sleeps.

There is a basic problem with the efficient market viewpoint, however: It just doesn't correspond to our experience, or at least not to our perceived experience. David Dreman, investment advisor and author, and perhaps the leading exponent of low-P/E strategies, expressed this idea succinctly when he quoted an anonymous investor who had been burned by glamour stocks in the early 1970s. Noting the 86 percent plunge in Disney between 1972 and 1974, this investor asked, "When was the market efficient? When it took Disney up to $119^1/8$, or when it put it back to $16^5/8$?" When, indeed?

We have already seen the deception involved in proof by anecdote. Besides, it *is* possible for Disney or any other stock to drop 86 percent in a perfectly efficient market. All it takes is a sufficient change in the outlook for the company or for stocks in general. We've also seen, in discussing the Dividend Discount Model, that changed growth expectations have a highly leveraged impact on valuations. Therefore, the mere fact that a stock (especially a growth stock, such as Disney) declined 86 percent does not in itself prove that the market is inefficient. Still, the suspicion remains that somewhere on the way up or down (or both), rationality was overcome by emotion. Perhaps the smart money wasn't so smart.

THE OVERREACTION HYPOTHESIS

A great deal of research confirms this suspicion. Psychologists refer to the *availability heuristic*. This formidable term refers to the way in which we process information to draw conclusions and formulate strategies. Not surprisingly, the information and experience that have the most impact on our decision making are the kinds that are most available to us. What's most available, in a psychological sense, are recent events or events that are unusual and startling enough to stick in the memory. In other words, our minds sort and filter our experiences, but the sorting and filtering process is flawed, leading to distorted ideas and images of reality.

The prices of all stocks reflect the expectations that investors have for them, but what if those expectations are wrong in some consistent (i.e., nonrandom) manner? If so, the market will not be perfectly efficient (returns will be related to more than just risk), and we ought to be able to formulate one or more strategies to outperform a simple buy-and-hold strategy. You may be surprised to hear that one of these successful strategies can be found in a very obvious place.

PRICE/EARNINGS (P/E) RATIOS

The most common standard of value in the stock market is the price/earnings ratio (price per share divided by annual earnings per share). The P/E simply measures how much the market says a dollar of any company's earnings is worth. The widely varying P/Es that we see in the market reflect investors' belief that some companies are worth a lot more than others, not only absolutely but also relatively.

Why would investors be willing to pay three or four dollars for a dollar of one company's earnings, but thirty or forty dollars for a dollar of another's? Clearly, investors are looking to the future. For whatever reasons, a more expensive stock (in terms of P/E) is perceived to have better prospects than a cheaper stock. (In terms of the Dividend Discount Model, one stock is more highly valued because the pattern of expected future earnings and dividends looks better.) Stocks in companies that are expected to achieve high rates of growth typically sell at high P/Es relative to the market, and relative to stocks of companies whose prospects are considered mediocre or worse.

None of this is news; it is intuitively obvious that different stocks should sell for different P/Es. But how different? If the market is efficient, we can find the answer easily. If we use the Dividend Discount Model, we see that the different P/Es of different stocks make the risk-adjusted rates of return equal. Stocks with high market risk must have higher expected (average) returns. After we adjust for that risk, the returns from all stocks must be equal—if the market is efficient. Stock prices—hence, P/E ratios—continually undergo adjustment so that expected rates of return are equal. In other words, if the market is perfectly efficient, no differences in rates of return can be attributed to P/E ratios.

It turns out that the reverse is true: Studies have confirmed repeatedly that returns *are* related to P/Es. To put the matter succinctly, *low-P/E stocks outperform high-P/E stocks*. When we consider how fundamental and accessible a measure of value the price/earnings ratio is, this finding is a rather severe blow to the efficient market theory.

Low P/E Strategies

The most important study of the significance of P/Es was published by Sanjoy Basu in 1977. It is still the most extensive, sophisticated, and complete research on the subject. It covered New York Stock Exchange (NYSE) industrial companies over a fourteen-year period (1957–1971), an average of about 500 stocks annually. Basu calculated the year-end P/Es for all the stocks and formed hypothetical portfolios by dividing the stocks into five groups according to P/E. One portfolio consisted of the 20 percent of the stocks with the highest P/Es, the next portfolio of the 20 percent with the second-highest P/Es, and so on. The study assumed that equal investments were made in each stock. The portfolios were rebalanced each year, and the annual returns were calculated. Because of this restructuring, a particular stock could be in one P/E group portfolio one year but in another the next.

The results are shown in Table 10.1. Portfolio A consists of the highest P/E group, and E contains the lowest. Portfolio A* is the same as A except that stocks with negative earnings (losses) are omitted. For a company with

TABLE 10.1 Performance of Common Stocks by Price/Earnings Ratios NYSE, April 1957–March 1971

	P/E Portfolios					
	A	A*	B	C	D	E
Median P/E	35.8	30.5	19.1	15.0	12.8	9.8
Average annual rate of return	9.3%	9.5%	9.3%	11.7%	13.6%	16.3%
Excess return	5.6%	5.8%	5.6%	8.0%	9.9%	12.6%
Market risk (beta)	1.11	1.06	1.04	.97	.94	.99

SOURCE: Basu, 1977.

a loss, the P/E is infinite; all such stocks necessarily end up in port-folio A. A* eliminates any bias that might arise from including money-losing companies.

The table shows both total returns and excess returns, which simply represent the difference between total return and the risk-free return available at the time (the T-Bill rate). High P/Es are clearly associated with lower returns and low P/Es with higher returns. The difference between the highest and lowest groups averages about 7 percent per year.

This difference cannot be explained by differences in risk. On the con-trary, lower P/Es are generally accompanied by lower risk (beta), not higher. The conclusion is inescapable: Stocks that the market views as inferior (on the basis of P/E valuations) produce superior returns. Investors seem to ex-aggerate both the strengths of high-P/E stocks and the weaknesses of low-P/E stocks. In other words, there is systematic misvaluation.

The comparisons in Table 10.1 are incomplete. A low-P/E strategy re-quires more activity than a simple buy-and-hold strategy. Higher transac-tion costs and taxes accompany increased trading activity. Basu recalculated his results to take account of these factors. After these adjustments, the dif-ferences between the P/E groups were not so large. After every conceivable adjustment, however, the conclusion still stood: Low-P/E stocks outperform high-P/E stocks, and a low-P/E strategy not only outperforms a buy-and-hold strategy, it also beats the market.

Basu is not the only person to have studied the P/E question. Many others have conducted similar research, varying either the time periods or the stocks considered. The results have all been the same.

David Dremen, the efficient-market debunker we met at the beginning of this chapter, tracked more than 1200 stocks from 1968 to 1977. These in-cluded more than 70 percent of the stocks on the NYSE, plus large Amex and over-the-counter companies. Like Basu, Dremen divided the stocks in-to portfolios by P/E, in this case into ten groups, or deciles. He tested his hypothesis with different switching intervals, which included reconstruct-ing portfolios every three months and holding original portfolios for the en-tire nine-year period.

Dremen's most significant results are shown in Table 10.2. Like Basu's, they present clear and dramatic evidence of the P/E effect. Regard-less of the switching interval, the returns line up almost perfectly inversely to P/E.

Dremen's results are impressive, but he made none of the adjustments for taxes and transaction costs that Basu did. Frequent portfolio switching certainly would diminish reported returns; thus, one of Dreman's most im-portant findings is the extent to which a low-P/E strategy works over long holding periods. Indeed, a nine-year buy-and-hold approach, in which the

TABLE 10.2 Annualized Compound Rates of Return by Price/Earnings Ratios—NYSE, Amex, OTC, August 1968–August 1977

	Switching After Each			Holding Original Portfolio
P/E DECILE	6 MOS.	1 YEAR	3 YEARS	9 YEARS
1 (highest)	−1.06%	−1.13%	−1.43%	.33%
2	1.62	0.56	−0.28	1.27
3	0.62	1.63	0.85	3.30
4	3.42	3.31	4.87	5.36
5	4.46	2.93	5.02	3.72
6	5.33	6.70	4.82	4.52
7	6.07	6.85	5.89	6.08
8	8.24	8.56	7.78	6.35
9	8.40	6.08	7.73	6.40
10 (lowest)	11.68	10.26	10.89	7.89

Average return of entire sample = 4.75%

SOURCE: Dreman, 1982.

original portfolios were *never* recast, was able to differentiate performance clearly by P/E ratios.

In Chapter 3, we saw some of the problems that can arise from the choice of a particular period to study. Since different periods seem to have different characters, research results can be biased right from the beginning. Dreman dealt with this potential bias straightforwardly: He broke the nine-year period into subperiods. In that way, he was able to test the P/E effect in bull and bear markets alike, from one market peak to the next, from peak to trough and from trough to peak. These further results (not shown) did nothing to contradict the conclusion that low-P/E stocks are superior performers. Dreman's results held up in every period, including the infamous two-tier market of the early 1970s, when glamour stocks, with their high P/Es, were most in vogue and were popularly thought to be the outstanding performers.

P/Es Within Industries

P/Es vary not only from stock to stock but also from industry to industry. When P/E seems to be a significant determinant of stock performance, we may be seeing not only the effects of P/E but also industry effects. Even if there are no industry effects, we may wonder whether the findings about P/E ratios apply to all industry groups or only to some.

We don't have a comprehensive answer, but a recent study is very suggestive. Peavy and Goodman, following the earlier procedure, divided stocks into five groups, or quintiles, by P/E ratios. Instead of using a sampling of the entire market, however, they studied three industry groups. From 1970 to 1980, they tracked 40 stocks each in electronics, paper/containers, and food. They selected industries to span a range of riskiness. Electronics stocks are generally a high-risk, high-beta group, while paper stocks have about average risk. Food stocks are low-risk, defensive stocks with low betas.

Peavy and Goodman's results are shown in Table 10.3. Returns are quarterly, not annual, and are based on quarterly restructuring of the portfolios. The results confirm what we've observed before: Within each industry, returns decline as P/Es rise, and not by small amounts. The difference between the highest- and lowest-P/E groups hovers around 20 percent per year. Again, we see that the higher returns available in low-P/E stocks do not result from higher risk. Risk and P/E are not correlated, except in the electronics industry, where higher P/Es are associated with higher risk.

The Price of Popularity

A stock's P/E ratio is a measure of investors' opinions about the stock. In a rational world, P/E embodies the considered judgment of the financial community. In a less ideal world, P/E may be largely a measure of popularity.

The Dividend Discount Model gives us a precise value (and hence a P/E) for a stock, once we have projected future growth, but we've already seen how volatile the valuations are. Slight changes or differences in growth projections cause dramatic changes in valuation. We've also seen the danger inherent in the situation: It is easy to come up with so-called reasonable growth assumptions to justify virtually any price and price/earnings ratio. Thus, there are really two sources of inaccurate valuations: simple error (the most rational and meticulous analysis turns out to be incorrect) and the psychological factor (we tend to exaggerate what we perceive as trends, whether positive or negative).

Picture how this volatility operates in the market. A company exhibits high growth in a growing, glamorous field, and its stock has been doing correspondingly well. The natural assumption is that both the company and its stock will continue to excel. The assumption is fine, as far as it goes, but there is something crucial that we must also recognize: This assumption of continued success will *already be reflected* in the price of the stock. The stock carries a high P/E ratio because of what the company has already done and because investors assume that the pattern will continue. If expectations prove exaggerated or go unfulfilled, shareholders are bound to suffer.

The inherent uncertainty of forecasting, and the human tendency to misperceive and exaggerate reality, work together in an insidious and often costly way. If positive prospects for favored stocks are exaggerated, then most surprises will be negative—and we know that surprises are the rule, since forecasting is inherently error-prone. Conversely, if negative outlooks

TABLE 10.3 Quarterly Returns by Price/Earnings Ratios January 1970–July 1980

INDUSTRY	Quintile 1	2	3	4	5	INDUSTRY MEAN
Electronics						
Number of Stocks	8	8	8	8	8	
Mean P/E Ratio	7.1	10.3	13.4	17.4	25.5	14.7
Mean Qtrly Return	9.2%	5.4%	5.1%	3.0%	2.2%	5.0%
Mean Beta	1.15	1.12	1.13	1.19	1.29	1.18
Paper/Containers						
Number of Stocks	8	8	8	8	8	
Mean P/E Ratio	6.7	8.5	10.2	12.4	20.2	11.6
Mean Qtrly Return	5.4%	3.4%	4.0%	2.4%	0.9%	3.4%
Mean Beta	1.02	1.02	1.00	1.03	1.02	1.02
Food						
Number of Stocks	8	8	8	8	8	
Mean P/E Ratio	7.2	9.5	11.1	12.8	16.8	11.5
Mean Qtrly Return	5.5%	3.8%	2.7%	0.8%	0.6%	2.8%
Mean Beta	0.90	0.85	0.86	0.86	0.90	0.87

SOURCE: Peavy and Goodman, 1983.

for the out-of-favor stocks are similarly exaggerated, then most surprises will be positive.

Dreman succinctly states the basic proposition underlying the low-P/E strategy: "If one cannot forecast [earnings] with any degree of accuracy, then the range between high and low P/E multiples should be much narrower" (p. 163). The studies we've looked at, as well as many others, confirm this idea. If the range were not so wide, low-P/E strategies would not work.

BUYING THE PRESENT, NOT THE PROSPECTS

Price/earnings ratios measure how the market evaluates companies' futures. In a real sense, the future is what creates present value, but there is another logical way to look at present value: to focus on the present, what we have here and now. To do this, we look at the balance sheet—what a company owns and what it owes, assets and liabilities, its financial status today.

Most of today's investors grew up in an era when analysis focused on earnings and especially on growth, but analysis has not always done so. Benjamin Graham, the pioneer of security analysis, placed great emphasis on the balance sheet in determining stock values. He considered what he called a company's "earnings power," and he developed methods for evaluating it. Nevertheless, he focused less on how much we should pay for a dollar of earnings than on how much we should pay for a dollar of net assets (total assets minus liabilities, i.e., net worth). To Graham, current value was at least as important as prospective value.

Assets, liabilities, and earnings are related. All companies try to use their assets and manage their liabilities to create earnings, and as much as possible. But since earnings seem to be so inconsistent and unpredictable, the company's balance sheet may provide a more stable and reliable measure of the value of its stock, and the price of a stock in relation to net assets may be a good measure of the stock's popularity. If there is systematic misvaluation of stocks, it may show up in terms of both assets and earnings.

Some recent studies have tested this idea, all based on Graham's "bargain issue" strategy, which is a model of simplicity. Graham focused on *liquidation value,* which is the same as net assets (book value) except that it includes only liquid assets; such assets as land, buildings, equipment, and goodwill are omitted. Liquidation value is a conservative estimate of what a company could be liquidated for immediately. Graham suggested that investors purchase stocks with market prices lower than two-thirds of the liquidation value per share. He also recommended that investors choose companies that have positive earnings and pay dividends, and he stressed that this approach requires holding a diversified portfolio.

Table 10.4 summarizes a nine-year study of NYSE, Amex, and OTC bargain stocks. For each year between 1970 and 1979, a portfolio was created from stocks that met Graham's liquidation-value criterion at the end of the preceding year. At the end of the next year, those stocks were replaced by stocks that met the criterion at that time. The table shows average monthly returns over the nine years. The performance of the entire portfolio is compared with a value-weighted index of all NYSE/Amex stocks. Moreover, the stocks are organized into subgroups according to where they are traded. These subgroups are compared with relevant market measures.

The results confirm Graham's ideas. In every comparison, the bargain issues are the clear winners, and by very wide margins. The figures may not seem very dramatic because they are reported on a monthly basis. Nevertheless, the difference in monthly returns between the entire group of bargain stocks and the NYSE/Amex index, to give one example, implies an *annual* difference of more than 25 percent.

The betas for the bargain stocks are shown in relation to the respective benchmarks, and we can see that the bargain issues are riskier than average. Still, the difference in riskiness doesn't explain the difference in performance. The last column of the table shows the average monthly return premium. This is a measure of the rate at which, every month, the bargain stocks outperform the benchmarks *after* adjustment for the bargain stocks' higher market risk. The results remain impressive.*

Table 10.5 tracks the bargain stocks in a different way. Many investors tend to hold stocks for much longer than a year. This table assumes that stocks are held for 30 months. The table gives results for each 30-month period, starting with December 31, 1970. Thus, the periods overlap. This table is for the entire group of bargain stocks and is not broken down by market. Again, the returns are shown in comparison to the benchmark of the NYSE/Amex index, and once again the betas of the bargain-issue portfolios are shown in relation to the benchmark, along with the return premiums.

The results support the bargain-issues strategy. In eight of the nine periods, this strategy would have significantly outdistanced the market—in most cases, by very hefty margins.

It's interesting to note how much variation there is in beta. For the 30-month periods beginning December 31, 1970, and December 31, 1974,

---

*Oppenheimer and Schlarbaum, the authors of this study, also made separate calculations for stocks that had positive and negative earnings. The average returns for the two groups were virtually identical, a finding that suggests Graham's requirement that companies be profitable may not be important. Bargain stocks in money-losing companies, however, were considerably riskier (they had higher betas); risk-adjusted returns are higher for stocks with positive earnings. On the question of dividends, the research revealed that nonpaying stocks tend, if anything, to outperform the dividend payers.

TABLE 10.4 "Bargain Issue" Returns December 1970–December 1979

Mean Monthly Returns

SAMPLE	BARGAIN ISSUES	MARKET BENCHMARK	BETA	MONTHLY RETURN PREMIUM
All bargain issues vs. NYSE/Amex index	2.85%	0.90%	1.27	1.85%
NYSE issues vs. S&P 500	2.43	0.34	1.42	1.97
Amex issues vs. Amex index	2.59	1.78	1.26	0.51
OTC issues vs. NASD index	2.94	0.94	1.11	1.96

Note: Monthly return premium is the difference between the actual return and the return implied by beta. The premium will be less than the nominal difference in returns for betas greater than 1.00. *SOURCE:* Oppenheimer and Schlarbaum, 1985.

TABLE 10.5 "Bargain Issue" Returns vs. NYSE/Amex Index (30-Month Holding Periods)

Mean Monthly Returns

PURCHASE DATE (DECEMBER 31)	BARGAIN ISSUES	MARKET BENCHMARK	BETA	MONTHLY RETURN PREMIUM
1970	0.50%	0.57%	1.64	− 0.20%
1971	0.01	− 0.38	1.24	0.60
1972	0.92	− 0.56	1.16	1.66
1973	3.57	0.73	1.19	2.61
1974	5.52	1.94	1.73	2.49
1975	3.69	0.88	1.24	2.70
1976	2.81	0.53	1.02	2.29
1977	2.65	1.35	1.36	1.09
1978	2.85	1.79	0.91	1.13

SOURCE: Oppenheimer and Schlarbaum, 1985.

the bargain-issue portfolio betas are well over 1.50, extremely high for diversified portfolios. In contrast, for the period beginning in 1978, the bargain stocks were actually less risky than the general market. The character of bargain stocks seems to vary considerably over time.

If stocks selling at low P/Es, as well as those selling cheaply in relation to asset values, both tend to outperform the market, a strategy combining both criteria might seem promising, and what evidence we have confirms this promise.

The findings on bargain stocks are ironic. As we noted in Chapter 6, Benjamin Graham eventually abandoned his own methods and threw his opinion on the side of the efficient market theorists. His capitulation may have been premature.

ANOTHER LOOK AT POPULARITY

We've looked at popularity from two standpoints: how much investors pay for a dollar of earnings and how much they pay for a dollar of net assets. A third approach has also been proposed: looking at the price/sales ratio (P/S), that is, how much is paid for a dollar of sales, rather than earnings.

The leading proponent of this approach is Kenneth Fisher, who details it in his 1984 book, *Super Stocks*. According to Fisher, sales are a more stable measure of a company's growth and performance than earnings are; changes in earnings are much more volatile than changes in sales. Fisher has many reasons for saying so, but one certainly is that earnings tend to be leveraged on sales. Managers plan and budget on the basis of sales forecasts. If actual sales are significantly higher or lower than those that are forecast, the effect on earnings will be magnified, because the indirect costs (overhead, research and development, etc.) will not adjust instantly to the change in sales.

Fisher also focuses on sales as a way of eliminating a common source of confusion about earnings growth: changing profit margins. Many companies experience periods of rapid earnings growth that are fueled not so much by rising sales as by widening margins. This phenomenon is certainly not negative; all managers strive to increase profit margins. Fisher rightly points out, however, that a competitive world places inevitable limits on how far margins can expand. Rapid growth caused by rising margins is self-limiting. For investors, it may be an impending disaster.

From his research, Fisher has developed a set of P/S standards that can be applied to stock valuation. These standards vary according to the type of stock or industry being considered, but they fall into three fundamental categories. The standards are shown in Table 10.6.

The standards are considerably different from one another because businesses have very different characteristics. A dollar of sales of an inherently low-margin, low-growth company would not be worth the same as for a company with higher margins and more growth potential. Furthermore, the standards—and, indeed, the whole P/S concept—do not apply to industries whose profits are not based on sales, in the conventional sense. Banks, securities firms, and utilities, for example, could not be evaluated on this basis.

TABLE 10.6   Popularity and Price/Sales Ratios

TYPE OF STOCK	Very Unpopular P/S BELOW	Accepted P/S OVER	Very Popular P/S OVER
Small, Growth, Technology	0.75	1.50	3.00
Multibillion in Sales, or Without Growth Characteristics	0.20	0.40	0.80
Low-Margin Industries, e.g., Supermarkets	0.03	0.06	0.12

SOURCE: Fisher, 1984.

How do we use these standards? We buy the very unpopular stocks and avoid the very popular ones.

Fisher has assembled some apparently impressive evidence to support his ideas. For example, he examined the 20 top-performing industrial stocks from 1979 to 1983. Of those 20, 11 started 1979 with P/Ss of less than 0.20; only two started with ratios greater than 0.75. In addition, Fisher cites numerous examples of sound companies that, because of short-term reversals and consequent unpopularity, have seen their stock prices fall to very low levels in relation to sales. These stocks later scored spectacular advances, as the market took them from unpopular to accepted and often to very popular (i.e., overvalued) status.

Fisher admittedly did not set out to produce scientific validation of strategies based on P/S ratios. Most of his evidence is essentially proof by anecdote, with examples chosen by hindsight. It is not hard to find examples of stocks that have been beaten down, only to come roaring back; many of these would show up on a P/S screen. But what about similarly undervalued stocks that went on to become even more undervalued or to vanish altogether? One of Fisher's low-P/S success stories concerned Applied Magnetics (APM). In the bear market of the early 1970s, APM was severely hammered, eventually reaching a buy-point P/S of 0.75 in early 1974. Purchasers at that level, however, would have had to endure a *further* price drop of *80 percent* before APM could be turned around, something Fisher failed to note.

Academic researchers have tested the P/S theory in several studies (most of them unpublished at this writing). Using the same type of analysis we saw earlier with P/Es, they divided stocks into quintiles or deciles based on P/S and tracked risk and return over time. Fisher has never proposed that people invest solely on the basis of P/S, much less P/S quintiles or deciles.

Moreover, most of the more recent studies have ignored Fisher's caveat that different standards be applied to different types of companies; many of the studies have included stocks to which Fisher feels the P/S theory does not apply. All the same, the results of these studies have strongly supported the P/S theory: Low-P/S stocks outperform high-P/S stocks.

Some researchers have tried to determine whether P/Ss are superior to P/Es for discriminating among stocks. The results have varied considerably, depending on samples, periods, and inclusion of certain stock categories. Some comparative studies have eliminated stocks of money-losing companies, since P/E is meaningless for them, while Fisher specifically states that P/S *does* apply. It appears that in general, and on the basis of simple return, P/S works at least as well as P/E. But low-P/E stocks tend also to be low-beta stocks, while low-P/S stocks tend to have high betas. On a risk-adjusted basis, P/S seems to be equal to or slightly worse than P/E as a stock screen.

Returns on low-P/S stocks seem more variable than returns on low-P/E stocks. This suggests the need for more diversification. There is more stability in low-P/S stocks, however, and so less turnover is required to maintain a low-P/S strategy.

Given the present state of our knowledge, we may do best if we use Fisher's standards the way Fisher himself recommends: not so much for finding stocks to purchase as for finding those to avoid.

OVERREACTION REVISITED

Study after study has reached the same conclusion: Cheap stocks outperform expensive stocks. No matter which measure of cheapness we use, we cannot refute this proposition. For whatever reasons, investors tend to exaggerate stocks' prospects, whether those prospects are positive or negative.

In Chapter 4, we considered the Dividend Discount Model and a hypothetical growth stock named HYPE. We saw that revisions in earnings and dividend forecasts have a very leveraged effect on valuations, which explains why a stock like HYPE (or Disney, to answer Dreman's unhappy investor) can plummet if its earnings are lower than expected: Analysts and investors lower their forecasts for the future, on the basis of the current disappointment. How much should they lower their expectations, if they should lower them at all? Does this quarter's problem signal a permanent change in the company's prospects, or just the inevitable vagaries and uncertainties of doing business? The evidence that we've seen shows that investors overestimate the importance of what they are seeing. They price good stocks too high and bad stocks too low.

A diagram from Fisher's *Super Stocks* illustrates overreaction very well. Figure 10.1 plots sales, profits, and price for a stock over time. The example is of a rapidly growing company that suffers temporary difficulty followed by resumed growth.

As we begin to look at the stock (left side of the figure), sales and profits are growing rapidly—profits more rapidly than sales, because margins are expanding. Earnings are growing at an increasing rate, and investors respond by rapidly bidding up the stock's price. In fact, however, they are overreacting, and the stock becomes overvalued.

After a time, sales growth begins to slow, perhaps because of increased competition or market saturation. Profit growth follows suit. Typically, the stock price begins to decline, because analysts and some investors hear about these changes even before the actual announcement of results. As the news spreads, wholesale reevaluation (also known as panic) ensues. The onetime darling of the market becomes a pariah. Sales decline modestly, but profits decline rapidly and perhaps even vanish. Once analysts praised the company's management; now they question its ability to pull the company out of the dive. What began as a focus on the positive quickly becomes quite

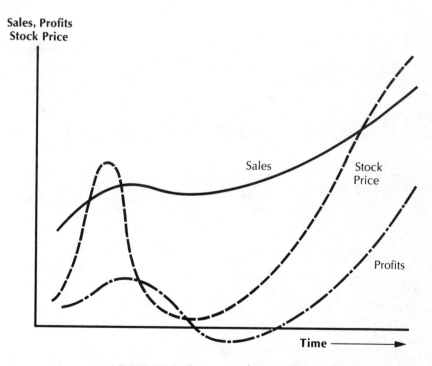

FIGURE 10.1 The process of overreaction

the opposite. Once again, the investment community overreacts, driving the stock down to undervalued levels. At this point (or somewhere near it), one or more of our value screens (P/E, P/S, etc.) presumably will tell us to buy the stock.

In Figure 10.1, happily, the company overcomes its setbacks, gets its house in order, resumes healthy growth, and sees a dramatic turnaround in profits. As always, investors react. Before long, they have overreacted once again, repeating the same mistakes. The cause is always the same: People pay too much attention to recent events and expect short-term trends to continue indefinitely. One of the oldest sayings on Wall Street is "No tree grows to the sky." It seems that not many people have been listening.

Little Stocks:
Is Ignorance Bliss?

SMALL STOCKS, BIG PROFITS

The investment and academic communities were both disturbed by evidence that out-of-favor stocks tend to outperform the market. This disturbance was minor compared to the uproar over the so-called small-stock effect. The proposition developed by Rolf Banz and Marc Reinganum at the University of Chicago was very simple: Stock market performance is strongly influenced by company size, with small companies doing better than large ones. They did not define size by a conventional measure, such as sales or assets; they measured it by market capitalization: the number of outstanding shares in a company, multiplied by the market price per share.

Banz and Reinganum conducted several studies, and the results were impressive, to say the least. One of the most dramatic findings was published by Reinganum in 1983. He studied the total returns (appreciation plus dividends) of all the stocks traded on the New York and American Stock Exchanges from 1963 through 1980. He divided the stocks into ten groups according to market value. For the beginning of each year, ten portfolios were formed, with the smallest 10 percent of the companies making up the portfolio "MV1" and the largest 10 percent making up "MV10." Eight intermediate portfolios were also created. This process was repeated for every year. Thus, the 1975 portfolios were created by the market values at the end of 1974. At the beginning of 1976, new portfolios were created, based on values at the end of 1975.

Reinganum's findings are shown in Table 11.1. The portfolios are listed in order in the far left column. On the far right are the average annual returns for the portfolios; these are not compound rates of return, but simply the mean (average) annual returns. The size effect is startlingly clear: The average annual returns of the smallest stocks are more than triple those of the largest ones. The relation between size and returns is also perfectly consistent. Each time we move to a larger capitalization group, the returns decline.

Other characteristics of the stock groups show up in the table. Low-capitalization stocks tend to be low-priced. There is also a clear correlation between size, price, and listing on either the American or New York exchanges. (This correlation makes sense, given the greater prestige and more stringent listing requirements of the New York Stock Exchange.)

We should also note the enormous spread between the largest and the smallest stocks. The average capitalization of the MV10 stocks was over $1 billion during this period, but the average for the small group MV1 was less than $5 million. The smallest stocks are very small indeed.

Extremely small stocks may not interest many investors, but this study shows that the size effect operates through the full range of capitalizations. For example, if we look at a medium-size group, MV5, we see that the average annual return is double that of the largest stocks, yet the latter have substantial capitalization, and almost 80 percent of them are listed on the New York Stock Exchange. Even just moving from MV10 to MV9, where we are still in the realm of huge companies, we see substantial increases in average returns.*

Another way to see the extent of the size effect is to study the growth in value of investments in different sizes of stocks. Table 11.2 shows this growth. The table assumes that portfolios are rebalanced annually by capitalization and that at the beginning of each year equal amounts are invested in each stock in a particular group. The results are dramatic: cumulative returns in group MV1 of 4528 percent. A dollar invested in 1963 would have grown to more than $46 through 1980 (as usual, no adjustments have been made for transaction costs or for taxes on either dividends or appreciation). In contrast, investing only in the largest stocks would have resulted in a cumulative return of only 312 percent, with a dollar growing only to slightly more than $4. These results, too, are quite consistent as we move from group to group. Once more, even among the largest companies (say, groups MV7 and up), the size effect is very pronounced.

Recreating and rebalancing portfolios annually is not practical for many investors. Transaction costs are incurred, and taxes must be paid on

*The median market values are averaged over the entire 1963–1980 period. Over time, average size has increased across the board. Thus, a capitalization of $50 million could be considered medium for purposes of Reinganum's study, but $50 million would generally be considered to represent a small stock today.

TABLE 11.1   Characteristics by Market Value Portfolios

All NYSE and Amex Stocks 1963–1980

PORTFOLIO	($ MILLIONS) AVERAGE MEDIAN VALUE	MEDIAN SHARE PRICE	AVERAGE PERCENT ON AMEX	AVERAGE ANNUAL RETURN
MV1	$ 4.6	$ 5.24	92	32.77%
MV2	10.8	9.52	77	23.51
MV3	19.3	12.89	52	22.98
MV4	30.7	16.19	34	20.24
MV5	47.2	19.22	21	19.08
MV6	74.2	22.59	13	18.30
MV7	119.1	26.44	8	15.64
MV8	209.7	30.83	5	14.24
MV9	434.6	34.43	3	13.00
MV10	1102.6	44.94	2	9.47

SOURCE: Reinganum, 1983.

TABLE 11.2   Cumulative Returns with Annual Updating (Selected Periods)

Cumulative Returns 1963 Through:

PORTFOLIO	1965	1968	1971	1974	1977	1980
MV1	120	1166	829	451	1788	4528
MV2	104	599	433	156	696	1850
MV3	128	472	392	177	839	2016
MV4	95	355	248	84	490	1395
MV5	83	303	249	94	463	1179
MV6	94	268	248	90	442	1168
MV7	74	200	179	59	308	782
MV8	74	166	167	61	295	650
MV9	74	152	164	64	250	570
MV10	54	89	99	53	141	312

SOURCE: Reinganum, 1983.

realized gains. For these reasons, Reinganum ran a different test, this one based on starting the portfolios at the beginning of 1963 and never changing them. Thus, for example, a stock that started in group MV5 remained there, regardless of whether it grew or shrank relative to the rest of the market. In effect, Reinganum tested a totally passive strategy.

Table 11.3 shows that the size effect was strong enough to differentiate performance over almost two decades, with no changes in the original

**TABLE 11.3   Cumulative Returns Without Annual Updating
(Selected Portfolios and Periods)**

	Cumulative Returns 1963 Through:					
PORTFOLIO	1965	1968	1971	1974	1977	1980
MV1	120	628	426	196	528	1026
MV3	114	377	345	182	470	923
MV6	88	232	203	109	314	603
MV8	70	153	159	74	239	414
MV10	55	93	105	60	182	328

SOURCE: Reinganum, 1983.

portfolios. A dollar invested in portfolio MV1 in 1963 became more than $11 in 1980, while a dollar invested in MV10 grew to only a little more than $4. Again, the results are very consistent from portfolio to portfolio.

A Rocky Road

A small-stock strategy may be a road to riches in the market, but this road is also liable to lead to sleepless nights. The owners of small stocks apparently have a very bumpy ride; Reinganum's data shows clearly that smaller stocks are more volatile. From groups MV10 to MV1, the portfolio betas rose consistently, from 0.96 to 1.58. Small stocks also outperform their big brothers inconsistently. The middle years of the study (1969–1974) were bear market years. All stocks suffered during this period, but while the largest stocks (MV10) lost a cumulative 19 percent over the six years, group MV5 and all the smaller groups lost more than 50 percent of their value. Even though small stocks were superior investments over the long haul, this road to riches certainly wasn't a one-way street.

Table 11.4 illustrates the volatility and inconsistency of small stocks in yet another way. Here the mean (average) returns for the different portfolios are shown along with the performance of the 10th and 90th percentile members of each group. The 10th percentile is simply the dividing line between the worst 10 percent and the rest of a group; the 90th percentile divides the best 10 percent from the rest. The spread between the 10th and 90th percentiles gets much larger as stocks get smaller. Among small stocks, the best do much better, but the worst do much worse.

In addition to the mean annual returns for the size groups, the median returns are shown. These are the middle returns for each group (the 50th percentile); that is, half the returns are higher than the median and half are lower. Here, there is no consistent or dramatic difference in performance figures. This configuration demonstrates what is really going on in the small-stock effect. It is not attributable to superior performance by small stocks

TABLE 11.4 Distribution of One-Year Holding Period Returns

Portfolio	Tenth Percentile	Ninetieth Percentile	Mean	Median
MV1	– 43.90%	120.59%	31.77%	10.94%
MV2	– 42.95	98.64	23.66	9.99
MV3	– 40.00	95.59	23.52	11.85
MV4	– 38.45	89.40	21.24	11.67
MV5	– 37.08	82.25	19.77	11.53
MV6	– 35.48	76.48	19.12	11.93
MV7	– 33.10	72.21	16.45	9.99
MV8	– 29.23	62.53	14.86	10.28
MV9	– 27.06	58.73	13.42	8.94
MV10	– 25.44	44.46	9.57	7.17

SOURCE: Reinganum, 1983.

generally; the typical small stock does not outperform the market. Rather, the small-stock effect results from spectacular performance by a very few small stocks.

On the Bandwagon

Reinganum's study clearly illustrates all that's involved in the small-stock effect, but his is not the only study to have documented the effect of stock size on returns. A similar study, conducted by Ibbotson and Sinquefield, compared the performance of the smallest quintile of the NYSE to the S&P 500 from 1932 to 1981. The annual compound rate of return for the small NYSE stocks was 16.8 percent, compared to 10.6 percent for the S&P 500.

William Sharpe studied NYSE returns from 1931 to 1979. Using a highly sophisticated multifactor model, he confirmed the same phenomena we've just seen. He found that for each tenfold increase in stock size (market value), the average annual rate of return dropped 5.6 percent. Thus, for example, stocks with average market values of $50 million might have average annual returns 5.6 percentage points higher than stocks with market values of $500 million.

I don't want to be a spoilsport, but I must tell you something not generally acknowledged by these researchers: Reinganum's choice of 1963 as his starting point was rather serendipitous, because 1963 just happens to be when the small-stock effect began! Ibbotson and Sinquefield's data shows that small and large stocks had been essentially equal performers for the previous four decades, each group in turn having its day in the sun. Overall, the small-stock advantage during the period for which data is available (1926 to the present) can be attributed entirely to the period that began in

1963. The small-stock effect may be a 60-year phenomenon statistically, but it does not continue reliably decade after decade.

Is It Real?

Study after study confirmed not only the existence but the strength of the small-stock effect. Where big money or big reputations are at stake, however, nothing goes unchallenged for long, and soon the challenges began to appear.

All of the studies we've examined use the price of the last transaction as the basis for computing returns. For example, to calculate returns for a stock in 1981, the closing price at the end of 1980 would be our base price. It would be more logical to use the *first*-sale price for the new year. Unfortunately, the historical data is not available. For stocks with an active, liquid market, the difference between sale prices is probably insignificant; for small stocks, this difference can distort the picture. The spreads between bid and ask prices are often quite large, and so the price of the first sale one day can be quite different from the price of the last sale the day before. Because many very small stocks do not trade at all for days on end, the distortion becomes even worse. Furthermore, it may be impossible to buy or sell many shares of thinly traded stocks without accepting prices much less favorable than the quoted bid or ask prices.

Reinganum's data indicates that the difference in returns between the largest and the smallest stocks would be wiped out if the additional transaction costs in small stocks consumed 15 percent of capital per year. Longer-term studies suggest that a 6 percent price penalty would eliminate the benefits of investing in small stocks. Especially for institutional investors, this scenario may not be too farfetched. A study by Thomas Loeb (Wells Fargo Investment Advisors) examined the full round-trip trading cost (commissions plus spreads) according to both size of transaction and capitalization of the stock being bought or sold. He found, for example, that for a $500,000 block of a $60 million stock, trading costs would average 17 percent (see Table 11.5). Even for transaction sizes common among individual investors, however, the extra costs of trading in small stocks are significant. The small-stock effect may exist statistically, but the practical realities of the market may severely reduce our ability to profit from it.

Some critics have argued that the returns on small stocks weren't what they appeared to be; others have claimed that the risks weren't, either. We know that small stocks are riskier than large ones, but their superior performance was confirmed in every study, even after adjustments for differences in risk. The measure of risk used in making the adjustments was beta. As we've seen, beta is an appropriate measure of a well-diversified portfolio's risk, because diversification eliminates all but general market risk.

TABLE 11.5   Institutional Round-Trip Trading Costs (Commissions plus Spreads)—Selected Transaction Sizes and Stock Capitalizations

Capitalization of stock (000,000 omitted)	Transaction Size (000 omitted)			
	$25	$250	$500	$1000
$ 25–50	7.6%	18.8%	25.9%	30.0%
50–75	5.8	9.6	16.9	25.4
100–500	2.1	3.2	4.4	5.6
1000–1500	1.9	2.7	3.3	4.6

SOURCE: Loeb, 1983.

A group of small stocks, however, is not a well-diversified portfolio, because it spans only one sector of the market. Diversification eliminates risk associated with individual small stocks, but not that of small stocks as a group. The upshot is that beta underestimates the risk inherent in a small-stock strategy. Many critics have argued that if we fully accounted for such risk, the small stock effect would vanish, and that the higher returns in small stocks are due to correspondingly higher risk, just as theory would suggest.

THE IGNORANCE EFFECT

Debates about the precise definition and measurement of return and risk for small stocks have become very technical and will probably go on for a very long time. Instead of technicalities, perhaps we should focus on understanding the cause of the small-stock effect.

We know that an efficient market needs effective competition: not only a large number of competitors, but also information and analysis to keep prices in line with values. In the case of small stocks, this need may be unmet, and it's easy to see why. Developing information and performing analysis are time-consuming, expensive activities that will be performed only if there is sufficient demand. Someone must be willing to pay, either directly (fees) or indirectly (commissions on transactions). Smaller stocks may not have enough of a market to support much research or analysis. If not, then the small-stock sector of the market may also be the uninformed sector, and the small-stock effect may really be an ignorance effect.

Avner Arbel and Paul Strebel probed this question in two studies. In the first one, they tracked every stock in the S&P 500 from 1970 to 1979. They divided the stocks into three groups according to market value. They also divided them into three groups according to the number of security analysts following the stocks. "Neglected" stocks were followed by zero or one analyst, "highly followed" stocks were covered by four or more analysts, and stocks in between were "moderately followed." Portfolios were formed on the basis of size and analysis groupings. Because analysts frequently change the stocks they cover, the portfolios were recompiled every six months.

As we might have suspected, the less stocks were analyzed, the better they performed. Over the ten-year period, the average annualized return for the neglected stocks was 16.4 percent, compared to a 12.7 percent return for moderately followed and 9.4 percent for highly followed stocks.

The results get even more interesting when we look at the size and coverage groupings simultaneously, as shown in Table 11.6. Reading across the bottom of the table, we see overall that returns do decrease as company size increases. This phenomenon seems to confirm the existence of the small-company effect, but if we look at the effects of size *within* each of the three coverage groups, we see no consistent relationship between size and returns. Given a certain amount of coverage by analysts, size seems to have no effect on returns. In contrast, every size grouping shows a clear relationship between coverage and returns. The implication is clear and important: Small stocks don't perform well because they are *small;* they perform well because they are *ignored.* Indeed, the lowest returns were those of highly followed small stocks. Neglected stocks do well no matter what their size.

Because this study was based on the S&P 500, even the small stocks were large, established companies. Arbel and Strebel's second study, conducted with Steven Carvell, was much broader. It used random samples of 170 stocks each from the New York and American exchanges and the over-the-counter market. Again, the stocks were divided into three groups based on size and three groups based on degree of neglect. In this second study, neglect was defined by how many institutional investors (e.g., pension funds, bank trust departments) held stock in each company.

Table 11.7 confirms the earlier findings. Regardless of company size, degree of institutional ownership is strongly related to returns. For a given

TABLE 11.6 Average Returns by Company Size and Analyst Coverage 1970–1979

	Company Size		
DEGREE OF COVERAGE	SMALL	MEDIUM	LARGE
1. Highly followed	5.0%	7.4%	8.4%
2. Moderately followed	13.2	11.0	10.2
3. Neglected	15.8	13.9	15.3
Mean*	13.5	10.7	9.8

*Weighted by number of companies in each category.
SOURCE: Arbel and Strebel, 1983.

TABLE 11.7 Average Returns by Company Size and Institutional Holdings 1971–1980

		Company Size	
DEGREE OF HOLDINGS	SMALL	MEDIUM	LARGE
1. Intensively held (13+ holders)	N/A	8.6%	10.9%
2. Moderately held (2–12 holders)	14.7	17.3	23.2
3. Neglected (0 or 1 holder)	20.1	26.0	N/A
Mean*	18.4	16.3	12.2

*Weighted by number of companies in each category.
N/A = not enough stocks for meaningful figures.
SOURCE: Arbel, Carvell, and Strebel, 1983.

degree of institutional participation, there is no evidence that small stocks perform particularly well. On the contrary, they seem to perform worse than their big brothers.

A SHOT IN THE DARK

One of the difficulties of studying the stock market is that important-looking factors may actually be proxies for still other factors. The small-stock effect seems to be a case in point. What is really at work is probably an information effect (or, conversely, an ignorance effect). It shows up as a size effect because there is generally less information, research, and analysis available on small stocks than on large ones.

Investors face an uncomfortable dilemma: It seems there is little to gain from buying small stocks that are widely followed by the professional investment community. Superior performance requires a shot in the dark— the purchase of stocks that neither we nor anyone else knows much about. I doubt that this approach is intuitively attractive to most investors.

12

Still More Anomalies

The efficient market theory tells us that we should not be able to use publicly available information to create market-beating strategies, but in the last two chapters we saw some severe challenges to the theory. Several stock-selection techniques were shown to produce superior returns. They were all based on information that is very easily obtained by any investor, and the challenges kept on coming.

A fundamental proposition of the efficient market hypothesis is that the market's adjustment to new information is very rapid, so that by the time news is out, it is too late to profit from it. We have seen evidence to support that idea, but there is a contradiction in a surprising area.

The most eagerly awaited piece of information on any stock is the latest quarterly earnings. It is also the most analyzed and forecast piece of information, because earnings are the cornerstone of stock valuation. Accordingly, earnings announcements are publicized quickly and widely to the investment community. Via the Dow Jones news wire and other news services, they are available across the nation—indeed, around the world—within a matter of minutes. Thus, if the stock market is efficient, it certainly ought to be efficient with respect to earnings announcements, responding very rapidly to whatever surprises are contained in the quarterly reports.

But what if the market is not so efficient?

SWEET SUEs

Various researchers have studied what happens to stocks of companies that have earnings surprises, in the form of what are called Standardized Unexpected Earnings (SUEs). It's a bit complicated mathematically, but it amounts to this: By means of a statistical method called linear regression, past earnings trends are projected into the future, providing a forecast of the next quarter's earnings. This is a purely mathematical projection, not the result of any form of security analysis. Actual earnings are then compared to the projection to determine the extent to which the actual earnings are unexpected. The standardized aspect of this is that the unexpected earnings are adjusted according to the past variability of each company's earnings. If a company has a history of erratic earnings, it requires more deviation from expected earnings for actual earnings to be considered surprises.

Table 12.1 summarizes some of the results of a major study of SUEs. The vast majority of all listed stocks were tracked from the third quarter of 1971 (the earliest date for which sufficient data was available) through mid-1980. The stocks were grouped into ten portfolios each quarter according to their SUEs (largest negative surprises in portfolio #1, largest positive ones in #10). SUE is calculated when actual quarterly earnings are announced. The study tracked the stocks for the 20 days preceding and the 90 days following the announcement. The method was to calculate the excess returns: the difference between the individual stocks' performance and that of an equally weighted NYSE/Amex index.

The table shows that the process of adjustment to earnings surprises is not quite what the efficient market theory would predict. As expected, there is a great deal of anticipation of the announcement, the result of ongoing news and analysis, and there is the expected instant reaction to the

TABLE 12.1 Summary of Excess Returns by Earnings "Surprises" 36 Quarters, 1971–1980

DAYS RELATIVE TO ANNOUNCEMENT	SUE Categories					
	EARNINGS LESS THAN EXPECTED			EARNINGS MORE THAN EXPECTED		
	1	2	4	7	9	10
− 20 to − 1	− 3.3	− 3.1	− 1.4	0.9	2.2	2.4
Announcement day	− 1.4	− 1.0	− 0.2	0.6	1.3	1.3
+ 1 to + 90	− 4.0	− 3.2	− 1.8	1.2	3.4	4.3
− 20 to + 90 (total)	− 8.7	− 7.3	− 3.6	2.8	6.9	8.0

SOURCE: Jones, Rendleman, and Latane, 1984.

earnings news: for the extreme groups, the average adjustment is more than 1 percent on the announcement day. Nevertheless, for unexpectedly good and poor earnings alike, the revaluation process continues far beyond this. Roughly half of the adjustment takes place in the 90 days following the announcement, and it occurs gradually, not suddenly. This is contrary to the efficient market theory and has been confirmed by other studies that used different stocks and different periods.

SUE research has uncovered another interesting phenomenon. There is a tendency for stocks that have high (or low) SUEs in one period to have high (or low) SUEs in the next. In short, there is some persistence in earnings patterns.

A SUE-based investment strategy is not a very plausible approach for real-world individual investors. The gains that could be expected from it would be swamped by the costs of trading and the cost of obtaining and processing the needed information. Why bring it up? First, the SUE research increases our understanding of how the market functions. Second, a variation of the SUE strategy is an important element of a successful investment approach that is widely available to individual investors. We will look at that approach shortly.

RELATIVE STRENGTH: RELATIVELY STRONG DEBATE

One of the precepts of technical analysis is that stocks move in discernible trends and that we can identify these trends early enough to profit from them. One natural approach to this is to use filter rules, but no rules have been found that produce superior returns after trading expenses. Another approach to trend following has shown more promise: *relative strength*.

The theory of relative strength is straightforward: Stocks that have done comparatively well in one period are expected to do comparatively well in the next. A major effort to verify this was made by Robert Levy. He studied a sample of 200 NYSE stocks for a five-year period in the early 1960s. The stocks were ranked each week according to their relative strength over the prior 26 weeks. The stock that had done the best (highest returns) would be ranked #1, and so on through #200. A model portfolio was then created from the top-rated stocks.

Levy experimented with different standards for determining which stocks would qualify for the portfolio and for determining the point at which they subsequently would have to be eliminated. He settled on including at the outset stocks in the top 10 percent of the relative-strength rankings. A stock would not be cast out, however, until it had fallen into the bottom fourth of the rankings. At that point, it would be replaced by stocks then meeting the top 10 percent standard.

Superior results seemed to come from this procedure. The most successful screens showed rates of return almost double those of a simple, equally weighted average of the 200 stocks, even after allowing for the transaction costs involved in implementing the strategy.*

Levy's results flew in the face of the random walk theory and were laboriously attacked by Michael Jensen, one of the preeminent proponents of the theory. Jensen's arguments were mostly technical, having to do with the measurement of risk and return. By applying what he felt were correct standards, he eliminated virtually all of the excess returns from the relative-strength strategy.

Jensen also suggested that the remaining positive results were nothing more than a statistical aberration, the result of the kind of "mucking around in the data" we referred to in Chapter 3. To test this, Jensen applied Levy's standards to 200-stock samples over other five-year periods, from 1931 to 1965. His results: In some periods the relative strength method would have worked, in others not. Overall, the approach would not have outperformed a buy-and-hold strategy, once trading commissions were taken into account.

Regardless of the merits, Levy's original reports excited technical analysts. Relative-strength measurements have become a part of many of their analyses, and the major stock chart services now include some type of relative-strength measure for the stocks they cover.

The debate over relative strength is far from over. Studies continue to be produced, with widely varying results. How well the approach works seems to depend on when we look and what we compare it to. For now, about the most we can say is that using relative strength is sometimes helpful, sometimes not. Like chicken soup, it may not help, but it can't hurt.

THE AMAZING MR. BERNHARD

While this book is not designed to be an advertisement for anyone, truth is where you find it, and it would be less than honest to ignore a successful approach to the market simply because it is commercial. One of the most commercial is apparently one of the most successful. More important for our purposes, it also provides an excellent model for understanding what is and is not possible in the market.

---

*Because the standard for including stocks is different from the standard for casting them out, by the time a stock is eliminated, there will be several qualified stocks awaiting admission. Thus, the portfolio tends to expand. In Levy's five-year study, the portfolio started with 10 percent of the stocks but ended with 36 percent of them. Thus, a direct application of Levy's methods is not practical.

Founded by Arnold Bernhard in the mid-1930s, Value Line spent decades not only dispensing stock market advice but also conducting an extensive search for a system for valuing stocks. This culminated in 1965 with the introduction of the Value Line ranking system. The system and methodology have remained essentially unchanged since then.

Value Line, in its weekly *Investment Survey*, covers 1700 stocks. The stocks are ranked according to their "timeliness," Value Line's estimate of their prospects for the next 12 months. There are five ranking groups, 100 stocks in the best and worst categories (1 and 5), 300 each in groups 2 and 4, and 900 in the middle group. All of the stocks are ranked each week.

The Value Line system is notable both for its record and for its methodology. The record is shown in a couple of ways. Figure 12.1 shows the 20-year cumulative percentage changes in each of the five groups, beginning in 1965 (dividends are not included). This corresponds to a strategy of investing in the respective groups. The accompanying table gives the year-by-year figures.

The figure provides dramatic visual evidence that the ranking system effectively discriminates among the stocks. Group 1 stocks have increased roughly 68-fold in 20 years. Over the same period, the NYSE Composite index and the S&P 500 roughly doubled. To look at it another way, the S&P 500 grew at a compound rate of about 3 percent per year; Value Line's group 1 grew at a compound rate of over 23 percent! Meanwhile, the group 5 stocks collectively have all but vanished.

This record is impressive, but no allowance has been made for commissions and taxes, both of which would cut heavily into the returns. Figure 12.1 is also based on adjusting the portfolios weekly to keep up with changing rankings. Value Line confirms that, in general, maintaining a pure group 1 portfolio requires turning over the portfolio about two and one-half to three times per year. This could easily cost an investor 6 to 10 percent per year in commissions. Of course, taxes also would have been due on the gains, reducing the amount available for reinvestment. Given the high turnover, the bulk of the gains would have been taxed at short-term (ordinary income) tax rates under the tax laws of the time.

Not even Value Line recommends reacting to these rankings changes on a weekly basis. A more conservative and more realistic view of performance by rankings is presented in Figure 12.2. Here, the assumption is that the portfolios are constructed at the beginning of each year and held to the end of the year, regardless of the changes in rankings that occur in the interim. It is thus a one-year buy-and-hold strategy. Again, commissions, taxes, and dividends are ignored.

Two points can be made about the second set of results. First, the rankings still effectively discriminate among the stocks. Second, the value of the rankings appears to be greatly diminished by this more restrictive use. The

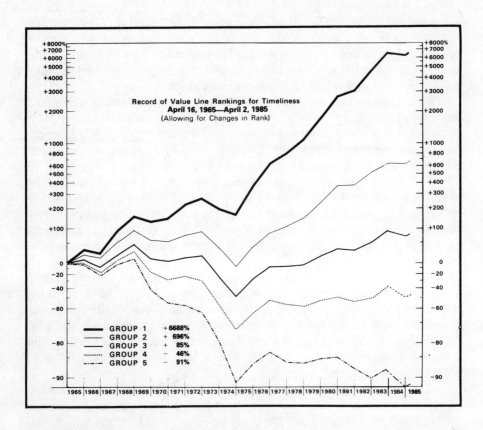

Record of Value Line Rankings For Timeliness (Allowing for Changes In Rank)
April 16, 1965—April 2, 1985

Group	1965*	1966	1967	1968	1969	1970	1971	1972	1973	1974	1975
1	+28.8%	− 5.5%	+53.4%	+37.1%	−10.4%	+ 7.3%	+30.6%	+12.6%	−19.1%	−11.1%	+75.6%
2	+18.5	− 6.2	+36.1	+26.9	−17.5	− 3.2	+13.7	+ 7.4	−28.9	−29.5	+47.4
3	+ 6.7	−13.9	+27.1	+24.0	−23.8	− 8.0	+ 9.3	+ 3.5	−33.6	−34.1	+40.7
4	− 0.4	−15.7	+23.8	+20.9	−33.3	−16.3	+ 8.4	− 7.1	−37.9	−40.6	+39.3
5	− 3.2	−18.2	+21.5	+11.8	−44.9	−23.3	− 5.5	−13.4	−43.8	−55.7	+40.9

Group	1976	1977	1978	1979	1980	1981	1982	1983	1984	Apr. 16, 1965 to Apr. 2, 1985
1	+54.0%	+26.6%	+32.6%	+54.7%	+52.6%	+13.6%	+50.6%	+40.9%	− 2.1%	+6688%
2	+31.2	+13.4	+18.3	+38.0	+35.7	+ 1.8	+31.0	+19.1	− 0.8	+ 696%
3	+29.0	+ 1.3	+ 3.0	+20.7	+15.4	− 3.3	+17.9	+20.2	− 5.6	+ 85%
4	+28.8	− 6.9	− 3.8	+12.8	+ 7.4	− 8.7	+ 5.1	+25.0	−17.4	− 46%
5	+26.7	−17.6	− 3.2	+10.4	+ 2.9	−21.4	−10.9	+19.0	−31.0	− 91%

*April through December

FIGURE 12.1 Record of Value Line rankings for timeliness (allowing for changes in rank) April 16, 1965–April 2, 1985.
SOURCE: Value Line, *Selection and Opinion,* April 19,1985.

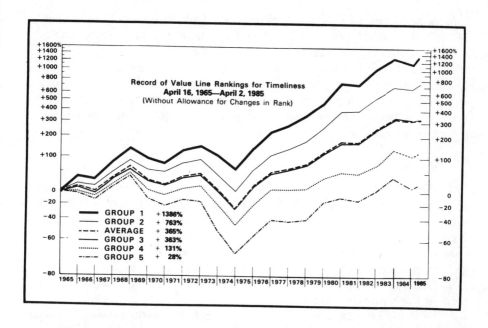

Record of Value Line Rankings For Timeliness (Without Allowance for Changes In Rank)
April 16, 1965—April 2, 1985

Group	1965*	1966	1967	1968	1969	1970	1971	1972	1973	1974	1975
1	+33.6%	− 3.1%	+39.2%	+31.2%	−17.7%	− 8.9%	+26.5%	+10.1%	−17.1%	−23.1%	+51.6%
2	+18.9	− 6.0	+31.9	+26.3	−16.3	− 4.0	+17.4	+ 7.5	−26.2	−27.8	+53.0
3	+ 8.9	− 9.7	+30.1	+21.4	−20.7	− 5.5	+12.2	+ 6.2	−27.0	−28.5	+52.9
4	+ 0.8	− 7.2	+25.1	+25.1	−26.8	−11.7	+14.2	+ 3.2	−29.1	−33.6	+48.4
5	− 1.2	−12.4	+28.4	+25.9	−35.7	−13.1	+10.5	+ 2.9	−43.1	−36.8	+42.1
Avg	+10.1	− 7.9	+29.9	+24.6	−22.1	− 7.5	+14.9	+ 5.5	−27.7	−29.6	+51.2

Group	1976	1977	1978	1979	1980	1981	1982	1983	1984	Apr. 16, 1965 to Apr. 2, 1985
1	+35.3%	+15.8%	+19.8%	+25.6%	+50.2%	− 1.9%	+33.7%	+25.2%	− 8.6%	+1386%
2	+36.3	+12.7	+16.1	+30.8	+37.4	+ 0.7	+29.0	+22.2	− 0.1	+ 763%
3	+33.8	+ 5.2	+ 9.2	+27.6	+20.8	+ 2.7	+25.5	+26.7	− 1.6	+ 363%
4	+36.1	− 0.2	+ 2.4	+23.1	+13.2	− 0.9	+18.5	+35.2	−12.3	+ 131%
5	+38.2	− 2.8	+ 4.0	+39.9	+ 8.4	− 4.2	+19.9	+30.0	−17.1	+ 28%
Avg	+35.1	+ 5.8	+ 9.6	+28.0	+23.4	+ 0.9	+25.0	+27.5	− 4.7	+ 365%
							Dow Jones Industrials			+ 39%
							N.Y. Stock Exchange Composite			+ 120%

*April through December

FIGURE 12.2 Record of Value Line rankings for timeliness (without allowances for changes in rank) April 16, 1965–April 2, 1985.
SOURCE: Value Line, 1985.

compounded annual rate of return of group 1 stocks on this basis is about 14 percent, a good 9 points below the returns from a continuously updated group 1 portfolio (but still 10 points better than the S&P 500). The costs of implementing the conservative strategy, however, are much lower. The portfolio will turn over at most once a year, and so it is doubtful that commissions would eat up more than 3 or 4 percent of the returns. All gains would have been taxed at long-term capital gains rates. Thus, the two approaches are not directly comparable.

How Do They Do It?

Value Line has been able to clearly and consistently differentiate stocks according to their market prospects, an apparent contradiction of the efficient market hypothesis. This is interesting in itself, but what is more interesting is how the Value Line analysts do it, for it turns out that they use the very anomalies that we have discussed in the past three chapters. Moreover, they have been using them since before any of the research evidence that we have looked at was produced. In other words, Value Line discovered and verified the anomalies independently.

The Value Line system has not been revealed in minute detail, but the important elements are widely known. It is based on *cross-sectional analysis*. It doesn't analyze each stock in isolation to forecast its prospects. Rather, it looks at each stock in relation to all the others—a comparative approach. Value Line's goal is not to predict returns, but simply to rank the stocks.

The Value Line system has five elements, all based on earnings and stock prices, tracked over the prior 10 years. Stocks showing higher last-12-month earnings and price in relation to 10-year average earnings and price (compared to the other stocks) are given a high rank. Stocks with comparatively low P/E ratios also gain high rankings. Recent strong price momentum is considered positive, and an acceleration of recent earnings growth is similarly positive. Finally, there is an earnings-surprise factor, which gives a stock additional points if the most recent earnings exceed analysts' estimates.

What Value Line does, in effect, is use the low-P/E approach, both short-term and long-term relative strength, earnings trends, and the unexpected-earnings effect, all of which we have looked at.

Value Line's ranking system does not rely on predictions, projections, or forecasts of any kind. It uses nothing but historical data. This may not be at all obvious to a reader of Value Line's weekly survey. On a rotating basis, each of the 1700 stocks receives a full-page report, which is not only full of factual information but also contains analysis and opinion about the outlook for the company. Value Line employs dozens of security analysts to produce this, but the analysis and opinion do not go into the rankings. The system is entirely backward-looking.

Beating the Market

The graphs we've looked at attest to the validity of the Value Line ranking system. One of the things we noted was the performance of high-ranked stocks compared to the NYSE Composite or the S&P 500, but if we look a little closer, we see something quite interesting. Value Line's group 4 stocks ("below average") also outperform the NYSE Composite! Moreover, the average Value Line stock has had roughly three times the cumulative 20-year appreciation of the NYSE Composite.

This is a manifestation of yet another anomaly: the small-stock effect. It works in two ways. First, Value Line's universe of stocks is much broader than the S&P 500 and contains many stocks that are too small to be included in that index. Second, Value Line's calculation of returns is based on equal weighting, as if a portfolio had been constructed by investing equal amounts of money in each stock in a group. The NYSE Composite and the S&P 500 are value-weighted indexes, giving more weight to bigger companies.

Since we know that small stocks have far outperformed the market over the past 20 years, it is not any great feat that Value Line has beaten the market; an equally weighted portfolio of 100 or 500 or 1700 stocks chosen at random would have beaten the market since 1965. There are two aspects to Value Line's record: the ability to discriminate among the stocks followed, and the choice of a broad universe in the first place. A small-stock strategy is not part of the ranking system, but we must recognize that a small-stock effect is operating when we compare Value Line to a market index such as the S&P 500.*

Now You See It, Now You Don't

Unfortunately, being able to pick good stocks and making extraordinary profits are not the same thing. We presented the record of Value Line's ranking groups without any allowance for commissions or taxes. This is the way most stock market results and research are reported, but the result is an incomplete, distorted view of the benefits that we can actually realize from an investment strategy—all the more so when that strategy is highly active and requires considerable trading.

When we look at Figures 12.1 and 12.2, it is tempting to assume that the results are so clearly extraordinary that they would dwarf any plausible cost and tax effects. Well, let's see.

---

*This "broad universe effect," a variant of the small stock effect, explains why both the S&P 500 and professional portfolio managers have usually come out second best when matched against dart-throwers, apes, and infants in the stock-picking contests that newspaper columnists conduct and report on with such relish.

   Since Value Line's recommendations are public and unambiguous, someone could track every single ranking change over the past 20 years, make assumptions about commissions and tax rates, and recreate the actual experience of an investor following a so-called Value Line strategy. This has not been done, because of the enormous amount of data that would have to be gathered and processed, but there is a simpler, looser, and yet still useful way that we can approach the problem.

   I have conducted a simple simulation of three alternative strategies based on Value Line. The first is to maintain continuously a portfolio of group 1 stocks. This corresponds to Figure 12.1, and requires weekly updating—replacing stocks that have dropped out of group 1 with newly upgraded ones (since the group always contains 100 stocks, one is added whenever one is dropped). The second strategy is to create a portfolio of the stocks ranked #1 at the beginning of the year and hold them for the full year, even if the rankings change during the year. This corresponds to Figure 12.2. In either of these strategies, the portfolio would have to be rebalanced at the beginning of each period (so that it would be equally weighted) to correspond to the way Value Line calculates returns. But weekly rebalancing of the continuously updated portfolio is preposterously costly as a practical matter, and I ignore it. Instead, I have made an allowance only for costs associated with replacing stocks, plus an allowance for rebalancing the portfolio at the end of each year. The final strategy is to hold a portfolio that corresponds to what Value Line reports as the average stock (see Figure 12.2). This is roughly a strategy of buying all 1700 stocks (or a random sample of them) in 1965 and holding the portfolio for 20 years.

   Table 12.2 shows the compound annual rates of return for the strategies under three different measurements. First are the gross returns, without commissions or taxes, corresponding to the figures published by Value Line. Second are the returns after an allowance for trading costs on the assumed turnover. I have used a rate of 1.25 percent per transaction. Thus, selling a stock and replacing it with another would cause a "leakage" of 2.5 percent. Finally, we see the returns available when commissions and taxes are both considered (a tax rate of 40 percent for ordinary income is used, and 16 percent for long-term capital gains).*

---

*A cost of 1.25 percent per transaction will not be appropriate for all investors and all circumstances, of course. Most customers of full-service brokers will pay a good deal more than this, while discount brokers may charge less. Commissions are not the only cost of trading. There is also the spread. Evidence suggest that this will cost at least 0.6 percent per transaction (e.g., ¼ point on a $40 stock). Thus, an assumed total trading cost of 1.25 percent per transaction is very conservative, something that probably only an investor dealing in large lots and using a discount broker could achieve. The assumptions regarding tax rates may seem inappropriate after the passage of the 1986 Tax Reform Act, but please see Chapter 13.

TABLE 12.2   Simulated Returns From Alternative Strategies Using Value Line Rankings (April 1965–April 1985)

	Compounded Annual Rates of Return		
STRATEGY	WITHOUT COSTS OR TAXES	AFTER COSTS @1.25%	AFTER COSTS AND TAXES
Continuously updated, group 1	23.47%	14.54%	9.75%
12-month buy-and-hold, group 1	14.44	11.90	10.00
20-year buy-and-hold, "average" VL stock	7.99	7.85	7.14

NOTES:
1. Dividends not included in any calculations.
2. Turnover in continuously updated portfolio is assumed to be three times per year, with one-third of gains long-term for tax purposes.
3. Turnover in 12-month buy-and-hold portfolio is assumed to be 90 percent per year.
4. The only assumed transactions for the 20-year buy-and-hold strategy are at the beginning (when the portfolio is purchased) and at the end (when it is sold).
5. Assumed tax rate = 40 percent (16 percent for long-term capital gains).

The results are eye-opening. For the aggressive strategy of continuous updating, our once-startling return of 23.5 percent has fallen to 14.5 percent after trading costs and to 9.8 percent after taxes. In fact, the strategy has completely lost its 9-point lead over the 12-month buy-and-hold approach, and both active strategies outperform the long-term buy-and-hold approach by less than 3 percent per year.

Another view of this is presented in Table 12.3, where these rates of return are translated into wealth ratios (simply the cumulative growth of one dollar invested in each of the strategies). Here, we see the effect of compounding on these lowered rates of return. We saw earlier that a pure group 1 strategy would have resulted in multiplying our investment 68-fold, ignoring commissions and taxes. Now these results are drastically slashed.

Seeing cumulative returns reduced to less than 7-fold from 68-fold (or 15-fold, in the case of the 12-month buy-and-hold strategy) may be difficult to accept, but all of the returns are calculated with the compound annual rates of return reported by Value Line—23.5 percent for continuously updated portfolios, 14.4 percent for 12-month buy-and-hold portfolios. The returns are sharply reduced because commissions and taxes reduce the amount of money on which the reported returns are working. Suppose that a group 1 stock were bought for $100 and owned for four months before

TABLE 12.3 Simulated Returns From Alternative Strategies Using Value Line Rankings (April 1965–April 1985)

	Terminal Value of $1.00		
STRATEGY	WITHOUT COSTS OR TAXES	AFTER COSTS @1.25%	AFTER COSTS AND TAXES
Continuously updated, group 1	$67.80	$15.11	$6.43
12-month buy-and-hold, group 1	14.84	9.48	6.73
20-year buy-and-hold, "average" VL stock	4.65	4.53	3.97

NOTE: All assumptions identical to Table 12.2.

it fell in ranking and had to be replaced. It was appreciating at an annual rate of 23.5 percent (a 4-month rate of 7.3 percent), and so at the end of four months, it was worth $107.30. Did this $107.30 get put to work in the new group 1 stock, again compounding at a rate of 23.5 percent? No. A commission of $1.34 was paid to sell the first stock. A tax of $2.38 was paid on the net gain (.4($7.30 − $1.34)). This left $103.58, which, after commission, would buy $102.30 worth of the new group 1 stock. It is this $102.30—not the original $107.30—that would be compounding at a 23.5 percent gross annual rate in the next period.

If we had assumed a total one-way trading cost (commission plus spread) of 2.5 percent (5 percent round-trip), which is probably realistic for most customers of full-service brokers, the performance of the 12-month strategy would be essentially indistinguishable from the 20-year buy-and-hold results. Furthermore, the performance of the continuously updated strategy would be substantially worse than either of the other strategies.

Some Final Thoughts

We have spent a good many pages discussing Value Line because of the length, completeness, and clarity of its record and because of its apparent success. It serves as a laboratory for studying active investment strategies. Our look at it yields some important conclusions.

Value Line has made use of many of the anomalies that have been uncovered in the market. The ranking system itself has proved to be an anomaly, a refutation of the efficient market hypothesis. Everything that goes into the rankings is public information, as are the rankings themselves, and so there is market inefficiency operating on two levels. If the market were truly efficient, the rankings wouldn't work in the first place. Further, if the market were efficient, it would react to rankings changes instantly, rendering them useless even if they were based on underlying inefficiencies.

Not surprisingly, Value Line's results have attracted a great deal of interest, not only from investors but also from researchers. Since Value Line was building its record at the same time that the efficient market idea was gaining strength and credence, most of the researchers were predisposed to find fault with Value Line, to somehow reconcile it with their theories—in short, to show that Value Line's results weren't what they seemed to be. Thus far, they have largely failed, and one conclusion seems inescapable: Value Line is able to effectively differentiate the prospects of the stocks it covers. Yet it is also clear that even a system so apparently successful may not be highly profitable in the real world of costs and taxes.

A WARNING

Almost all research, advertising, and advice aimed at individual investors reports returns on a gross basis, ignoring costs. This problem plagues us, because it both exaggerates the potential in different investment strategies and biases the comparisons between them.

A typical example is *Fortune*'s special issue, ''The 1986 Investor's Guide.'' The average annual total returns of several hypothetical market-beating strategies were shown in a large, multicolor graph, along with the returns from the S&P 500, over the six years from 1979 to 1984. The S&P 500's return is reported as 15 percent. Others include high-dividend stocks (return of 22.1 percent), low-P/E stocks (22.5 percent), low-price/book value stocks (23.3 percent), and small stocks (33.3 percent). The graphics are eye-catching and impress us with the obvious success of these strategies, but deep in the text of the article lurks a caveat: The figures don't allow for trading commissions. Unstated, but obvious, is the fact that they don't allow for spreads or taxes, either.

These are major problems. First, the use of average annual returns is biased. Compounded rates of return are what are relevant, and these are always lower than average returns. Worse, using average returns exaggerates the *differences* between the strategies.

The failure to account for costs and taxes is even more prejudicial. Following any of these strategies requires more trading than just buying and holding the S&P 500. This implies not only greater commissions, but also higher taxes, which must be paid along the way. Thus, the comparison with the S&P 500 is not on an equal basis. The article doesn't provide enough information to try to adjust for these factors, but it is not at all certain that the strategies would have held up as significant winners in the real world of commissions, spreads, and taxes. It exactly parallels the Value Line situation: What you see is not what you get.

This discussion is not intended to denigrate Value Line, whose achievements are remarkable. Value Line's stock rankings stand up, and these analysts certainly are not the only people to report results without considering costs and taxes. I have no doubt that they have found and exploited some real market inefficiencies. Nor do I wish to disparage *Fortune*, which followed standard industry practice. Rather, it is an object lesson for all of us when relevant costs are omitted from the reported results of active trading strategies. Such costs may seem trifling at first glance, when in fact they have enormous impacts on the returns that can actually be achieved.

The efficient market theory says that we can expect returns commensurate only with the level of market risk we assume, but in the last three chapters we have seen a variety of areas in which the theory seems to break down. It now seems possible to take publicly available information and create strategies that yield returns in excess of those that can be attributed to risk, even if those returns may be exaggerated in the popular press. It appears that the real market is not quite the tidy risk/return world of the capital market theorists.

13

Capital Gains Taxes:
Past, Present, Future

The taxation of capital gains has varied considerably through time. For decades, preference was given to long-term gains, though the degree of preference and the definition of *long-term* changed from time to time. For most of the past quarter-century, long-term gains benefited from a 60 percent exclusion, thus making the effective rate on long-term gains only 40 percent of a taxpayer's rate on ordinary income. The holding period required to qualify for the preferential treatment was usually 6 months, but there were times when it was 12.

The 1986 Tax Reform Act marked a watershed. For the first time since the 1920s, all preference for capital gains was eliminated. After the transitional year 1987, capital gains (and losses) are to be treated identically to any other source of income or loss, regardless of the holding period. This equalization is achieved by reducing the rates on ordinary income (and short-term gains) for most taxpayers while increasing them on long-term capital transactions.

This is pretty straightforward, and many observers have concluded that the effects and implications are equally straightforward. They are not quite as simple as they might appear, however.

LOWER RATES: A BOON TO TRADERS?

The most obvious effects of the new law are that investors will no longer have a tax incentive to hold a position six months, and most short-term traders will face lower tax rates than previously. Both effects imply that short-term trading will increase (which doubtless explains why the brokerage industry did not lobby against the new provisions).

On the face of it, it would seem that lower short-term tax rates would be a boon to short-term traders. Nevertheless, the situation is anything but clearcut, because it is likely that the new tax law will reduce the pretax returns from profitable but highly active strategies.

To illustrate, let's consider again the Value Line ranking system and the strategy of continuous updating to maintain a pure group 1 portfolio. The Value Line system is primarily dependent on company earnings reports. Each time a company issues new earnings figures, it is a likely candidate for a new ranking. By the nature of the publishing business, however, Value Line's subscribers receive notice of a new ranking a week or more after the actual earnings report. It is clear that one of the keys to Value Line's apparent success is that investors do not react immediately or fully to earnings announcements. This inefficiency gives Value Line a window of opportunity. Yet one of the reasons why active investors have not eliminated the inefficiency and closed the window may be the high tax cost of short-term activity.

Lower short-term rates and the lack of a reason to hold positions until they are long-term will increase the incentive to respond to earnings reports or any other information bearing on stock values. This will increase the market's short-run efficiency with respect to new information. There is no way to predict the size or extent of this effect. For many stocks, prices may be established at the margin by tax-exempt investors (pension and endowment funds) and by investors who don't care much about taxes (mutual funds). Just the same, strategies that depend on delayed responses to information are likely to become less profitable.

This leads to yet another warning about research and analysis designed to justify or promote highly active investment strategies. I could have conducted the Value Line-based simulations in Chapter 12 using the new tax rates, rather than ones based on the tax situation as it actually existed from 1965 to 1985. The results would have been different and more favorable to the high-turnover strategies, but they would also have been utterly misrepresentative. We cannot assume that the strategies would have achieved the same pretax returns in a different tax environment, because we cannot be sure that investors would have behaved the same. I am afraid, however, that we will soon be subjected to a great deal of so-called research based on back-testing, in which the new tax rates are applied to returns from periods before the new rates went into effect. This is a trap.

Since the 1986 tax law eliminated the rate difference between short-term and long-term gains, many have concluded that this equalizes the merits of strategies that have inherently different holding periods. This is not true, and it is easy to demonstrate. Consider the ten-year results from two alternative strategies, A and B. Both achieve steady pretax rates of return of 12 percent per year. For simplicity, let's assume that there are no dividends, and so all of the return comes in the form of capital gains. Assume round-trip trading costs of 2.5 percent and a marginal tax rate of 28 percent. The only difference between the two strategies is that A requires a completely new portfolio at the end of each year (turnover of 100 percent per year), while B is based on holding the original portfolio the entire ten years. At the end of ten years, $10,000 invested in strategy A would have grown to $19,014 after all commissions and taxes (including final liquidation and taxes), but the same investment in B would be worth $24,607. The after-tax compound rate of return for B is 9.4 percent, while for A it is only 6.6 percent. The reasons? Not only are commissions eroding the returns from A, but so are the taxes—not because they are higher, but because they are paid more frequently, each time reducing the amount available for reinvestment. Therefore, strategies based on active trading will still require significantly higher gross returns to compete with more passive ones.

Will It Last?

Many observers have acted as if the 1986 Tax Reform Act would somehow be the last. In reality, there is good reason to think that the elimination of preferential treatment for long-term gains will be reversed, because it is a mistake by all three important standards: fairness, effect on economic growth, and revenue yield. In each area, there is reason to give preference to long-term gains. Americans tend to feel that investors are better than speculators and should be treated better—as a matter of fairness. Economic growth requires investment and so requires a willingness to put capital at risk over long periods. This is certainly spurred by preferential tax treatment.

Perhaps most important from a political standpoint, raising the tax rates on long-term capital gains will result in lower tax revenue, not higher, because of the lock-in effect. Faced with higher tax rates, many investors will hold on to profitable positions longer in order to delay paying taxes. The higher the tax rate, the better a prospective new investment must be in order to justify paying the taxes to get out of an existing position, because higher taxes reduce the amount available for reinvestment in the new one.

We should also remember that the tax rate has increased enormously under the 1986 act. Many have commented that the maximum rate on long-term gains has gone from 20 percent to 28 percent. This is true, but it understates the actual situation, because the new 28 percent rate starts at a much lower income level than the old 20 percent rate. For a great many investors, the change will be to 28 percent from around 16 percent. That is a powerful lock-in, and there is considerable research evidence that it will significantly reduce tax revenues. When this begins to become obvious, there will be great pressure to reinstate the tax preference.

When major changes are made in our tax code, there are two dangers. The first is that there are usually unintended consequences. In the case of the 1986 act, these are likely to result in the eventual reversal of the change in capital gains taxation. The second danger is that analysts may jump to erroneous conclusions about the economic and investment implications of the new laws. In this case, it seems obvious that the new code will make short-term trading more profitable and long-term investing less profitable. In fact, this is not at all certain. Even if it turns out to be true to some degree, it will not eliminate the built-in advantage held by strategies based on long holding periods.

Part Five
The Real Stock Market

14

What's Really Going On?

The central conclusion of the efficient market theory is that investors can expect returns commensurate only with the amount of risk they are willing to take on. Risk is nothing more than the variability of returns over time (volatility). This risk can be broken into two parts; only market risk will be rewarded, because specific risk (the risk associated with particular, individual stocks) can be diversified away. Since beta measures the riskiness of a well-diversified portfolio, a diversified portfolio's returns should relate to beta and nothing else (given the performance of the market as a whole). Beta should be a complete description of the risk and return characteristics of the portfolio.

There is only one problem with this: It doesn't seem to work! We have seen many examples in which returns are not explained by beta, in which there are positive risk-adjusted returns. That is, we have found strategies that yield returns that are significantly greater than they should be, given the amount of risk incurred.

Something is wrong. In some respect or another, the efficient market model is flawed. It promised to fully explain the behavior of the market; it evidently doesn't do this.

Discovering that the market is not perfectly efficient may be interesting, but it is not enough. If we are trying to develop effective investment strategies, we need to have at least some idea of why the market is inefficient, the areas of the market where inefficiency exists, the extent of those

163

inefficiencies, and whether they are likely to persist. In short, we need to figure out what is really going on in the market.

DOUBTING THE ASSUMPTIONS

For the market to be efficient, we need a large number of well-informed, rational, risk-averse investors who attempt to determine the value of stocks, who are competent analysts, and who make portfolio decisions (buying and selling) in response to new information and changing prices and values. Let's look again at these assumptions and see what might result if one or more of them is invalid.

A few can be disposed of easily. There is certainly plenty of competition—a very large number of both individual and institutional investors. A great many investors make portfolio decisions on the basis of new information; this is obvious in the market response to the release of economic data, earnings announcements, and so on. Finally, there is no reason to doubt the assumption of aversion to risk. Historical data demonstrates that investors demand and receive higher returns for accepting greater risk.

More problematic are the assumptions that investors are well-informed and are competent analysts. This requires not only that investors receive relevant information, but also that they know what to make of it. We've seen considerable evidence that even professional security analysts are not able to forecast important figures, such as corporate earnings, with much accuracy. Economists, business executives, and financial analysts have equal difficulty in forecasting broader variables, such as interest rates, GNP, and inflation. We've also noted that the problem may not be as serious as it seems. The fact that forecasts are not accurate doesn't necessarily mean that the forecasters are incompetent; it is impossible to achieve great precision in the real world, even if analysis adds significantly to our knowledge. Further, inaccuracy won't matter, so long as the errors of different investor/analysts tend to offset each other. We know that the average errors of consensus estimates are much smaller than the average individual errors going into them.

In looking at the question of information and analysis, remember that the market is not a monolithic entity. The stock market of fledgling or struggling companies may have little in common with the stock market of such blue-chip behemoths as IBM. If the market for IBM is not efficient, it certainly isn't for lack of information and competent analysis. Scores of professional analysts scrutinize every scrap of fact and rumor concerning the company. But what of the little guys? We've already seen the answer, in

Chapter 11. Stocks that were not highly followed by professional analysts had higher returns than those that were.

It seems clear that an information effect operates in the market. While the availability of information and analysis is a continuum, we might say, loosely, that there is an informed sector of the market and an uninformed one. If that is the case, perhaps there is an efficient sector and an inefficient one. The informed sector would correspond to the stocks of interest to institutional investors: the 300 to 400 (mostly large) stocks that constitute their universe. This may be one of the reasons why these professionals don't do better in the market.*

Are Investors Rational?

Rationality is a broad word. In general, it refers to making decisions on the basis of self-interest and reasoned analysis, rather than emotion. We can expand on this in several ways. First, rational investors will make their decisions independently. A rational investor will not let the actions of other investors influence his own decisions unless he has reason to think that they know something he doesn't. Second, a rational investor will gather and process information in an unbiased way, giving each bit of information its appropriate weight in his analytical process. Finally, the rational investor will consider and understand both the relative returns and risks from alternative investments, choosing among them accordingly.

We've already seen suggestions and evidence that these descriptions of investor behavior are not very accurate. For example, cheap stocks (as measured by price/earnings, price/sales, or price/book ratios) have outperformed the market with a great deal of consistency, which implies that the valuation process is not rational. This is implicit in the overreaction hypothesis, which is predicated on the idea that investors don't gather and process information in an unbiased way. Rather, they attach undue importance to recent or extraordinary events, distorting reality in the process.

In addition, investors may attach undue or unexamined value to certain presumably desirable or undesirable characteristics. Andrew Tobias, in his modestly titled book *The Only Investment Guide You'll Ever Need*, recounts a conversation (p. 84) with a professional portfolio manager. This worthy's policy was to buy only stocks with above-average earnings growth prospects. Under Tobias's badgering, he admitted he would not buy companies with average or below-average earnings prospects, *regardless of price.*

---

*It has been documented that corporate insiders achieve excess returns. It is speculation on my part, but I wouldn't be surprised to find that these insiders do much better in companies in the uninformed sector than they do in the informed, institutional one. Information, like most things, is more valuable the scarcer it is.

Apparently, no price was too high for a growth stock, and no price was low enough for its less blessed cousin—hardly a rational approach to the market.

The efficient market theorists make the rather heroic assumption that the excessive optimism of Jones will be balanced out by the corresponding pessimism of Smith. It is equally plausible that crowd psychology—the herd instinct—operates in the market. We cannot prove this directly, but we have plenty of indications.

Many people have observed the groupthink that seems to pervade institutional investment management. Indeed, very few institutional investors deny it. If a clear example is needed, it is most easily found in the two-tier market of the early 1970s. During that period, investment professionals became enamored of what were called *one-decision stocks*. The term referred to the belief that the only decision that had to be made was to buy them. They would never need to be sold. As ludicrous as this is, the idea was that certain well-established growth companies (also known as the Nifty Fifty) could be bought at virtually any price, because subsequent earnings growth would make them bargains in retrospect. These companies (Avon, Polaroid, and yes, Disney, were a few) were thought to have such technical, managerial, and market dominance that they could maintain extraordinary growth forever. The portfolio manager cited by Tobias was interviewed during this period.

All of the Nifty Fifty were good and growing companies whose success had been deservedly recognized in the market. The problem came when recognition turned into concept and then into gospel. Investors failed to understand how much expected growth was already built into the stock prices (remember the Dividend Discount Model). As the Wall Street expression goes, the top-tier stocks were not only discounting the future, they were discounting the hereafter. For the record, when the bubble finally burst, Avon, Polaroid, and Disney all fell more than 85 percent from their highs.

Isolated, outrageous examples may be considered cheap shots, but another that has been cited by many others before me is irresistible. In early 1970, a gathering of 2000 institutional investors was held in New York. They were polled as to their favorite stocks for the year. The most popular choice was National Student Marketing, one of the preceding year's biggest stars. Reaching for 140 in February, NSM could be had for 7 by July. Professional portfolio managers had rushed in as a group and rushed out the same way.

The point of this is not that institutional money managers are fools. On the contrary: They may not always invest rationally, but they may *behave* rationally. The reason is simple: There is safety in numbers. Consider an astute institutional portfolio manager in 1971. He sees two things. First, the prices being paid for Nifty Fifty stocks imply future earnings growth that is so unlikely as to be preposterous. They are greatly overvalued. Second, his competitors are making money hand over fist in those same stocks. What is he to do? Chances are he will buy the stocks (or continue to hold them if he already has them). He can't risk being left behind in the competitive game. Even if his analysis is correct, he doesn't know when the glamour craze will end. If he heeds his own analysis and shuns the glamour stocks, but they keep on rising, his reputation and even his job are in jeopardy. He is in the worst possible position: failing to profit on a trend that is obvious both to his competitors and to his clients.

In contrast, suppose he sticks with the Nifty Fifty, his analysis proves correct, and the stocks plunge. The worst that will happen is that he will do about as poorly as his competitors, something he can live with. Thus, for an institutional manager, there was more risk in shunning the top tier than there was in embracing it, even if his analysis told him otherwise. If you go against the crowd, against the conventional wisdom, the penalties for being wrong are much greater than the rewards for being right.

Institutional portfolio managers are certainly not the only people subject to the allure and pressure of group thinking. I dare say it affects virtually all of us. The point is that not even professionals are immune. In a famous example, a group of 1000 children in New York were surveyed at a time when tonsillectomies were commonly performed. It was found that 61 percent of them had had their tonsils removed. The others were then examined by a group of doctors who concluded that 45 percent of these kids needed tonsillectomies. The shrinking group of "healthy" children was examined by another group of physicians, and 46 percent were diagnosed as needing the operation. When the survivors of this round (by now there were only 116) were examined by yet another group of doctors—you guessed it—45 percent of *them* needed their tonsils out.

Whether we are discussing doctors, investors, or security analysts, the behavior is understandable. By sticking close to consensus forecasts and current conventional wisdom, they reduce their professional risks. In short, it is the story of the emperior's new clothes. Scarcely anyone is immune, not even the presumably sophisticated, rational, hardheaded mavens of Wall Street. The market is populated not by automatons but by real people for whom fear and greed are inescapable. Both conformity and overreaction are inherent.

What Risks?

Rational and risk-averse investors are presumed to consider both the returns and the risks of potential investments, and they are presumed to understand that they can largely ignore risks that they can eliminate by diversification. But what if investors are not entirely rational? What if they don't know about market risk and specific risk, about diversification and beta?

The assumption that most investors are risk-averse is quite reasonable. As we've seen, if that is the case, then they will demand a premium (in returns) for taking on additional risk. What is important, however, may not be actual risk but *perceived* risk.

The best-documented cases of market inefficiency are of stocks that are somehow flawed. The companies are small, obscure, unknown, unanalyzed, or are of presumed low quality; they have erratic earnings, are recently unsuccessful, or are expected to be unsuccessful soon; the stocks are volatile, illiquid, or simply uninteresting. Stocks that are cheap aren't cheap for no reason; they are cheap because there is something wrong with them, something unappealing about them: They are loaded with negatives. It stands to reason that people won't want to own these stocks unless they can expect premium returns.

Most of these negatives can be thought of as perceived risk factors, but they are not the kinds of risk that we have talked about earlier. We haven't identified an obscurity risk or an erratic-earnings risk or even an illiquidity risk. All we have talked about is price variability and divided it into market risk and specific risk.

Where do these new risks fit in? To the extent that they are risks at all, they are largely specific risks and can be eliminated by diversification. As such, they shouldn't command a premium return. Since they do, the question is *Why?*

Evidently, it is perceived risk, diversifiable or not, for which investors demand compensation. Investors, amateur or professional, like to feel comfortable with their decisions and their positions. The kinds of stocks that achieve superior returns don't offer much in the way of comfort. Tobias's portfolio manager didn't want nongrowth stocks at any price. Another manager, appalled by the idea of buying out-of-favor stocks, said simply, "You don't know what's down there." It appears that reasonable compensation for real risk is not enough to induce many people to invest outside the market mainstream. Investors demand—and receive—compensation for perceived risks as well.

An obvious conclusion jumps out at us: If the market rewards diversifiable (specific) risks, then buy risky stocks and diversify. We should be careful here, though. For the most part, cheap stocks deserve to be cheap. The question is *how* cheap. Evidence suggests that they generally are priced cheaper than is warranted by nondiversifiable factors. In other words, they are bargains. But I need to repeat a warning given earlier: If we create a portfolio based on a particular strategy, then one form of specific risk will remain: the risk associated with the strategy itself. We saw this in Chapter 9 when we looked at the performance of two mutual funds in the 1973–1974 bear market (see Table 9.1). As compared to the S&P 500, one fund had adopted a cyclical-stock strategy, the other a growth-stock strategy. Even though both funds were widely diversified, in terms of numbers, and had almost identical betas, they had far different results, because their strategies carried their own risks, risks that could not be eliminated by any amount of diversification. We also noted this phenomenon with small stocks, in Chapter 11. For the period 1963–1980, they were very successful, far outperforming the market, but for a six-year stretch in the middle (the bear market years 1969–1974), they were failures, losing far more ground than large-capitalization stocks.

When a researcher finds some strategy (e.g., low capitalization) that yields returns that cannot be accounted for by market risk (beta), he usually says, "Aha! I have demonstrated that the market is inefficient." This is not quite true. Beta measures risk only in a well-diversified portfolio. The typical strategy is not well diversified; it is based on a particular characteristic. In that case, *beta will always understate the riskiness of the strategy*, a fact that is unfortunately often either unknown or ignored.

What is really going on? Demonstrable market-beating strategies are providing returns for risks that are more perceived than real and for risks that can be greatly reduced by diversification. The earlier conclusion still holds: Buy risky stocks and diversify. Still, those same winning strategies are significantly riskier than is implied by a naive use of beta as the measure of risk.

The Institutional Market

Institutional investors as a group do not outperform the market. Over the long run, most fail even to match the performance of the S&P 500. Whatever small advantage their expertise may give them is more than erased by their costs of trading and operations. Further, there are very few examples of particular professional managers achieving consistently superior performance. These facts conform to the theory of an efficient market, and they are taken as prima facie evidence of efficiency.

We have also suggested that institutional investors are just as vulnerable as individual investors to crowd psychology and just as prone to overreact to short-term developments. If that is the case, then the institutional market should be inefficient. What *is* really going on?

Let's remember that for a few hundred (mostly large) stocks, the institutions virtually *are* the market, accounting for the preponderance of both holdings and trading. If they are the market, then they can't possibly significantly outperform it or underperform it. Saying that the institutional market is efficient because institutions only match its performance is a little like saying that the National Football League is efficient because the teams, taken together, achieve only a .500 record. If we look only at institutions as a group, the market will look pretty efficient, whether it is or not!

What about the fact that so few individual institutions are able to outperform the market with any consistency? If the market were inefficient, wouldn't some managers be able to exploit it? In principle, yes, but there are enormous pressures for conformity in the investment profession. There are very few original thinkers in the institutional management business.

It seems to me that, for practical as well as psychological reasons, the following situation prevails in the institutional investment field: The vast majority of institutions are investing in the same few hundred stocks in which they dominate the market. They have access to the same information and they process and react to that information in essentially the same way. If this is a reasonably accurate description, then no one is going to achieve consistently superior (or inferior) results. Everyone will achieve consistently similar results. To put it baldly, everyone rises and falls with IBM.

Whether the institutional market is efficient is an open question. Given the motivation and behavior of institutional investors, it is likely that there is at least some inefficiency. The institutional market is a highly informed one, however. It is also highly liquid, and it is generally populated by good stocks, not "dogs." (When a stock falls into the dog category, it usually drops out of the institutional market.) In other words, it doesn't contain many of the perceived risks that seem to be rewarded in the market. It is the comfortable sector of the market. We have seen that stocks widely held by institutions have lower returns than those that are not. Thus, the institutional universe as a whole cannot be considered to be an area of overlooked value or unexploited opportunity. On the contrary, it is probably much easier to find an overvalued stock in the institutional market than an undervalued one. This fact alone suggests that there is much less potential for excess returns here than in the riskier stocks outside the institutional sector.

The institutional market doubtless offers opportunities for investors who can manage to immunize themselves against overreaction and hence profit from it. Nevertheless, both logic and facts suggest that for investors who are determined to beat the market, the institutional sector isn't a very plausible place to try to do it.

ABANDONING ANALYSIS

In Chapter 9, we noted that the Capital Assets Pricing Model (CAPM), based on the theory that the stock market is efficient, is a *replacement* for both fundamental and technical analysis. Neither type of analysis could produce excess returns, so both could be abandoned in favor of the CAPM model, which explained returns solely by the amount of market risk assumed.

Since then, we have seen several documented cases of apparent market inefficiency—strategies that would produce returns in excess of what could be predicted from their riskiness. The best-documented and most promising of these were based on such things as earnings changes, price/earnings and price/book value ratios, market capitalization, and institutional and analytical coverage. All of these measures are part of the fundamental analyst's bag of tricks. Are we now to conclude that fundamental analysis has been vindicated? *No.* While the winning strategies we have looked at make use of fundamental information, they are not based on fundamental analysis. This may be a subtle point, but it is an important one.

The fundamental analyst is in the business of forecasting. He forecasts product development and demand, competition, interest rates, management capabilities, labor trends, and the like. Ultimately, he forecasts the future profits of a company. From that, he can assess its value in relation to its price and come up with an appropriate recommendation. As we have seen, fundamental analysis is based on the premise that stock prices often diverge significantly from value. The job of the analyst is to find the stocks that are undervalued or overvalued in the market.

Let's look at it in terms of P/E ratios, the most common standard of value. As a result of his labors, an analyst will say that XYZ should be valued at 8 times earnings but is priced at 6 times; UVW should have a P/E of 12 but currently sells at 17 times earnings. One by one, the stocks are analyzed and evaluated.

Now consider the low-P/E strategy. It, too, is based on the assumption that some stocks are undervalued and others are overvalued. Yet someone using this approach doesn't do any analysis of what P/Es different stocks should sell for. He simply assumes that low-P/E stocks as a group are undervalued, period. He doesn't try to figure out which ones are undervalued or by how much. He simply plays the odds.

The data on small stocks developed by Reinganum provided an excellent illustration, one worth looking at again (see Table 12.4). He demonstrated that the smaller the size group, the higher the mean annual returns—the small-stock effect. Yet there was no relationship between size and *median* returns. That is, the typical small stock did no better than the typical large one. Finally, the worst-performing small stocks did far worse than the worst large stocks; the best-performing small stocks far outdistanced the best big ones. The conclusion from this information was clear: The small-stock strategy works not because all or even most small stocks are superior performers, but because a few perform spectacularly. Among small stocks, as among any other group of stocks, there are some that will prove to be excellent investments and others that will be very poor ones.

Faced with this situation, the fundamental analyst tries to figure out which are which. Reinganum doesn't. He just buys them all. No analysis is necessary, just the knowledge or belief that small stocks, *taken together*, are undervalued. Again, he is simply playing the odds.

David Dreman doesn't say that all low-P/E stocks are bargains or that all high-P/E stocks are overpriced. Can a stock with a P/E of 3 be overpriced? Can one with a P/E of 30 be underpriced? Of course. Marc Reinganum doesn't say that all small stocks are bargains or that all big ones are not. In fact, his data shows that the best 10 percent of the biggest stocks returned an average of 44 percent per year, while the worst 10 percent of the smallest stocks *lost* 44 percent. What Dreman and Reinganum do say is that the market has systematic biases in the way it values stocks, and that the key investment success is to understand and utilize those biases.

The idea that systematic errors in valuation occur in the market is a direct contradiction of the efficient market hypothesis. In a strange way, however, the two sides are allied. Both are saying that conventional analysis is unnecessary and that forecasting is not the route to market success.

15

Risk Again:
It's About Time

Arguments about market efficiency aside, return in the stock market is unquestionably related to risk. Innumerable studies have borne this out. As a result, investment professionals agree that return and risk must be evaluated together. The idea is not to measure returns in isolation, but rather in terms of the risks incurred to achieve them. Returns, as reported, and risk-adjusted performance can look very different.

Beta is the measure of risk that is normally used to compare the riskiness of different investments (or investment strategies). As we've seen, beta is a measure of the volatility of a stock or a portfolio in relation to the overall market. It measures the risk that cannot be eliminated by diversification. In fact, it measures the relative riskiness of a portfolio *after* it has been effectively diversified.

Since risk essentially means uncertainty, and volatility is a manifestation of uncertainty, beta is a very useful measure both for evaluating performance and for constructing portfolios. Nevertheless, it is not the be-all and end-all of risk measurement. Beta has severe limitations that are usually overlooked or misunderstood by investors. We have already noted that beta is an adequate measure of risk only for well-diversified portfolios. It will understate the riskiness of portfolios that are constructed on the basis of a particular strategy.

RISK AND TIME

An even more significant limitation to beta's usefulness is that it does not account for the relationship between risk and time. Beta is a short-term risk measure. Depending on who is calculating it, it is based on weekly or monthly returns. When we make investments, we may be concerned about what kind of ride we are in for, but what we care most about is how we end up, not how we get there. How we end up depends upon when we look. If we look far into the future, weekly or monthly variations in returns may have little or no relevance.

In Chapter 7, we said that if we compare two possible investments, A and B, and we see that A has both higher expected returns and lower risk than B, then we can say that A dominates B. If A has greater risk, along with the greater returns, then we face an inconclusive trade-off. Investors must make their own choices, based on their attitudes toward risk-taking. This is the situation we usually face.

Now consider this possibility: What if A has both higher expected returns and greater risk than B, but the *worst* possible return from A is higher than the *best* possible outcome from B? For example, suppose that B has two possible outcomes, a return of 10 percent or 12 percent. With A, the possible outcomes are returns of 15 percent or 25 percent. Investment A has a higher expected return. It also is riskier, because the variability of possible returns is greater than for B, but only a fool would fail to agree that A is the superior investment—that A dominates B.

Unfortunately, it is difficult if not impossible to find situations like this in the real world, at least in the short run. What about the long run? Does time have an effect? Most emphatically, yes. Using the data developed by Roger Ibbotson and Rex Sinquefield (see Chapter 2), I studied three possible investments over the period 1926 through 1984. The investments are T-Bills, the general stock market (as represented by the S&P 500), and small stocks. Since the S&P 500 is a value-weighted index, it represents a large-stock strategy. Small stocks are defined as the bottom 20 percent by total market value on the NYSE, with hypothetical portfolios put together on an equally weighted basis and reconstituted every five years. We look at each investment over 1-, 5-, 10-, 15-, and 20-year holding periods. Table 15.1 shows the average returns for each type of investment. For multiyear holding periods, the returns are for the period, not annual rates.

Regardless of the length of the holding period, T-Bills are outperformed *on average* by the S&P 500, which is in turn outperformed by the small stocks. The table also provides a measure of the risk involved in each investment, the standard deviation of returns. This is a better risk measure than beta, in this case, because it measures the total variability of returns, not just volatility in relation to the market. It eliminates the problem of beta's

TABLE 15.1 Average Returns, Risk, and Number of Losing Periods 1926–1984

	59 ONE-YEAR PERIODS	55 FIVE-YEAR PERIODS	50 TEN-YEAR PERIODS	45 FIFTEEN-YEAR PERIODS	40 TWENTY-YEAR PERIODS
T-Bills:					
Ave. Return	3.4%	17.7%	36.0%	56.9%	79.2%
Stand. Dev.	3.3%	18.0	36.4	57.9	N/A
Coeff. Variation	.97	1.02	1.01	1.02	N/A
# Loss Periods	0	0	0	0	0
S&P 500:					
Ave. Return	11.7%	64.8%	180.1%	396.6%	793.3%
Stand. Dev.	21.2%	57.8%	137.2%	304.5%	N/A
Coeff. Variation	1.81	.89	.76	.76	N/A
# Loss Periods	19	7	2	0	0
Small Stocks:					
Ave. Return	18.2%	131.2%	340.3%	761.1%	1,668.3%
Stand. Dev.	36.3%	153.8%	285.9%	529.7%	N/A
Coeff. Variation	1.99	1.17	.84	.70	N/A
# Loss Periods	19	9	2	3	0

SOURCE: Adapted from Ibbotson and Sinquefield, 1982, 1987.

understating the riskiness of the small-stock strategy. In addition, standard deviation is expressed in the same terms as returns, and so it can be used to make a direct calculation of return per unit of risk.

Risk is much higher in the S&P 500 than in T-Bills and higher yet in small stocks, corresponding to our intuitive understanding of these investments. (Betas for the various investments would show a similar pattern. The beta of the S&P 500 is 1.0, by definition, and that of small stocks is well above 1.0. Beta for T-Bills is approximately 0.) Further, for each investment, the longer the holding periods, the greater not only the returns but also the risks. This also makes sense: Investment returns vary more on a monthly basis than on a weekly one, still more on a yearly basis, and so on.

For stocks, both return and risk rise as holding periods lengthen. Nevertheless, longer holding periods do not make investing riskier! The reason is that risk and return are absolute measures. We are interested here in more than just the levels of risk and return; we're interested in the relationship between them.

For both types of stock investments, *relative risk* declines as holding periods lengthen. The measure of this is what is called the *coefficient of variation*, the standard deviation divided by the average return. It is thus a measure of risk per unit of return. For example, for the S&P 500, the standard deviation of returns is roughly twice the average return for 1-year holding periods. But by the time we get to 10-year periods, it is only about three-fourths of the average return. For small stocks, it is quite similar, but for T-Bills, the relative risk remains steady.

For stocks, while risk increases with longer holding periods, returns increase even more rapidly. This implies that the likelihood of losing money decreases as holding periods get longer, and Table 15.1 bears this out. Either stock investment would have resulted in losses in about one-third of the 1-year periods, but this rapidly decreases: Only two of the fifty 10-year periods were losers, and neither stock investment would have resulted in a loss over *any* 20-year period. By their nature, T-Bills never result in losses. For most purposes, they are considered a risk-free investment.*

How Much Loss?

It may be useful to know how likely a loss is for a given investment and a given holding period, but an equally important question is *How big a loss?* Table 15.2 helps answer that question by showing the worst performances in each category. Here, the riskiness of stocks, and especially of smaller stocks, is evident. An investor in the S&P 500 has lost as much as 45 percent over a 5-year period, the small stock investor 80 percent! Even on a

---

*The 20-year returns in T-Bills will vary, but all T-Bills mature in a year or less. Thus, a 20-year holding period is based on a string of 1-year returns, each of which is riskless.

TABLE 15.2 Worst Historical Returns by Holding Period 1926–1984

	59 ONE-YEAR PERIODS	55 FIVE-YEAR PERIODS	50 TEN-YEAR PERIODS	45 FIFTEEN-YEAR PERIODS	40 TWENTY-YEAR PERIODS
T-Bills:					
Worst Return	0.0%	0.4%	1.6%	3.5%	9.0%
(Ending Year)	(1939)	(1941)	(1942)	(1947)	(1950)
S&P 500:					
Worst Year	−43.4%	−44.9%	−8.6%	10.1%	84.4%
(Ending Year)	(1931)	(1933)	(1938)	(1943)	(1948)
Small Stocks:					
Worst Return	−58.1%	−80.0%	−44.5%	−17.8%	205.3%
(Ending Year)	(1937)	(1932)	(1938)	(1941)	(1948)

10-year basis, small stocks have suffered some truly grievous losses. (Incidentally, all of the "worsts" are from the distant past. If we used inflation-adjusted figures, however, the picture would change. Many of the worsts would be recent.)

As we move to the right on Table 15.2, we see something rather startling. For shorter holding periods, the worst of the S&P 500 is much worse than the worst of T-Bills. At 15 years, this reverses, and at 20 years, the lowest S&P return is many times as large as the lowest T-Bill return. In the case of small stocks, the reversal is even more dramatic. This is graphic evidence of the declining relative risk in risky investments as we move to longer and longer holding periods.

Table 15.3 presents direct comparisons among the three alternative investments, based on how often one investment beats another. Again, dramatic changes occur with longer holding periods. Stocks outperform T-Bills in only about 60 percent of the single-year periods. When we consider 10-year periods, stocks win about 85 percent of the time. Investing in either stock group would have been superior to a T-Bill investment in *every* 20-year period. Further, the riskier small stocks outperformed the S&P 500 in almost the same pattern.

One final comparison: The T-Bill investor never loses money. By contrast, the longest loss period in the S&P 500 was 14 years, from 1929 through 1942, but this reveals a crucial point. Without question, the worst possible time (on an annual basis) to invest in the stock market was the beginning of 1929. Investors holding T-Bills must have been congratulating themselves during the Great Crash and ensuing Depression. Yet, as bad as the Crash was, by the end of 1943 the stockholder was ahead of the T-Bill holder. By the end of 1984, this ill-timed investor in stocks would have achieved a wealth more than 15 times as great as the bill holder!

Time on Your Side

The implications of all this for investors are powerful, and they overturn some of the usual ideas about risk and return. By any standard measure, investing in stocks is riskier than investing in T-Bills. This includes 20 year holding periods. Still, how can we say that stocks are riskier if they outperform T-Bills in every period?

There is a caveat. Consider Rip Van Winkle. If he had invested all his money in the S&P 500 just before taking his nap, he would have checked the results when he woke up 20 years later. No matter when that was, he could only have been pleased with the results, at least if T-Bills had been the alternative. If he had invested in small stocks, he would have been happier yet (unless he had fallen asleep in 1945, 1946, or 1947, in which case he would have underperformed the S&P 500). He would neither have

TABLE 15.3 Alternative Investment Comparisons 1926–1984

	59 ONE-YEAR PERIODS	*55* FIVE-YEAR PERIODS	*50* TEN-YEAR PERIODS	*45* FIFTEEN-YEAR PERIODS	*40* TWENTY-YEAR PERIODS
S&P 500 versus T-Bills: Periods in which S&P 500 Superior					
Number	36	42	41	41	40
Percent	61%	76%	82%	91%	100%
Small Stocks versus T-Bills: Periods in which Small Stocks Superior					
Number	38	44	43	42	40
Percent	64%	80%	86%	93%	100%
Small Stocks versus S&P 500: Periods in which Small Stocks Superior					
Number	35	35	37	36	37
Percent	59%	64%	74%	80%	92%

known nor cared what had happened in the interim; he would have been blissfully ignorant of the bull and bear markets his money had been through. Real-life investors don't have this luxury. Many people who think they have long time horizons discover that their horizons shrink dramatically when times turn tough. *Saying* you are a 20-year investor and *being* one are two different things.

In preceding chapters, we have looked at several strategic approaches to the market that yielded returns that could not be explained by conventional risk measures. These approaches were long-term by nature. Now we have an idea of what the implications of long-term investing really are. We can see that whether beta fully explains the returns from different stocks may not really matter. Even if high long-term returns are fully explained or justified by high short-term risk, that risk may be largely irrelevant to a true long-term investor.

Here is a profound difference between individual and institutional investors: Quite simply, individuals can take a long view of investing. Institutional investors don't have this luxury. Theirs is a short-term competitive game and is appropriately defined by short-term measures of risk and return. Individuals can choose to ignore short-term risk and reap greater long-term rewards. This is their single greatest advantage in today's institutionally dominated market.

We are typically advised to think in terms of return and risk. To this, we must add a third factor: time. Time has a profound impact on the risk/reward profile of investments. In particular, it affects the *comparative* merits of different investments. Conventional studies of risk and return are based on the premise that risk is negative, something to which we investors are supposed to be averse. Yet short-term risk may be our long-term friend, offering both opportunity and safety. Short-term risk measures, such as beta and standard deviation, may not have great relevance for long-term investors, except perhaps in reverse. The longer our time horizons, the more we should welcome risk, not avoid it.

16

Market Timing

Stock selection is the major concern of most investors; owning winning stocks and avoiding losers is what beating the market is all about. Whether it is finding the next Xerox, takeover targets, or the market leaders of the next three months, differentiating the prospects of stocks is the most traditional and common activity on Wall Street. Another approach to beating the market has equal allure: the prospect of being heavily invested while the market is rising but resting smugly on the sidelines while it is falling—market timing.

Market timing became increasingly popular in the last couple of decades, for two reasons. First, investors perceived that the market had become more volatile while not getting anywhere in the long run. When they looked at the Dow Jones Industrial Average, they saw that overall growth was insignificant from the mid-1960s to the mid-1980s. Yet there were several major bear and bull markets, as well as some dramatic intermediate-term swoops and swoons. The potential in successful timing, as compared to buy-and-hold approaches, was obvious. Second, there was some highly publicized success in market timing. The best-known case was that of Joe Granville, who not only had a great gift for self-promotion but also racked up an eye-popping and odds-defying record, successfully calling a succession of market turns from 1978 to 1981. This came a cropper in 1982, with his subscribers caught in short positions when an enormous market rise began. In succeeding years, of course, various other analysts, primarily technicians, have enjoyed periods of seemingly uncanny success.

Stock pickers and market timers are clearly opposed. The former like to say that no one can predict the overall market: "It's not a stock market, anyway, it's a market of stocks" (remember that movements of the general market account for only about 30 percent of the movements of individual stocks). That may be true, say the market timers, but when the market is rising, the majority of the stocks will rise; when it is falling, most stocks will fall. My own research indicates that in significant intermediate-term bull moves, roughly 85 percent of all stocks will rise. In declines, 90 percent will fall. Correct timing puts the odds heavily on your side.

In a strange way, the timers are allied with the efficient market theorists and the Capital Assets Pricing Model: If you hold a well-diversified portfolio, your results will be determined almost entirely by the moves of the overall market (all the risk is market risk), and so market timing is the *only* way to beat the market. This is as far as the parallel goes, of course, because the efficient market theorists don't believe that consistently accurate market timing is possible.

AN ODDS-AGAINST PROPOSITION

Market timing may have allure and potential, but a recent study shows that the numbers are not in your favor. To beat the market with timing, you will have to be a very good timer indeed. Robert Jeffrey, a professional investment manager, examined the effects of both successful and unsuccessful hypothetical timing efforts from 1926 through 1982. The premise was that in the best case, an investor would be 100 percent invested in the S&P 500 during periods when that index outperformed T-Bills, and in T-Bills during periods when they proved to be the superior investment. The worst case (unsuccessful timing) was the reverse—getting it exactly backwards. Jeffrey calculated *net return*, which he defined as the actual return less the T-Bill rate (during periods that an investor is in T-Bills, net return is thus zero). He assumed trading costs of 1 percent per transaction, but there was no allowance for taxes. He studied different time periods, using both annual and quarterly timing intervals. In a quarterly model, for example, the decision between stocks and T-Bills is made each calendar quarter. The returns were compared with a passive strategy of simply holding the S&P 500 through thick and thin.

Jeffrey's results are instructive. Consider the period from 1975 to 1982. An investor with perfect timing (on a quarterly basis) would have achieved an annualized net rate of return of 15.9 percent. In contrast, one who always zigged when he should have zagged would have realized −11.9 percent per year. The buy-and-hold investor, holding the S&P 500 throughout, would have had an annual return of 5.7 percent. Perfect timing offered the prospect of *incremental* net returns of 10.2 percent per year (15.9 percent less 5.7 percent). Perfectly *wrong* timing reduced the annual rate of return by 17.6 percent (5.7 percent plus 11.9 percent). In other words, the prospects weren't symmetrical. There was more to be lost by being wrong than there was to be gained by being right.

Success in market timing has two elements: how often you are right, and being right when it most matters. For example, in the 32 quarters making up the 1975–1982 period, the three best (first quarter 1975, fourth quarter 1982, second quarter 1975, in descending order) accounted for *all* of the eight-year return in the S&P 500. Missing one of those periods would have cut heavily into the returns from timing that was otherwise almost perfect.

Figure 16.1 illustrates the two elements on an annual timing interval over the 1926–1982 period. The figure is a bit complicated but worth understanding. On the left vertical axis, we see the real (inflation-adjusted) growth of an invested dollar over the period, using the T-Bill rate as a proxy for the inflation rate. (Based on the data in Chapter 2, this is a reasonable assumption.) On the right vertical axis, we see the corresponding annualized real rates of return. The horizontal axis shows timing accuracy rates between 50 percent and 75 percent (with a 75 percent rate, you would have made the right choice between stocks and T-Bills in 75 percent of the years). Two lines are plotted—the best and worst cases—along with the results of buying and holding the S&P 500 for the entire 57 years. The best-case line is based on the assumption that the times you are wrong will be the years when it least matters, when the returns on stocks and T-Bills are quite close. The worst-case line is the opposite, being wrong when it counts—in stocks when the market is plunging, in T-Bills when it is soaring.

The lengths of the vectors (the arrows above and below the dotted line, which represents the S&P 500) indicate the potential gains and losses from good and bad timing, as compared to simply holding the S&P 500 for 57 years. If, for a given accuracy rate, the vectors were of equal length, then the gain in annual return from best timing is equal to the loss in annual rate of return from the worst.

The figure demonstrates what market timers are up against. For example, if we assume that it is simply a matter of chance *which* times you are correct, then you will have to be correct about 70 percent of the time to have an expected return better than a simple buy-and-hold strategy. Even if you are correct three-fourths of the time, your expected returns are barely superior. Or suppose that you are right only half the time. Unless you have the knack of being right when it most matters, you are likely to far underperform the buy-and-hold investor.

Why would 50 percent accuracy lead to below-average performance? Why isn't the figure symmetrical? Because stocks have higher average returns than T-Bills and outperform T-Bills in more than 60 percent of the

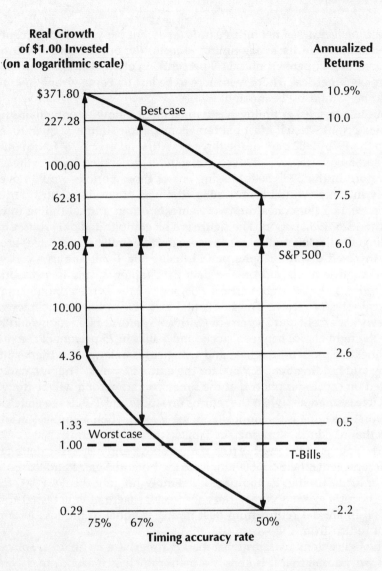

FIGURE 16.1 Market timing accuracy and real returns (yearly timing 1926–1982) *SOURCE:* Jeffrey, 1985.

years. The two investments are not created equal, and there is an inherent bias that favors the buy-and-hold investor. In the long run, there is more risk in being out of the market than in it. Our figure would be symmetrical if, over time, stocks and T-Bills had equal returns.

The real picture is actually worse than indicated by Figure 16.1, because Jeffrey makes no allowance for taxes. Successful market timing will result in gains on which taxes will be due. As we've seen, this reduces the amount of money available for reinvestment, and so tax erosion works on a cumulative basis. By contrast, a buy-and-hold investor has virtually no interim transactions other than reinvesting dividends. Taxes have a much greater impact on the timer.

Mucking Around

The basic nature of the market makes successful market timing an odds-against proposition, but that hasn't kept people from trying. A recent effort by an academician not only demonstrates how difficult it is but also illustrates many of the statistical deceptions we discussed in Chapter 3, especially the perils of developing investment strategies on the basis of back-testing.

Edward Renshaw looked for trading rules using the S&P industrial index. He developed both an annual and a quarterly rule. Under the annual rule, an annual (calendar year) decline of 5 percent in the index constitutes a buy signal. A sell signal comes if there are two annual increases of 5 percent that are not interrupted by a 5 percent annual decline. The quarterly rules are similar: A buy signal results from a 7 percent one-quarter decline. A sell signal is generated if there are three 7 percent rises that are not interrupted by a 7 percent decline. Thus, both trading rules are based on cyclical market behavior.

Renshaw's results are shown in Table 16.1. The record of the annual trading rule is on the left side of the table, that of the quarterly rule on the right.

At first glance, the results appear impressive, suggesting that Renshaw has developed a powerful tool for market timing. In fact, he has done nothing of the sort. All he has done is "muck around in the data" to find a set of rules that *would have worked* in a past period. As we've noted, this is no difficult feat. With a little effort, it can always be accomplished, because it amounts to nothing more than developing questions to match answers that are already known.

It is also noteworthy that his results begin in 1953 in one case, in 1957 in the other, despite the fact that he had more than five decades' worth of data. Why? Because the rules would not have been successful prior to those two dates. (Now, that's a good way to resolve difficulties. Just throw away the data that contradicts your thesis!)

The test of a strategy based on back-testing is how it performs after it is developed, so let's take a look. When Renshaw left off, the annual rule had given a buy signal at the end of 1981, with the S&P 500 at 122.55. A

TABLE 16.1 Percentage Changes Associated With Trading Rules

SIGNAL YEAR		% Change after		SIGNAL QUARTER		% Change after	
		BUY SIGNAL	SELL SIGNAL			BUY SIGNAL	SELL SIGNAL
1953	B	94.8		1957–3rd	B	28.8	
1955	S		−11.5	1958–4th	S		.1
1957	B	50.5		1960–1st	B	28.3	
1959	S		2.3	1961–4th	S		−24.3
1962	B	35.8		1962–2nd	B	88.9	
1964	S		−4.9	1968–2nd	S		−26.2
1966	B	32.6		1970–2nd	B	38.2	
1968	S		−10.2	1971–1st	S		−1.2
1969	B	29.9		1973–4th	B	−2.1	
1972	S		−17.2	1975–2nd	S		−12.1
1973	B	9.5		1975–3rd	B	30.0	
1976	S		−12.3	1979–3rd	S		6.5
1977	B	47.5		1981–3rd	B		
1980	S		−11.2				
1981	B						
Mean Price Change		42.9	−9.3			35.4	−9.5

SOURCE: Adapted from Renshaw, 1983.

sell signal came at the end of 1983, with the index at 164.93, a two-year gain of 35 percent. Not bad, but I am writing this in the spring of 1987, and there has been no buy signal. The S&P 500 is at 301, and Renshaw's rule has missed a gain to this point of 82 percent.

The results are better with the quarterly model. A sell signal came at the end of the third quarter of 1983, after a 43 percent rise in the S&P 500. A buy signal was given in September 1986, but a 39 percent rise had been missed in the interim.

Ironically, Renshaw foresaw what would undo his strategy. "The great worry in following the mechanical trading rule," he wrote, "is that some unusual circumstance, such as a decline in long-term interest rates, might lead to a rather prolonged bull market that would make it unprofitable to move out of the market after only two good years in a row." This, of course, is exactly what happened. If we think about it for a moment, however, we see that Renshaw is saying, in effect, "This method will work until it doesn't. As long as the market continues to behave identically to the period from which I created rules to fit the results, the rules will continue to work." I am afraid that most market timers whose methods stem from back-testing unwittingly fall into this questionable logic.

Is It Worth the Effort?

Market timing clearly has the potential to produce exceptional returns. Presumably, investors wouldn't engage in it if they didn't feel that they (or their advisors) could do significantly better than 50-50. Nevertheless, the evidence suggests that they are going to have to do a lot better than 50 percent to make the effort pay.

We do not have comprehensive evidence on whether they succeed, but one observation should give us pause. Mark Hulbert is the publisher of the *Hulbert Financial Digest* and a columnist for the *AAII* (American Association of Individual Investors) *Journal*. It says something about the hopes and frustrations of investors that Hulbert has had great success with his newsletter, which exists solely to measure and rate the quality of advice given by *other* advisory letters. Hulbert has produced some insightful research into their records, the most thorough evaluations yet of their merits.*

Hulbert studied the ability of advisory letters to correctly call the three massive market rallies of August 1982, August 1984, and January 1985. After determining the six letters (out of more than eight times that many) that had been most accurate in January 1985, he looked at how they had performed in the previous two cases. All six were well-known technical services. *None* had called all three major rallies. In fact, only one had

---

*Hulbert's letter was not the source of the outrageous misuse of statistics cited in Chapter 3.

been so much as 50 percent invested at the beginning of even one of the two prior rallies. On the basis of this and other research, Hulbert wrote:

> [O]ne is led to suspect that a significant number of short-term trading strategies will underperform those taking a buy-and-hold approach over long periods of time.... If no trading newsletters can consistently catch explosive market rallies, and if at least some buy-and-hold newsletters are able to profit enough from market rallies to make up for losses incurred at other times, then one would expect [to find] a disproportionate number of buy-and-hold approaches beating the short-term approaches over long periods of time.... Performance figures from the *Hulbert Financial Digest* confirm this.

17

Facing Reality

Most of the market-beating strategies that have been documented are long-term. This point may have been obscured by the fact that the research evidence was presented in terms of average short-term (e.g., quarterly) returns. There are even studies in which the results are expressed in daily returns, but it really doesn't matter how we express the results. What determines whether a strategy is long-term or short is partly how often a portfolio is reconstructed (what the average holding period is) but, more important, how long the strategy will be utilized.

Suppose we are going to follow a low-P/E strategy. The first thing we need to do is set up a criterion for low-P/E, to determine whether a stock qualifies for our portfolio. Then we must decide how often the stocks will be reviewed, to determine if they still qualify and/or if new ones qualify. We might do this quarterly, every six months, annually, every two years, every five, and so on. Frequent reconstruction of the portfolio ensures a purer strategy (at the cost of commissions, spreads, taxes, and bother), because stocks that no longer meet the criterion will be weeded out sooner. But reconstructing a portfolio quarterly, for example, does not mean that a stock is given only one quarter to perform. And it certainly doesn't mean that, from the moment a stock qualifies under this strategy, it is expected to soar. It only means that *some time* while it meets the low-P/E criterion, the *average* low-P/E stock is expected to outperform the market.

What really determines whether a strategy is long-term is whether it is applied over a long period of time. Investing in low-capitalization stocks, for example, can be a long-term proposition, even if it requires a lot of turn-over. The research suggests that it had *better* be a long-term proposition. Trying out the strategy for a few months is a misapplication of the research findings. I have repeatedly stressed that every strategy carries its own risk: Regardless of the long-run results, the market sometimes rewards and sometimes punishes small stocks *as a group*. A short flirtation with a small-stock strategy does nothing more than expose us to how investors happen to feel about small stocks at the moment. The same can be said of every successful investment strategy. Low-P/E stocks don't outperform the market each quarter or each year. Neither do stocks ranked highest by Value Line, or Benjamin Graham's "bargain stocks," or any other categories of stocks that have been identified as superior performers.

If we try to convert inherently long-term strategies into short-term ones, we are moving into an entirely different realm of analysis: predicting how the market will value a particular characteristic in the near future. It is one thing to have confidence that small stocks will outperform the market over a period of 20 years, but quite another to think that we will know *when* during the period that will happen.

As newspapers often do, the San Jose (California) *Mercury News* runs an annual stock-picking contest among local stockbrokers and analysts. I happened across the 1984 results. In the heart of Silicon Valley, the contestants were apparently disposed to small high-tech stocks. Their portfolios were loaded with them, although the contest did not require it. In 1984, the Dow Industrials lost about 4 percent, but it was a very poor year for small high-tech stocks, and so the contestants didn't fare well. The *winner* underperformed the Dow, and the others all lost more than 25 percent. What caused these poor results? Most of the participants blamed the companies: "The stock market will not abide a growth company hemorrhaging money the way these guys did." One was more analytical. "The key indicator was that in the last two years, it was very easy to make money in high-tech stocks," he said. "When it gets that easy, it should be a warning to pull in your horns and take great care" ("All Players...," 1984). This wisdom apparently wasn't available to him at the beginning of the year, however. With a portfolio of high-tech stocks, he finished last, with a loss of 40 percent.

There was a much better statement that this fellow could have made. He could have said, "I believe that small, high-tech stocks will generally have superior long-term performance, for reasons X, Y, and Z. My strategy is to own stocks of this type over many years. This strategy will be richly rewarded in some years and severely punished in others. 1984 turned out to be one of the latter, but over a multiyear period, I feel that the strategy will result in superior returns. I don't believe that I can tell in advance which years will be good and which ones bad, so there is more to be lost by being out of these stocks than in them."

I imagine that is exactly what this man does believe. He got caught up in confusing the long-term game with the short-term one. Actually, he got trapped—maybe *seduced* is a better word—by the newspaper into playing a prediction game. And he paid the price.

WHAT ABOUT SKILL?

A better understanding of the workings of the market, the ways in which prices and values are established, and the relationship between risk and reward should make you a more skillful investor. But this is not what comes to most people's minds when they think of skill. What comes to mind is making better judgments than other people: getting into the market just as a bull market starts; loading up on oil stocks in the late 1970s; avoiding small high-tech stocks in 1984. In short, being smarter about both timing and selection.

This kind of skill is part of the prediction game. We can also call it the analysis game. It has to do with getting better information or getting it sooner, making superior forecasts and better decisions than other investors. As such, it is part of the competitive, winning-and-losing game, and it is certainly part of the short-term game.

It would seem obvious on the face of it that some people would have more skill than others. There are differences in skill among people in every other field of endeavor. Everyone isn't equally good at playing basketball, laying carpet, writing novels, managing businesses, performing surgery, and so on. Even at the highest levels, skill differences are apparent. Out of the millions of boys who play basketball, only a few hundred make it to the NBA. Within the NBA, they are still not equal. So why, we can ask, should investing be any different?

The efficient market theorists tell us that skill is negated by the competitive forces of the market: Information is available to all, and all information is rapidly incorporated into stock prices. But somehow this is not an intuitively appealing answer. We feel that some people should be better at forecasting company profits, market cycles, and economic trends than others. It doesn't stand to reason that the stock market would be different from other fields.

Some Doubts

Personally, I don't doubt that some people are smarter than others in the investment field, but there are difficulties in making use of that belief. I also have some strong doubts about the efficacy of skill and the wisdom of basing investment decisions on it. Superior skill is hard to define, hard to find, and harder yet to preserve.

The first problem is in knowing skill when we see it. A host of brokers, analysts, and advisors on Wall Street is engaged in what amounts to a mammoth, never-ending stock-picking contest. Let's suppose that this is an annual game, a game of skill, and that there are significant differences in the skillfulness of the players. The result will be differences in their performances. We are likely to see a few outstandingly good (and bad) results, with the bulk of them concentrated close to the average (the familiar bell curve).

Now, however, suppose that all the investors in fact have equal skill, or that the market is so efficient that no one can get an edge on anyone else. In this case there will still be differences in performance. We will still see the bell curve, because investors do not hold pefectly diversified portfolios, and so they incur significant specific risk. This means that they will achieve different results. But in this case, the differences will be the result of pure chance.

On "Wall Street Week," they have an annual stock-picking contest among the regular panelists. At the beginning of the year they list their portfolios; at the end they are held up for praise, needling, or something in between. One year, I took a casual look at the results. For the year, the market had been up, and most of the panelists' portfolios had been, too. But some did quite a bit better than the market, some quite a bit worse. Were the winners smart, the losers stupid? Perhaps. But on the basis of the numbers of stocks in the portfolios and the character of those stocks, I made a rough estimate of the standard deviation of portfolio returns. Guess what: The pattern of actual results corresponded to what was predicted by this calculation. In other words, the results could reasonably be ascribed to nothing more than luck.

Michael Jensen found the same phenomenon when he studied mutual fund performance (see Chapter 6). The funds did not achieve identical returns. Some beat the market, and most did not, but the pattern of returns was perfectly consistent with the hypothesis that chance, not skill, was controlling the outcomes. These illustrations do not *prove* that luck governs the game, but if the results that are presumably attributable to skill cannot be distinguished from the results from chance, it is reasonable to question the role of skill in determining investment success.

It is difficult for most of us to accept the idea that chance is the primary factor in an activity in which the participants are clearly applying their efforts and abilities. We have to remember, though, that in every game that is designed to have a winner, there will be a winner. Finding the winner may or may not have any significance, because someone will win, *even if skill is not a factor.* Consider a large tennis tournament with a 256-player field. It will take eight rounds to determine a winner: At the end of the tournament, one player will have won eight straight matches. We know that tennis is a game of skill, but just suppose that in this tournament all the players are equal, and the result of each match is just a matter of luck. Does that mean that no one will win eight straight matches (and the tournament)? Of course not. Someone will win, because someone has to win. Our natural inclination is to conclude that the winner is the best player, but this would obviously be a mistake. It could be an expensive mistake, if we were to stake our money on the belief that the winner of this tournament has a better than 1-in-256 chance to win the next one.

Have You Got It?

In a psychological experiment, lottery tickets were sold to workers in an office for a dollar apiece. The workers were divided into two groups. Those in the first group were permitted to select the numbers they wanted. Those in the second received theirs at random. This lottery was a zero-sum game (all the revenue was distributed as prizes), so the true, actuarial value of a ticket was one dollar. Just before the drawing was held, the ticket holders were offered the opportunity to sell their tickets back. Each was asked the price he would be willing to take for his ticket. The average price demanded by the people who had gotten their tickets randomly was $1.96 (which certainly demonstrates why people buy lottery tickets), but those who had selected their own numbers asked an average of $8.67! Apparently they believed that they had brought skill to a random process, so much skill that a self-selected ticket was more than four times as likely to win as a randomly selected one.

We know that beating the market in the short-term prediction/analysis game is a negative-sum proposition. Thus we know that most investors are losing, and most investors are always going to lose. Nevertheless, this game is played by the vast majority of all investors. A belief in superior ability is implicit in playing, and so a very large number of people evidently think they possess it.

Superior skill does exist in the stock market. In some people, it doubtless exists to such a degree that they can consistently and significantly win in the prediction game, but that level of skill is, by definition, extremely rare. The problem is that we all want to believe it exists in ourselves, our advisors, or our brokers, when in fact it probably doesn't.

FIRST PRINCIPLES

In the physical sciences there is an enviable precision. If we combine hydrogen and oxygen in a particular way, we will get water—every time. In the social sciences, including the study of the stock market, we do not have assurances. Research, no matter how extensive and meticulous, does not provide a set of neat formulas for stock market success. It is impossible to state with certainty that if we do a, b, and c, the result will be z. All we have are probabilities. Perfect? No. Useful? Absolutely.

I recall a discussion I had with one investor. He showed great interest in both the concept and the evidence behind the low-P/E strategy. When we were finished, however, he only said, "Yes, but under that strategy you would never have bought Hewlett-Packard." My reaction was "So what?" While many investors made a good deal of money in Hewlett-Packard over the years, many more earned below-market or negative returns in other high-P/E stocks. Owning Hewlett-Packard was never a requirement for investment success, but I was looking to the rule, while my friend was looking for the exception, determined to defy the odds.

This exemplifies the first principle of investing: Invest on the basis of what is probable, not what is possible. There is plenty of money in going with the rules; don't seek the exceptions.

What are the probabilities and the rules? By now we have a pretty good idea of how the real stock market operates.

1. The market is much more efficient than most investors, brokers, and advisors would like to believe. This is especially true for the few hundred major stocks that constitute the bulk of the market's value. Conventional predictive analysis, whether fundamental or technical, is unlikely to beat the market for established, widely held stocks. Investors who believe that they can consistently reap extraordinary returns by outwitting the collective wisdom of the market are deluding themselves.

2. The reported profits from highly active trading strategies are greatly exaggerated, since they are calculated without any consideration of the effects of costs or taxes. Once these leakages are accounted for, there is little evidence that many, if any, of these strategies yield returns significantly higher than those of simple buy-and-hold approaches of similar riskiness.

3. The market is fundamentally a risk/reward system. Market risk is rewarded, and it can be measured and controlled by investors. Most specific risk is not rewarded and can be eliminated by diversification without reducing expected returns. Conversely, the failure to diversify does not increase expected returns; it only increases the uncertainty and variability of returns. To the extent that investors do not diversify, they are relying on skill or (more plausibly) luck to determine their returns as compared to the market.

4. To outperform the market averages over time, investors must take on greater than average risk. One method is to create portfolios with high market risk (high betas). Another is to accept one or more of the perceived risks that we have looked at. These are largely specific risks and can be reduced through diversification, but a portfolio designed on the basis of one of these perceived risks will still be riskier than one of similar beta that is diversified over the full range of stocks.

5. Risk and time are connected. All conventional risk measures are short-term. Short-term risk is rewarded in the long run. Thus investment strategies must be based not only on investors' attitudes toward risk but also on their time horizons.

DO YOU REALLY NEED TO BEAT THE MARKET?

Investors and researchers of all sorts are focused on one idea: beating the market. But beating the market means something quite different to an economist or a finance professor than it does to an individual investor. The latter thinks of it as achieving higher average or cumulative returns than a common index, such as the S&P 500. This avoids the issue of risk, however. This is where the academics step in, and we get the concept of risk-adjusted returns. Now, beating the market means achieving returns that are disproportionate to the amount of risk assumed. Simply achieving high returns has no particular significance. It is entirely possible to beat the market with returns that are lower than the market (with a successful but low-risk strategy), or to underperform the market with returns that exceed it (with a high-risk one).

Using risk-adjusted returns enables the academics to evaluate the relative merits of different investors, different types of stocks, and different strategies. When they find significant excess risk-adjusted returns, they have found the holy grail: market inefficiency, otherwise known as the free lunch.

To some people, the issues of market efficiency, valid risk measures, and risk-adjusted returns are vitally important. They must be of concern to the academic researcher, whose interest is scholarship, not making money in the market. They are thrust upon the institutional investment manager, because his performance is evaluated on the basis of risk-adjusted returns. It is the measuring rod of the competition.

What about the rest of us? Are risk-adjusted returns and demonstrated inefficiencies all there is? No! While we are all happy to find a free lunch, our goal is not to achieve excess risk-adjusted returns, but to achieve satisfactory results. Let's think about the apparent inefficiencies that we have seen. For the sake of argument, let's suppose that the market is in fact perfectly efficient. It just appeared inefficient because we didn't have an accurate measure of true risk, and the alleged market-beating strategies didn't beat the market after all, if their true riskiness was allowed for.

This might seem like discouraging news (no free lunch after all), but is it really? We don't live in a world of risk-adjusted returns. We don't report risk-adjusted returns on our tax returns. We don't get statements from a mutual fund saying, "Actual returns were $1.68 per share, but your distribution is $1.32, risk-adjusted." No: We receive actual returns, and we incur actual risk. For the academic or the institutional portfolio manager, they must be combined into risk-adjusted returns, but we are under no such constraint.

When we refer to market inefficiencies, we are talking about beating the market in an academic sense, not in the sense of simply beating the Dow or the S&P 500. Inefficiencies may not have much relevance to what you are really trying to accomplish. A very low-risk strategy that yields excess, but still low, returns is irrelevant to you if you are determined to achieve high rates of return. A very high-risk strategy that also yields excess returns is of no use if you are not willing to accept the high risks in the first place. There is much more to sucessful investing than excess risk-adjusted returns. In the real world, I doubt that one investor in a thousand knows what *risk-adjusted returns* means, that one in ten thousand cares what his risk-adjusted returns are, or that one in a hundred thousand would know how to calculate them, much less go through the work of actually doing so.

We don't need a free lunch to achieve satisfactory results in the market. If the market were perfectly efficient, it would be impossible to beat the market in an academic sense, but there would still be ample opportunity to achieve any reasonable investment goal. We should not lose sight of what we saw in Chapter 2: Simply *matching* the market over time yields not inconsiderable returns, returns that are in fact not achieved by most investors, professional or amateur. In contrast, if our goal is to beat the market in the everyday sense of attaining higher returns than the S&P 500, the route seems obvious: Buy risky stocks, diversify, minimize trading expenses, and stay in the market for a long time. If the market is efficient, we will be fairly rewarded and achieve our goal. If it is not, we will probably reap a pleasant bonus to boot. But, even if the market is not perfectly efficient, it is still *primarily* a risk/reward game. Free lunch is a small part of the overall returns from investing.

Part Six
Into Action

18

Using Your
Knowledge

Armed with sound theory and strong evidence of how the stock market really works, it is time to get down to business: developing practical applications of what we've learned. This involves two steps. First, investors must determine what their basic strategies will be. Second, those strategies must be put into workable forms.

At this point, we know that the stock market rewards risk taking, that time is on our side in investing, and that diversification can eliminate a great deal of risk without sacrificing return. We know that the market *primarily* rewards market risk, but that certain types of discomfort—what we have labelled *perceived risks*—are rewarded as well.

This knowledge is sufficient for you to determine your investment strategies, because strategy is essentially nothing more than the answers to two questions: How *much* risk will you accept? *What* risks will you accept? All you need do now is engage in a little introspection about your goals, your feelings about risk, your current position, and your time horizons.

I cannot tell you what is appropriate for you, because that is inherently personal, but I will offer my judgments about what are and are not plausible strategies for individual investors, based on what we know of the market.

Many apparently successful strategies that spring from academic research are not practical in the real world. For example, the use of standardized unexpected earnings as an investment criterion (Chapter 12) requires doing linear regression analysis to forecast earnings and standard deviation analysis to calibrate the degree to which actual results are unexpected. This may be feasible for a professor with a large grant, access to a mainframe computer, and a cadre of research assistants, but it is well beyond the capabilities of the rest of us. Many of the more mundane approaches are impractical or implausible as well. We have seen many strategies that succeed only in a world of zero taxes and negligible transaction costs. Unfortunately, that is a world very few of us live in.

In my opinion, there are three basic workable strategies that are plausible for most individual investors: the out-of-favor stock strategy, the small/neglected stock strategy, and what I will call the market risk strategy. Following a discussion of each of them, we'll look at sources for the information needed to put them into practice.

GOING WITH THE FLOW: THE MARKET RISK STRATEGY

The simplest and easiest investment approach is just to put together a well-diversified portfolio that doesn't reflect any particular notion of which stocks will beat the market and which won't. This is an essentially passive strategy, and if you are a confirmed believer in the efficient market, it is the only strategy that makes any sense. It is based on the proposition that the only risk you wish to take—and perhaps the only risk worth taking—is market risk, the risk associated with the market as a whole.

Under this approach, the only decision you have to make is how much market risk to take on. This is determined by how much money you invest and by the character of the stocks in your portfolio. Some stocks are more responsive to the action of the general market than others. This can be measured (using beta) so that you can control the relative market risk of a portfolio.

Using Beta

Beta can be a very useful tool for investors, and it has the added virtue of being simple. To calculate the beta of your portfolio, you only need to weight the individual stocks' betas by the amount of money you have invested in them. For example, suppose you have a portfolio of three stocks: 200 shares Black & Decker (ticker symbol BDK), 100 Digital Equipment (DEC), and 200 Texaco (TX). The calculation of beta is shown below (the prices used will not be current when you read this).

In this example, the beta of 1.11 indicates that the portfolio is slightly aggressive. The investment of $21,600 represents $23,976 of market risk (21600 × 1.11).*

---

*In this example, beta would not be a valid or reliable risk measure, because three stocks hardly represents effective diversification. The small portfolio was chosen to keep the example simple.

STOCK	# SHARES	PRICE	VALUE	VALUE % TOTAL	BETA	WEIGHTED BETA
BDK	200	21	4200	.194	1.15	.22
DEC	100	98	9800	.454	1.25	.57
TX	200	38	7600	.352	.90	.32
	Total		21600			

Portfolio beta = sum of weighted betas = 1.11.

Calculating the beta of a portfolio is simple and quick, but one thing should be kept in mind. The portfolio beta depends on the weighting, and the weighting depends on the relative dollar values of the various stocks. Portfolio beta will change as the stocks rise or fall, because the weightings will change. In our example, if DEC rises relative to the other two stocks, the portfolio beta will rise, because DEC's weighting will increase. Thus, even if the composition of your portfolio doesn't change, it's a good idea to recalculate its beta periodically. Both the individual betas and their weightings may have changed.

Finding betas for your stocks can be simple, or it can be impossible. Between the *Value Line Investment Survey* and the Standard & Poor's monthly *Stock Reports*, both of which are commonly available in libraries, you can find betas for about 3000 stocks. If your taste runs to very small or new OTC issues, however, you will be out of luck, because betas are unlikely to be available. Of course, if you get beyond the top 3000, it's obvious that you are not following a strategy based on market risk!

The Special Case

It is possible to create diversified portfolios of widely differing betas, but many investors want a portfolio beta of 1.0 or very close to it. In other words, they want a general participation in the market. This is a special case, not for any theoretical reason, but because there is a cheap, efficient shortcut available: the index fund. As we've seen, this is a fund that invests in the stocks that make up the S&P 500 index, and it holds them in proportion to their weighting in the index. Thus it is a replica of the index and tracks it essentially perfectly.

To my knowledge, there is only one substantial index fund that is offered to individual investors: the Vanguard Index Trust.* It has no sales charges and very low expenses. Vanguard will even let you exchange any S&P 500 stocks for shares in the fund, eliminating the commission you would normally incur to liquidate the stocks.

*Vanguard Group, Vanguard Financial Center, Valley Forge, PA 19482; 1-800-662-7447.

There is no way for an individual to replicate or even approximate the index fund without incurring much higher costs. Even if you believe in the index strategy, however, you shouldn't necessarily liquidate your portfolio to go into the fund. The reason is taxes. As I am writing, the market is at historic highs, so that anyone who has held a diversified portfolio for a reasonable time has significant unrealized capital gains. Liquidating the portfolio would result in a large tax liability, reducing the funds available for reinvestment in the index fund. If your portfolio is already reasonably well diversified, you may be better off holding the portfolio you have.

Some people scoff at the index strategy because it represents guaranteed mediocrity. It certainly takes much of the thrill out of investing, but index investors tend to get the last laugh, because very few professionally managed funds outperform the S&P 500 over time. Fewer yet do so without incurring significantly greater risk.

You will never beat the market in an index fund, if the market is defined as the S&P 500. If you use a market risk strategy with a high beta, you are likely to outperform the market in the everyday sense of achieving higher returns than the S&P 500, but this will reflect the excess risk incurred, not market inefficiency.

This is the only problem with the market risk approach, and especially with index funds. The S&P 500 represents about 70 percent of the market's value, but it is the remaining 30 percent that contains the kinds of stocks (and risks) that have been shown to generate excess returns: the less efficient sector of the market. If you are determined to significantly beat the market, the market risk strategy is not the one for you.

CONTRARY THINKING: OUT-OF-FAVOR STOCKS

We have seen consistent evidence that cheap stocks outperform expensive ones, regardless of whether cheapness is defined in relation to earnings, sales, or book value. In principle, portfolio criteria can be established in terms of any of these value measures.

Under any approach, standards must be set for adding a stock to a portfolio and for later removing it. Most of the academic studies have been conducted on the basis of quintiles or deciles: dividing stocks into five or ten groups based on the characteristic being studied. This is a logical research procedure, but it is purely arbitrary and has no magic qualities for real-world investors.

You can set your standard anywhere you want: bottom 10 percent, bottom quarter, third, half, and so on, but whatever the standard, a good deal of work awaits you. To find, for example, the bottom third in terms of price/sales ratio (P/S), you will have to compute the P/S for all stocks in your universe and then rank them to find the bottom third. You could shorten the job by taking a sample of, say, 100 stocks to find the cutoff point, but even that is a big job.

A far simpler approach is quite adequate: You can set up a standard in relation to the average value. For example, you would buy a stock only if it was selling at a P/E ratio no greater than 80 percent of the average market P/E. This would be roughly equivalent to a bottom-third standard.

P/E ratios are available from innumerable sources, including most daily newspapers. Average P/Es for the S&P 500 or other broad measures of the market are also reported regularly. P/S data will require a little more effort. You can get the sales for thousands of public companies from Standard & Poor's *Stock Reports* (see below), but these are not reported on a per-share basis. Value Line gives sales per share for the 1700 stocks it covers.

Depending on your source, you may have to make two computations for each stock: dividing sales by shares outstanding, and dividing this figure into the price per share to get the P/S ratio. The situation is similar for price-to-book value information. Once you do this, more computations will be needed: In order to set up your portfolio standard, you must average all the individual stock data to determine the market average P/S or P/BV.

If you have a personal computer, this process is much easier. You can obtain sales and balance sheet information from subscription or on-line data services. It is simple to process that information into the form you want and to screen the stocks according to various characteristics, but for most investors, the low-P/E approach remains the most convenient of all the strategies designed to find out-of-favor, undervalued stocks.*

Setting Criteria

The first step in the low-P/E strategy is to set the purchase standard. More restrictive standards may give purer or more aggressive strategies. They also give you fewer stocks from which to choose. It also often happens that entire industries are showing very low P/Es. This can make proper diversification difficult. If the only stocks meeting your standard are steel stocks, for example, then you are not pursuing a low-P/E strategy as much as a steel-stock strategy. If the standard is highly restrictive, you may also find that the only qualifiers are stocks that look so bad they make your skin crawl.

---

*The relative ease of obtaining information on earnings, sales, and book value may be a mixed blessing. The more people attempt to acquire out-of-favor stocks, the less out-of-favor they may become. This could undermine the value of the strategies, but the basic orientation of most investors makes this unlikely. Peter L. Bernstein, editor of the *Journal of Portfolio Management*, explains: "If most investors ever developed the necessary attitudes to be true long-term investors, the Benjamin Graham [and] low-P/E strategies would no longer earn excess returns. As long as uncertainty is such an important word in our vocabulary, however, that will be an unlikely outcome" (p. 1).

I think that, for most purposes, the standard I suggested above will be adequate: Select stocks with P/Es no higher than 80 percent of the market P/E.

Having defined your standard and found the stocks that meet it, all you really need to do is create a portfolio of stocks that spans many different industries. You can also control the beta of the portfolio. You will find that low-P/E stocks tend to be low-beta ones as well.

Your portfolio can be essentially random, requiring no real analysis. It is debatable whether analysis will help, anyway, but many people will be inclined to try to improve the strategy. Without getting into full-fledged security analysis, David Dreman, the leading exponent of the low-P/E strategy, has suggested trying to pick companies with relatively strong balance sheets and financial and operating ratios (e.g., current assets versus current liabilities, return on equity). Dreman also suggests that investors restrict themselves to stocks listed on the NYSE or Amex or to large OTC stocks, on two grounds. First, the research supporting the strategy is based on these stocks. Second, he feels that the accounting of very small companies is suspect: Earnings may not be what they appear to be.

At this point, it might also be useful to look at the P/Ss of the stocks. Most low-P/E stocks will also be low-P/S ones. What if you find one that has a high P/S? This implies that the company has very high profits in relation to sales. This is suspicious on the face of it and unlikely to be sustained for long.

Not only must we set standards for including a stock, we also must set standards for selling them later. In a way, this is considerably trickier, balancing the desire to fully exploit the strategy against the costs of frequent trading. We certainly don't want to buy a stock because its P/E is 79 percent of the market average, then quickly sell it because it has risen to 81 percent.

The research indicates that it is entirely plausible to take a buy-and-hold approach, setting up a low-P/E portfolio and sitting on it for years. Over time, of course, many of the stocks would cease to be low-P/E ones, either through declining earnings or (hopefully) soaring prices.

A purer strategy requires occasional updating, perhaps every year or two. At those times, a logical sell criterion would be a P/E above the current market average.*

INTO THE UNKNOWN: SMALL AND NEGLECTED STOCKS

The final strategy is based on what we've learned about small and neglected stocks. Aptly, they have been called *shadow stocks*, and they may offer risk-oriented investors their best hope for superior long-term performance.

*Dreman has some additional ideas about when to sell. Anyone seriously interested in the low-P/E strategy should read *The New Contrarian Investment Strategy*.

Computing quintiles or deciles based on market capitalization is difficult and time-consuming. It is much simpler just to set a market capitalization standard and create a diversified portfolio of the stocks that qualify. Where should you set your standard? The evidence suggests that the smaller you go, the higher the long-term returns will be. Unfortunately, as the average returns increase, so does their variability, while available information, analysis, and opinion plummet. It's a clear trade-off, and you must decide according to your own attitudes about risk, uncertainty, and ignorance. To capture much of the excess return associated with small stocks, I would say that you certainly must restrict yourself to capitalizations of less than $200 million, and at least half your portfolio should be in under-$100 million stocks. These criteria will give you thousands of stocks from which to choose. The universe can be shrunk further with lower standards.

Remember that the small-stock effect is largely an ignorance effect. That means that in applying a small-stock strategy, you are in effect throwing darts at the stock list. Even if you think that you are making thoughtful choices of the individual stocks, there will be an inevitable randomness to the results. Ignorance doesn't mean ignorance on the part of everyone else but you.

Selling rules for the small-stock strategy depend upon the buying rules. A useful rule is that the sell standard should be twice the buy standard (if you bought stocks under $100 million, you would sell a stock when it reached $200 million).

Measuring Neglect

The best measure of neglect is probably the number of analysts covering a stock. Unfortunately, this information is essentially unavailable to individual investors, but two useful proxies are easy to find: the number of institutions owning a company's stock, and the percentage of a company's stock owned by institutions. Now we must establish some standards for what constitutes neglect.

From Standard & Poor's' publication (see below), I took samplings from the NYSE, Amex, and OTC markets (in the spring of 1987). I found that the mean percentages of shares owned by institutions were 38 percent, 20 percent, and 22 percent on the respective markets. The corresponding standard deviations were 19, 15, and 17.

If the distributions are reasonably symmetrical, about two-thirds of the observations will lie within one standard deviation (SD) of the mean. The remaining one-third will lie at the extremes (about one-sixth more than one SD above the mean, another one-sixth one SD below it). The bottom sixth would be a reasonable standard of neglect, and so all we need to do is subtract the SD from the mean for each market. This gives us our standards: no more than 19 percent institutional ownership for NYSE stocks, no more than 5 percent elsewhere. (An appropriate universal standard would be 5 percent. This would eliminate almost all NYSE stocks.)

I also looked at the number of institutional shareholders. The mean number of these holders was about 100 on the NYSE, 15 on the Amex, and 20 in the OTC market. The pattern is anything but symmetrical, and so standard deviation is meaningless. I calculated the medians, the numbers that divide the top halves from the bottom halves. They were 55, 15, and 19, respectively. I also found that the dividing lines for the lowest quintile (fifth) were 25, 5, and 5. Thus, if you wanted to buy stocks in the lowest quintile (by number of institutional shareholders) on the NYSE, you would restrict yourself to stocks with less than 25 institutional shareholders. Once again, a limit of 5 would be a more universal standard, but it would restrict you to non-NYSE stocks.

In applying a strategy based on neglect, how low you should go will depend on your temperament and how aggressively you wish to pursue the strategy. At the very least, you must go below the mean in terms of institutional shareholdings and the median in terms of the number of institutional shareholders.

IS THERE NO PLACE FOR STOCK PICKING?

Finding an effective investment strategy is the best route to long-term success. Once the strategy is set and the stocks that qualify are found, the only work remaining is to assemble a diversified portfolio. Actual stocks must be chosen. This can be a random process, but the question is: Can judicious stock-picking improve the situation and the results?

There is ample reason to be leery of the efficacy of analysis in finding superior stocks, especially in the well-informed, large-stock sector of the market. But what about the market shadows, the neglected sector? If ignorance is rampant, wouldn't your analytical efforts be likely to pay off?

There are three answers to that, two negative and one positive. First, asking individual investors to be security analysts is a bit ridiculous. You have a business or an occupation that commands your time and attention. I presume that if you had the ability, inclination, and training to be a security analyst, then you would actually be one.

Second, the neglected sector of the market is not just lacking in analysis, it is lacking in facts. Without an inordinate amount of effort, you will not be able to get the information on a shadow stock that you will on a better-established one. Even if you want to perform some security analysis, it may be difficult to get the necessary information.

The third answer is more encouraging. A little bit of information may give you an edge in the shadow market. You may occasionally find such information falling into your lap, through your business or social life. A dentist, for example, may encounter a promising shadow stock through the introduction of a new and important piece of dental equipment. A retailer may recognize the potential of a new product line. A wholesaler may be able to sense the health of retailers he services. This list could be extended infinitely. In some cases, it could even apply to large stocks. Security analysts have to concern themselves with the big picture, aggregate statistics. Individuals may sometimes see something far below the surface that has significant implications for the future. I suggest only that you keep your eyes, ears, and mind open. Chasing obscure, nonpublic information is not likely to be a profitable use of your time.

GETTING INFORMATION (AND A LITTLE HELP)

There are many sources of basic investment information, and many more sources of investment opinion. Since I am not a strong believer in the value of opinion, the following list is primarily one of factual resources. It is not exhaustive but should be sufficient.

Value Line Investment Survey (Value Line, Inc., 711 Third Ave., New York, NY 10017; weekly, $425 per year, available at most brokers and many public libraries).

Covers about 1700 stocks, mostly NYSE. Provides the Value Line rankings. For all stocks, gives P/E; beta; several years of sales, earnings, book value; multiyear rates of growth of various measures; capital structure; balance sheet data. Shows number of shares held by institutions and number of institutional buy and sell decisions, but not number of institutional shareholders. It is one of the only sources that shows sales per share and P/E relative to the market. It also regularly compiles useful stock screens (e.g., stocks trading below book value).

Standard & Poor's Security Owner's Stock Guide (Standard & Poor's Corp., 25 Broadway, New York, NY 10004; monthly, $88 per year, available from brokers and in many public libraries).

Covers more than 5000 stocks. Provides beta; quality ranking; P/E; number of institutional holders and shares held; balance sheet data, including capitalization. Five years of income data. Shows newly listed stocks.

Standard & Poor's Stock Reports (Available at brokerage houses and many public libraries).

Covers all NYSE, Amex, and about 1500 OTC stocks (a separate publication for each market). Issued quarterly; individual stock reports updated if new information is available. Gives beta, P/E, book value, quality ranking, percentage of shares held by institutions. Ten years of income and balance sheet data. Shows when the stock was listed if within the past seven years.

A related publication, *OTC Profiles*, provides earnings, capital structure, book value for about 650 small OTC stocks. Does not provide beta or institutional holdings.

In addition to these sources, daily and weekly publications, such as the *Wall Street Journal* and *Barron's*, provide trading data as well as P/E ratios. The various stock price chart services provide some fundamental data. In particular, many have data on institutional shareholdings. Almost all the sources cited here show a company's capital structure, including the number of common shares outstanding, but none calculate market capitalization. You'll have to do that yourself, multiplying the number of shares by the current price.

Advisory publications are so numerous and span such a range of investment styles and approaches that recommendations are superfluous. Nevertheless, I can wholeheartedly recommend an organization that provides more education than advice: the American Association of Individual Investors (612 N. Michigan Ave., Chicago IL 60611; annual dues of $48). Membership includes a subscription to the *AAII Journal* (10 issues per year), an annual financial planning guide, and an annual no-load mutual fund guide. The *AAII Journal* is an excellent vehicle for keeping up to date with current stock market theories and evidence. Its articles are in the forefront of modern research but are readable and nontechnical. The *AAII Journal* also covers investment areas other than the stock market. The association also offers various educational materials and seminars throughout the country.

MONEY MANAGEMENT

Every professional cardplayer knows that knowing probabilities is only the first step to success. No matter how much you know, you won't win every hand, and you won't win every night, every week, or every month. The key is not just to have the odds on your side, but to effectively manage your money, so that when things turn your way, you will be there to reap the profits.

It is no different in the stock market. We can put the odds on our side, but there is still an undeniable element of risk—luck, to be honest about it—that remains. Just like cardplayers, no investor wins every day, week, month, or year. So just like cardplayers, investors must look beyond strategy to money management.

Diversification

We have looked carefully at diversification, how it works, and what it can do for us. For most of us, the failure to diversify places an inappropriate reliance on skill or luck to determine our investment results.

There is little left to be said about diversification except to offer one piece of practical advice. The appropriate degree of diversification depends on your market strategy. If you are following a market risk strategy, creating a portfolio of well-established, large companies, 12 to 20 stocks should represent adequate diversification. If you move into the shadowland of tiny, neglected stocks, the picture changes considerably. The worst-performing small stocks do horribly. This is balanced by the fact that a small percentage of them perform spectacularly. The variability of results in this sector is enormous, and so prudence requires much more diversification. The amount will depend on how low you go in terms of size and neglect, but if you were to restrict yourself to, say, companies with capitalizations under $50 million, I would think you would want at least 25 stocks. If you were to go down to $25 million, you would want at least 40. In this sector of the market, the more the better.

This may seem unwieldy, but it doesn't have to be. Unless you are trying to play security analyst, there is little research to do, and unless you insist on heavy trading—a misapplication of the small-stock strategy—you won't have lots of gains and losses to account for each year. You also won't have a lot of dividends to keep track of. Most of the companies won't pay dividends.

Putting together a large portfolio can be expensive, too. If meeting the diversification standards requires buying odd lots, the commission costs soar, seriously reducing the potential returns. This may be less likely than it appears, however. Small stocks tend to be low-priced stocks. A portfolio of 40 stocks bought in 100-share lots at an average price of $10 would cost $40,000. By contrast, a 15-stock portfolio of blue chips averaging $40 would cost $60,000. On a percentage basis, the commissions on the low-priced stocks would be higher, but not enough to seriously deter you from purchasing them. If you cannot meet reasonable diversification standards, however, mutual funds may be a better choice.

Minimizing Costs

Many seemingly impressive investment strategies unravel once we look at the costs involved in implementing them. Those costs include commissions, spreads, and taxes. Every time we trade, these reduce the funds available for reinvestment. It is clear on the face of it that whatever our strategy, we should try to implement it in ways that minimize the frequency of trading.

Most of the promising strategies we have looked at have various manifestations, with widely varying trading implications. Whatever the strategy, we must occasionally review, restructure, and rebalance the portfolio. We could do this monthly, quarterly, annually, and so on. In most of the examples we've seen, the more frequent the reviews (the purer the strategy), the higher the *gross* returns.

Even if the higher gross returns from frequent trading exceed the costs of the trading, there is reason to be less aggressive. We know that no strategy will be a winner in every time period, and we know that there are no guarantees that any strategy will be a winner in the future. Suppose that you adopt a low-P/E strategy, one based on a quarterly portfolio review. Suppose further that, for the next few years, low-P/E stocks perform only as well as the general market. If you are trading frequently, constantly replacing stocks and rebalancing your portfolio, the costs will be enormous, and you will far underperform the market. If you have adopted a more conservative approach to the strategy—say, an annual or biannual review—your performance will scarcely be penalized. It is a classic risk/reward trade-off, but I think that caution is in order for most investors.

Hedging

The profusion of new stock-related products in the index and options markets has made it easy to hedge stock market investments. The simplest hedge is a put option. It gives you the right to sell a security at a fixed price for a fixed period. A classic hedge, then, would be to buy 100 shares of a stock and buy a put option that would give you the right to sell it at or about the price you paid for it. If the stock rose, you would reap the profits. If it fell, you would be protected. In either case, you are out the cost of the option.

You can also buy and sell options on some major market indexes. There are options contracts on the S&P 500, the NYSE Composite, and the Value Line Composite. There is an Amex option, and there are options on some market sector indexes (e.g., oil and technology). If one of these indexes approximates the character of your portfolio, it is a simple, convenient hedge.

Using stock index futures contracts, many institutional investors have begun to apply portfolio insurance. This is a hedging technique that is not applicable to most individual investors, but recently some mutual funds and banks have offered forms of this to retail customers. For example, Chase Manhattan has begun offering a certificate of deposit whose returns are tied to the performance of the S&P 500, but which guarantees a minimum return. Investors choose from a set of maturities, guarantees, and appreciation potential.

New products designed to limit or eliminate portfolio losses seem destined to proliferate at a rapid rate. The result is likely to be as much confusion as protection. Remember the key principle: Hedges of all sorts are forms of insurance. They are not cheap, either. Like all forms of insurance, they are designed to produce long-run profits for the insurer, not the insured. That does not mean they are necessarily bad buys. Hedging in the options market may make sense in some situations—for instance, if you intend to make a large market timing bet and want some protection—but endless hedging is not a plausible strategy, because it can easily reduce returns by half or more. There is little reason for true long-term investors to sacrifice a significant part of their returns for the sake of short-term protection.

19

Mutual Funds:
Help at a Price

The logic of investing via mutual funds seems compelling in terms of many of the things we have learned, and I dare say that mutual funds are the logical investment choice for many investors. They certainly have been the actual choice of a large and rapidly increasing number of investors, as sales of mutual fund shares have soared in recent years. In fact, some funds have seen such a deluge of arriving money that they have felt unable to effectively invest it all and have closed the funds to new investors.

The process of actually choosing and using funds bears some exploration. There are more benefits to mutual funds than are commonly understood. Unfortunately, there are misconceptions, difficulties, and drawbacks to be faced as well. Funds are certainly not the investment of choice for everyone.

SOME BASICS

Mutual funds are a large subject, and this will be anything but a complete discussion. A number of good books and guides are widely available, but a few basics are in order.

What Is a Fund?

The term *mutual fund* technically refers to several different types of invest-ment funds. Here, we are referring only to the most common and popular type: open-end stock funds operated by "diversified management com-panies" under the Investment Company Act of 1940. In a fund, each share-holder (investor) owns a pro rata share of all the assets of the fund. *Open-end* refers to the fact that fund shares are continuously offered to the public, and investors liquidate their shares by selling them back to the fund (redeem-ing them) at a price equal to the net asset value per share. Net asset value (NAV) is determined daily and is simply the total value of the fund's assets, divided by the number of shares outstanding.*

The board of directors of a mutual fund hires an investment advi-sory firm to manage the fund's portfolio. This firm, called the manage-ment company, sets the policies and strategies of the fund and makes the buying and selling decisions. Normally, the majority of the board members of the fund are principals in the management company, and so it's a foregone conclusion that the company will be selected to manage the fund and receive the fees for doing so. That's why the fund was estab-lished in the first place.

The Investment Company Act, which has been modified many times over the years, regulates many of the investment, accounting, custo-dial, and sales practices of the funds and the management companies. Most of the regulations are designed to ensure full disclosure and to discourage fraud and conflicts of interest. Beyond this, there are two sets of provisions that are important to investors. One regulates the maximum sales charges that can be levied. The other regulates how much a fund can invest in any one security and still qualify as a registered diversified investment company. This is to prevent concentration of the assets. In addition, a fund must qualify under the laws and regulations of the in-dividual states in which it is offered, further restricting the investment practices. There are a few nondiversified funds, in which greater concen-tration of investments is permitted by their charters, but this will be stated in their prospectuses.

---

*There are also some closed-end funds. In this case, a fixed number of shares is sold at the fund's inception. After that, no more shares are issued, and the shares of the fund are traded on the open market, just as individual stocks are. New investors must acquire their interest by buying it from existing investors. Correspondingly, investors wishing to liquidate must do so on the open market, not by redemption through the fund itself. Unlike open-end funds, which can always be sold at NAV, closed-end funds can and do trade at premiums or dis-counts to the underlying NAV. While there is nothing inherently inferior about closed-end funds, our interest here will be in open-end funds, because they account for the overwhelm-ing majority of funds available to the public.

Selling the Funds

Mutual funds traditionally are distributed in one of two ways. They are either sold directly to investors by the fund itself (at NAV), or they are sold via salesmen who receive commssions for doing so. The salesmen are usually stockbrokers, but some funds have their own sales forces, and many financial planners and investment advisors sell mutual funds as well. The sales commissions are paid out of the *load*, a sales charge levied on the investor. The different sales methods merely reflect different marketing strategies.

In recent years, the simple load/no-load distinction has broken down, and the whole subject of mutual fund fees charged to shareholders has become much more complex. Regrettably, most of the changes in fund practices have been expensive for investors.

CHOOSING AND USING MUTUAL FUNDS

The Question of Performance

Mutual funds publish their past results in their prospectuses. Of course, the ones who feel that their records are impressive publish them in advertisements as well. While past performance may be of interest, however, most investors place too much emphasis on it, often assuming that the funds that have shown superior past performance are the best investment candidates. Most people take the figures they see at face value, when a little critical thinking is necessary for making good investment decisions.

There are four primary issues involved in evaluating past performance. First, cumulative performance figures (the growth of investments over time), as seen in fund advertising, are, frankly, illusory. They are based on the assumption that all distributions are reinvested. Except in a pension plan, however, taxes are due on those distributions. Thus, as we noted in Chapter 3, reinvesting the distributions really means contributing additional capital to the extent of the taxes due. This problem affects all funds, but it doesn't affect them equally. Prior to the 1986 Tax Reform Act, it depended on the proportion of the returns that were in the form of ordinary income versus tax-favored long-term capital gains. Still, even without the tax preference for long-term gains, there is another penalty for a short-term orientation: The more frequently gains are realized, the more frequently taxes are incurred. Each time taxes are paid, the amount remaining for reinvestment is reduced. Other things being equal, a fund that holds its stocks for longer time periods will provide greater actual returns to tax-paying investors than one that has shorter holding periods, even if their reported returns are identical. Thus there are two deceptions: The reported performance of all funds is exaggerated, and comparisons among them are distorted.

Second, funds are highly selective in their advertising, carefully choosing the time periods for which they display their results. Quite naturally, they will select periods that make them look good. This is regulated to some extent, but plenty of flexibility remains. For example, a fund could use the last quarter, the last year, the last three years, the last ten years, the time since inception, and so on. Whatever time period you see in a fund advertisement, you may safely assume it was chosen not to best reflect but to reflect best on the fund's performance.

We have already referred to the third issue. Many funds reflect a singular characteristic that defines their strategies. Particularly good (or bad) results may not reflect on the manager's skill so much as they reflect the market's judgment of that characteristic during a given time period. There may be skill involved in selecting the individual stocks, but stocks in the same category tend to move together, and what happens to them as a group will be the primary factor in the fund's results. The fund should neither be blamed nor credited for how the investment community values a group in a given period.*

Apart from all of the above, funds haven't achieved equal performance. The fourth issue is what to make of this. Are some fund managers more skillful than others or just luckier?

There is a way to deal with this problem—a precise, scientific, mathematical one. A statistician can examine investment results, calculate returns (risk-adjusted, of course), compute standard deviations, and so on, and say, "Joe Smith's excess returns are statistically significant." This is a fancy way of saying that his excellent results cannot reasonably be explained by luck. This kind of measurement can be applied to anything. Can the record of Martina Navratilova be explained by luck? Any statistician could easily prove that it cannot.

This scientific approach is exactly what Michael Jensen followed in his study of mutual fund performance (see Chapter 6). He demonstrated that the pattern of fund results was compatible with the hypothesis that there is no significant difference in ability among fund managers.

Nevertheless, there is a problem with the scientific approach when it comes to investment results. Statistical significance depends upon differences

---

*A strong trend in recent years has been for mutual fund companies to create large numbers of very specialized *sector funds*. In principle, this should work to investors' benefit, by offering wider choice, but a profusion of specialized funds virtually guarantees that at least some of them will always be exceptional performers. The successful ones will be trumpeted in advertising, when their success may well be the result of nothing more than luck. As such, the sector-fund approach may be more a marketing ploy than a genuine maximizing of the fund managers' expertise.

in results, the number of observations (e.g., 10 annual results), and the amount of variability (standard deviation of annual returns). The narrower the performance differences and the greater the variability in results, the more observations will be required to demonstrate statistical significance. The unfortunate fact is that in the stock market these may not come together in a way that yields usable answers. In a recent article in the *Financial Analysts Journal*, Bob Boldt and Hal Arbit expressed the problem:

> For the 10-year period ending in June 1983, the spread in performance between the top performing fund...and the median fund was 7.1% [per year]. But superior performance of this magnitude would have to persist for 30 years before we could conclude with 95 percent certainty that this spread was not simply a measurement error! By that time the managers responsible for the early years of the performance record would have gone on to their just rewards, a new team would be in place and, although the results might finally be significant statistically, they may no longer be significant practically.

By the nature of the data, science is not able to take us very far in determining whether some mutual fund managers are better than others. The pattern of results cannot be distinguished from one generated by luck. But saying that we cannot prove that truly superior performance *does* exist is not the same as proving that it *doesn't* exist.

There is a practical way to deal with the problem. There are only two possibilities: Differences in fund performance are the result of either skill or luck. If they are the result of skill, then it makes sense to invest in funds that have shown superior performance. If they are the result of luck, then it cannot hurt to invest in those same funds, because they are as likely as the others to do well in the future (of course they are just as likely to do badly, too).

The bugaboo in this is the question of risk. Acting as if risk is irrelevant to either fund returns or investor concerns is both foolish and dangerous. Yet making explicit adjustments for risk is perilous at best, especially when different investors have dramatically different time horizons. We cannot go through a pile of mutual fund risk and return data and rank the funds in a way that would be unambiguously valid or universally relevant. Add the fact that much of fund performance is largely the result of how a particular strategy is rewarded over a particular period of time, and we can only conclude that performance records are not even a very reliable guide to the *past*, much less to the future.

This may seem very discouraging, but this should be our reaction only if we view mutual funds as nothing more than a vehicle for latching on to someone else's investment skill. In truth, this is the *least* of the benefits of mutual fund investing. The real advantages of funds are in areas of much more fundamental importance: risk management and strategy implementation.

Diversification

There are several advantages to investing through mutual funds, aside from the supposed benefits of professional management. The fund does all the necessary record keeping, processing of dividends, interest, splits, commissions, and so on. You receive a simple quarterly statement of your (and the fund's) position, as well as an annual statement of distributions that can go directly onto your tax return. In addition, you get liquidity. Except under the most unusual circumstances, a fund must redeem your shares on any day you wish at the current NAV. This can often be done by telephone.

These features undoubtedly have value, but another characteristic is far more important in both theory and practice: A mutual fund is by nature diversified.

The basic tool for risk management in the stock market is diversification, and it is here that the case for mutual funds quite rightly usually begins. Funds indeed provide instant diversification. As soon as you invest, you become the proportional owner of the fund's assets, usually consisting of a small amount of cash and short-term money market instruments and a large number of stocks. For many individual investors, it is not possible, as a practical matter, to achieve this degree of diversification, because the total investment required is too high. Suppose, for example, that an investor feels that he must have at least 15 stocks in his portfolio to achieve effective diversification. If he buys a round lot (100 shares) of each, and the average stock price is $30, he must invest $45,000 to meet his diversification standard. If he lacks the $45,000, a mutual fund is the logical choice. Of course, a person can buy 30 shares of one stock and 17 of another, but the commission costs on odd-lot transactions are prohibitive, even with discount brokers.

Mutual funds not only give us instant diversification when we purchase them, they also diversify our *sales*. Consider the person with the $45,000 investment in 15 stocks. Suppose that he wants to reduce his investment by 10 percent, selling $4,500 worth of stock. He must decide *which* stock or stocks to sell. In other words, he has to make a second decision that has nothing to do with his basic motive. His portfolio must be restructured just so that he can reduce his total commitment. But the mutual fund investor simply redeems 10 percent of his shares, reducing his holdings in the entire portfolio proportionately. He avoids the undesired second decision and maintains exactly the same diversification he started with, something that is impractical for many individual investors. The same benefit also applies to adding to an investment position and reinvesting dividends.

Little Boxes

Every mutual fund has a general orientation, and while each is unique to some degree, it is common to put funds into a few general classes, based on the types of stocks in which they invest. Thus we often see such descriptions as *capital appreciation, growth, growth and income,* and the like. Firms that measure and track mutual fund performance commonly divide funds into categories such as these, often compiling group performance indexes. Every book on mutual funds also features definitions of the various categories.

Implicit in these classifications is one purpose: to describe the risk and return characteristics of the funds. For example, capital appreciation funds tend to hold high-risk stocks in the hopes of achieving high returns, while growth and income funds tend to emphasize low-risk stocks, much of whose returns are expected to come in the form of dividends rather than capital gains.

Terms such as these give us a sense of how a fund is managed. In addition, every fund must include a statement of its objectives and policies in its prospectus. If its policy is to buy established growth stocks, the prospectus will say so. If it seeks stocks with unrecognized assets, small size, or high yield, the prospectus will state that. While some fund statements are vague, most give a good picture of the basic strategy of a fund and of what kinds of risk are being taken.

What a fund says it does and what it actually does may be quite different, and so it is worthwhile to do a little checking. Either in the prospectus or in a separate annual or quarterly report, funds will list their current holdings, by dollar value and by percentage. A casual look at a portfolio will give us an idea of its character. If we've never heard of any of the stocks, that tells us something. If they are all household names, such as IBM and GM, that tells us something, too. We can also estimate such things as the average P/E or capitalization of the fund's holdings.

We can look at the year-to-year volatility in a fund's results to get an idea of the fund's riskiness. We can also check the portfolio turnover to understand whether it takes a long-term or an active trading approach to investing. In sum, we can get a pretty good idea of what principles are guiding the portfolio and whether they correspond to the fund's stated objectives and policies.

Getting Serious

Studying a mutual fund's statements, portfolio, and results gives us important insight into its character, but there are more sophisticated ways in which to deal with this.

Aggressive portfolios have betas in excess of 1.0, while defensive ones have betas lower than 1.0. Beta, then, serves to predict the extent to which a portfolio will exaggerate or mute the moves in the general market. As we have discussed, beta is not faultless on either a theoretical or a practical level, but it is an important summary of the character of any portfolio, and so it is a good starting point for serious risk management with mutual funds.

Beta is certainly not the ending point, however. We have already seen an example of two funds with dramatically different performance, even though they had almost identical betas. We saw the reason, too: Beta is only a sufficient risk measure for *effectively* diversified portfolios, ones whose makeup reflects the composition of the general market. Neither of the two funds was effectively diversified. As compared to the market, each was heavily weighted toward particular types of stocks. When a particular strategy is followed, beta is not a complete risk measure, because it doesn't account for the risk associated with the strategy itself.

There is a way to ameliorate this problem, with the measure *R-squared*, discussed in Chapter 8. This statistic, which can vary from 0.00 to 1.00, indicates what proportion of a portfolio's variation in returns is explained by the variations of the overall market. Thus it measures how much of a portfolio's total risk is what we've called market risk. For example, an R-squared of 0.85 means that the action of the market accounts for 85 percent of the action of the portfolio. The specific risk represented by the individual stocks accounts for the remaining 15 percent. A perfectly diversified portfolio has an R-squared of 1.00, which can be achieved only by buying the market (i.e., an index fund). Otherwise, even widely diversified funds will have R-squareds of less than 1.00.

R-squared is not a measure that translates easily into plain English. We cannot say, "R-squared of x means the portfolio has character y." Its best use is as a comparative measure: The higher the figure, the more a fund's performance is being governed by the general market—the more effectively it is diversified. The lower the R-squared, the less the fund's results will depend on the market. Turning this around, the lower the R-squared, the more the results will depend on the success of the fund's strategic approach and the investment manager's skill.*

Gold-oriented mutual funds illustrate this. To a degree, their performance will be affected by how capital assets in general are valued—that is, by the performance of the overall stock market—but the dominant factor in their results will be the behavior of the price of gold. Since there is no particular correlation between the stock market and gold prices, there is little correlation between the performance of gold funds and the performance

---

*Widely diversified funds that aren't structured to exploit a particular strategy generally have R-squared's between 0.85 and 0.90.

of the stock market. Mathematically, this means that the R-squared of gold funds should be extremely low, and this is the case. The low R-squared is just a formal way of expressing the fact that the success of a gold fund is predicated on the success of a gold strategy.

We should be clear on the idea that beta and R-squared are two different things. A portfolio can have a low R-squared and a high beta, a high R-squared and a high beta, and so on. Any fund or portfolio that is specialized by a particular characteristic is likely to have a low R-squared, regardless of its beta. For example, a fund specializing in utility stocks is apt to have a low R-squared and a low beta, because utility stocks are inherently low-beta, but a fund specializing in semiconductor stocks will have a low R-squared and a high beta.

Both beta and R-squared come from data on how a fund has behaved in the past—say, in the last five years. There can be no guarantee that the same pattern will continue, at least not with precision. Assuming, however, that a fund is reasonably diversified (the good old Law of Large Numbers) and that its basic orientation does not change, both of these measures will be reasonably stable.

Beta and R-squared are useful measures for mutual fund investors, providing a good picture of the risk characteristics of the funds. Unfortunately, they are not widely published. I have browsed through many otherwise good books on mutual fund investing. Most of these give a variety of information on individual funds—performance, size, objectives, and so on—but none gives either beta or R-squared or even mentions them. This seems like a sad commentary on the level of knowledge and sophistication of mutual fund investors. Or perhaps it is a sad commentary on how most so-called investment experts view the investing public.

Happily, there is an exception: the American Association of Individual Investors' *The Individual Investor's Guide to No-Load Mutual Funds* (see Chapter 18 for the address). In addition to all the usual information, this annual publication gives the betas for each of the scores of funds it covers. It also shows effective diversification, based on R-squared. The guide's only limitation is that it is restricted to no-load funds.

The key to risk management in investing is to recognize which risks exist in various possible investments and to know which risks we are willing to accept and which ones we want to control or eliminate. With mutual funds, a knowledge of beta and R-squared, combined with a look at the objectives and the actual portfolios, gives us the tools to do just that.

I must emphasize one thing about this: It is easy to confuse responsibility for decision making. A fund's responsibility is to decide on a basic strategy or orientation, make it clear to prospective investors, and implement it as well as possible. The fund sponsor's decision on the type of fund to offer is a judgment about investor interest and the fund's marketability, not the investment merits of the strategy. The judgment about whether it is a good or appropriate strategy lies with investors, not the fund.

Putting It Together

It is likely that, in choosing mutual funds, most investors look first at performance records and second at the kinds of stocks the funds invest in. Risk characteristics are considered third, if at all. *The process should be reversed.* Future results will be determined far more by the aggressiveness of the portfolio, and the degree to which it reflects a specialized strategy, than by the skill of the fund manager. If a specialized fund is what you want, look at the statements of objectives and policies and look at the portfolios. Find ones that match the strategy and the risks that *you* want to assume.

Once you have identified a group of funds meeting your basic risk and strategic criteria, *then* look at the performance records. This may seem contrary, but past performance is the least reliable guide to future performance.

Most people seem to be drawn into a not-so-tender trap. In an interview with the AAII *Journal*, Dean LeBaron, a leading institutional investment manager, was asked what disadvantages individual investors face. His response was enlightening: "They can be forced to exercise stock selection of individual issues, which is a small part of the overall return that comes from investing." In other words, most investors get it backwards: Strategy and risk management should come first in both time and priority. Asked about the stocks in his institutional portfolios, LeBaron's reply was telling: "I don't know much about individual stocks—it is part of a package." One virtue of mutual funds is that they allow us to turn our attention where it belongs.

THE FLIP SIDE

Thus far, I have presented an intentionally one-sided case for mutual fund investing. This is not to suggest that mutual funds are perfect. There are very few unmixed blessings in life.

Taxes

The taxation of mutual funds is a complex subject, one that we cannot deal with in depth here. The AAII guide and other books on funds deal with it, but a few problems and potential pitfalls must be mentioned.

When you sell mutual fund shares, you will realize a capital gain or loss. In addition, you will receive dividend and interest income while you hold the shares. These are all taxed as if the fund shares were shares of common stocks.

A mutual fund itself is exempt from taxes on the income distributed from the fund, if the fund passes at least 90% of its earnings through to the shareholders. Funds may retain realized capital gains but must pay taxes on them out of fund assets. The shareholders then get a tax credit for their share of the taxes paid. As a practical matter, most funds distribute all realized capital gains, in addition to the required 90% of ordinary income.

Fund shareholders are required to pay taxes on the distributions. For tax purposes, most distributions have the same character in the hands of the shareholder that they had in the hands of the fund. Thus, capital gains of the fund are distributed as capital gains of the shareholder (regardless of how long shares in the fund have been owned), and similarly with interest and dividend income.

The problem is that the funds don't—and can't—care about their shareholders' tax situations. A fund's primary interest is in maximizing its own performance record, which is calculated before taxes, not *your* performance record, which is calculated after them.

Individual investors can make portfolio decisions based on tax considerations. For example, selling a stock and realizing a gain could be postponed until it qualified for long-term tax treatment. The 1986 Tax Reform Act eliminated the preference for long-term gains, but an investor might still want to delay taking a gain, because realizing the gain subjects him to a tax liability that reduces the amount of money available for reinvestment. Or he can decide to delay in order to push a tax liability into the following year. Whatever the tax considerations, by investing via mutual funds, investors cede control of the decisions to the fund managers.

The 1986 tax bill held a nasty surprise for investors. Investment expenses, such as advisory fees, publications, and custodial services, are no longer deductible except to the extent that they exceed 2 percent of adjusted gross income. This also applies to mutual fund expenses that are passed on to shareholders, such that investors will now be taxed on gross income while receiving only net income. To illustrate, suppose that a fund has gross income from dividends and interest of $1.00 per share, and expenses of $0.60 to pass on to shareholders. The actual distribution will be $0.40. In the past, investors would simply report the $0.40 as income on their tax returns. Under the 1986 law, they will receive $0.40, must report income of $1.00, and won't be able to deduct the $0.60 per share unless they have passed the 2 percent threshold.

Fund distributions offer another tax pitfall for investors. If you buy shares just before an income distribution, you will in effect have some of your capital handed back to you—and be forced to pay income tax on it!

There are other tax matters that are beyond the scope of our interest here. They have to do with the timing and identification of fund shares when sold, and the tax accounting for reinvested dividends. Virtually any book on mutual funds will explain these. There are pitfalls for the unwary or uninformed, and it is important to understand them before redeeming mutual fund shares.

Trading Costs

Fund investors bear two types of costs: the costs of actually buying and selling the stocks in the funds' portfolios, and the sales, management, and operating costs of the funds that are charged to the investors in the form of various fees.

Trading costs are not shown in fund financial data (although turnover is), because commission costs are capitalized, not expensed, for accounting and tax purposes. Proponents of mutual funds often claim that one of their benefits is low trading costs. This is true, if we consider commissions only, but buying or selling large quantities of stock may force funds to accept prices far from the current quote or the last sale price. There is considerable evidence that funds actually incur *higher* trading costs than individual investors do, especially in the case of smaller stocks, as we saw in Chapter 11.

The performance record of any fund will be net of all costs, including trading costs. Thus the record of a fund with a great deal of turnover and high trading costs will already reflect those costs. But there is a danger in high-turnover funds. In periods in which the fund managers are unsuccessful in their trading, the costs will make a mediocre performance much worse.

Marketing and Management Costs

Until recently, funds that sold directly to the public had no sales charges (no-load funds), while those that sold through salesmen had a specified *front load*. This charge was simply taken out of an investor's initial investment, thus representing a one-time reduction of his capital. Typically, the load was 8.5 percent of the investment, though some funds had smaller loads, and many charged on a sliding scale, with larger investments incurring lower charges. Part of the load would go to the salesmen, part to a middleman (the fund distributor, who acts as a marketing agent of the fund, handling advertising and promotion). Many of these "plain vanilla" front-load funds still exist, but there is a new scheme that has rapidly gained popularity. Under a *12b-1* plan (named for the SEC rule permitting it), fund sponsors may annually charge the *fund* for marketing expenses. This annual charge is commonly 1 percent of net assets and runs as high as 1.25 percent with some funds. Since it is the fund itself that is bearing this charge, it is a direct reduction of each investor's annual returns. Thus it is quite a bit different from a charge that is levied specifically on the person making an investment in the fund. Some funds have *both* a front load and a 12b-1 charge.

The 12b-1 plans sound insidious, usually giving investors a break on the load but extracting a fee every year. Such plans are not necessarily so bad, though, at least if an 8.5 percent front load is the alternative. The biggest problem is that funds aren't very forthcoming about their use of the 12b-1 plans, burying them very deep in the prospectuses. Investors may not be aware of them until they receive annual statements and even then may assume that they are simply a part of the normal deduction for expenses.*

Even worse, many no-load funds have been imposing 12b-1 charges. Since the SEC generally considers these charges reimbursement of indirect marketing expenses, rather than sales charges, these funds go right on advertising themselves as no-load funds. At the end of 1985, roughly 40 percent of all no-load stock funds imposed 12b-1 charges, and the number will undoubtedly increase. (An existing fund cannot adopt a 12b-1 plan without a vote of the shareholders.)

Another recent innovation in marketing charges is the *deferred contingent sales charge*—in effect a redemption charge, a back-end load. This has become quite common, almost always in combination with a 12b-1 plan. Funds generally charge in the area of 4 percent, but this is usually on a sliding scale, based on how long the investor has been in the fund. The redemption charge typically decreases to zero or near zero in four to seven years. The redemption charge is normally based on the amount invested, not on the value at redemption.

Sales charges do not buy investment advice or expertise. The fund's management company receives a fee for this under any sales structure. The management fee and various other nonmarketing expenses are charged periodically against the fund's assets. Logic suggests that sales charges would not contribute to performance, and the facts bear this out. There is no evidence that investors gain anything by buying load funds except the convenience of being able to buy them from their stockbrokers. In general, investments in load funds seem to underperform those in no-load ones by amounts that roughly correspond to the size of the load, just as we would expect.

Apart from sales and management charges, every fund is charged for various operating costs—for example, legal, accounting, and auditing expenses. All these are outlined in the prospectus and listed in the quarterly and annual financial data.

An 8.5 percent front load is unlikely to be overlooked by a reasonably alert investor, but 12b-1 charges and redemption fees are much less

*Information about a 12b-1 charge and other expenses is sometimes omitted from the prospectuses that investors are routinely sent and is placed in a statement of additional information. This is not sent except on specific request.

obvious. Even when noticed, they may seem trivial individually—hence their increasing popularity among fund sponsors—but when annual and deferred sales charges are combined with the management and maintenance fees, the package can be substantial indeed. Many investors are unknowingly being nickeled and dimed to death. In a fund with a 12b-1 charge of 1.25 percent, operations charges of .25 percent, and an advisory fee of 1 percent, fund investors are giving up 2.5 percent per year, a hefty cut in a market that historically has returned only slightly more than 10 percent per year. In addition, they might well be subject to a 3 percent or 4 percent fee if they redeem shares within a few years, cutting their annual returns by another percentage point or so. In a reasonably efficient market, it is unlikely that professional skill will overcome the fee handicap. Thus it is not surprising that mutual funds as a group consistently underperform the overall market.

The whole matter of mutual fund sales and marketing charges is in a state of flux. Funds no longer fall neatly into two categories, and your fund may be changing right before your eyes. In the era of deregulation, the government takes the position that virtually anything goes, so long as there is full disclosure. It is essential to read the prospectuses (and proxy material) carefully.

It appears that in the face of rising popularity, mutual fund sponsors have become progressively greedier. Not long ago, it was easy to find true no-load funds with total annual costs of less than 1 percent. Now such funds are very scarce and getting scarcer. In short, mutual funds have become much more expensive, and a good deal has become a good deal worse. As a result, the number of investors for whom funds are the best choice has considerably decreased.

Impurities

We have looked at several successful investment strategies in previous chapters, and funds exist to attempt to exploit some of these apparent market inefficiencies. There are funds specializing in small stocks, as well as value-oriented funds that purport to invest on the basis of low P/E, low price-to-book value, and so on. But it is difficult to find any fund that is applying any of these strategies in a pure form. For example, several funds that say they invest in small stocks don't really do so. I have seen examples of such funds, in which less than a quarter of the assets were actually invested in stocks that could reasonably be considered small (say, less than $100 million market value)—a very good reason to look at a fund's portfolio, not just its words.

More common is what may be called the "Yes, but..." syndrome: Yes, we invest in low P/E stocks, but only in stocks likely to grow at least as fast as the economy. Yes, we invest in stocks with low price-to-sales ratios, but not in companies we think likely to go bankrupt. Yes, we invest in stocks with low prices in relation to book value, but only if they have positive earnings. Yes, we invest in small stocks, but only in industries likely to show above-average growth.

This is not just a hypothetical problem. David Booth, a director of one of the "purest" small-stock funds, told Solveig Jansson in 1982, "If World Airways comes out and says, as it did earlier this year, that it will have to renegotiate a union contract—or else file for Chapter 11—at that point, the stock starts trading on speculation and the company's ability to survive. *We won't buy*" [p. 147; emphasis added]. He also stated that stocks would be bought on the basis of size but sold on the basis of "tape watching"!

All these "buts" represent a backing away from the basic strategy. The funds are in effect distorting the strategy by adding one or more layers of additional analysis. At that point, we must merely assume either that it will still work in its altered form or that the fund manager's skill will carry the day. Worst, most fund prospectuses will not specify all the "buts."

In sum, among mutual funds, it may not be possible to find very pure applications of many of the most promising strategies we have seen. A do-it-yourself approach is the route to pure strategies if you have sufficient assets to achieve the required diversification.

YOUR OWN FUND?

It is debatable (at best) whether mutual funds yield performance superior to what the individual investor could achieve on his own. A few funds undoubtedly have, but predicting which ones will in the future is another matter. On top of this inherent uncertainty, you have to pay them to manage your money for you. Fund managers have to be paid, as do salesmen, lawyers, accountants, transfer agents, and many others. It can easily cost you 3 to 4 percent per year, all to create a diversified portfolio that approximates your investment ideas. Why not do it yourself and save the expenses?

There are several issues involved. We have seen the first. It takes a reasonable amount of capital to make diversified individual investing practical. The shareowner survey conducted by the New York Stock Exchange in mid-1985 determined that the median portfolio size was $6,200. This indicates that most individual investors cannot practically achieve effective diversification.

In looking at the costs of mutual fund investing, we must also remember that individual investing is hardly cost-free. Many investors spend a great deal of both money and time on investment publications and information services. After all, their ideas have to come from somewhere. In addition, there is paperwork to process, and there are records to keep and dividends to cash and reinvest. These are greatly simplified for fund investors, and so mutual funds may be a bargain for many small investors. For those with more substantial investment assets—say, $50,000 or more—2 to 4 percent per year in costs and fees may be a high price to pay for convenience.

Beyond costs, the real issues are strategy and risk management. Lacking either the information or the discipline necessary to maintain and manage a consistent strategy, many investors end up with portfolios that reflect no discernible strategy at all, or with ones whose implicit strategies are so short-lived as to be meaningless. Remedying this situation is the primary benefit of professional management. For many investors, the process of selecting a mutual fund will represent a great leap forward in strategic planning and risk management, whose benefits will outweigh the costs involved. In contrast, if an investor with sufficient funds has a strict, clearly defined strategy that he wishes to pursue, there is little doubt that he can create a purer manifestation of it with his own portfolio, while saving money to boot. Asking whether mutual fund investing is superior to individual investing is a little like asking whether French or Chinese food is better. The answer depends not so much on what they are as on who you are.

20

Epilogue:
Keep It Simple

If we consider a single company, what happens to its shareholders will not depend greatly on what happens to the economy or the stock market in general, nor will it depend very much on the riskiness of that stock. The results will depend almost entirely upon what hapens to the company itself through time. If the company is successful, shareholders will be rewarded. If not, they will be punished.

Given this obvious truth, most investors conclude that the key to investment success is selection. They seem to spend the bulk of their efforts on finding hot stocks, hot mutual funds, or hot investment advisors. They attempt to predict the future. What they actually find, of course, is what *has been* hot, not what *will be* hot. The whole endeavor is likely to be a costly and nerve-wracking exercise in futility, because a small degree of superiority in skill or effort will not overcome the costs of playing this game. And a small degree of superiority is all that most of us can ever hope to attain. The stock market may not be perfectly efficient, but it is efficient enough that the percentage of people who can outwit it significantly and consistently will be infinitesimal.

The problem is that most people see the market as a collection of individual and unrelated stocks, about which individual and unrelated judgments and decisions must be made. In truth, the stock market is a risk capital market, and it exists to attract and allocate risk capital among different enterprises. It is a competitive system, not just a collection of stocks.

It rewards the shareholders in successful companies and punishes the losers, but risk is the key element, and the market must reward risk taking if it is to perform its role. Its longevity is testimony to its continued ability to do this. The market is not perfectly efficient. It does not allocate capital perfectly, nor does it allocate rewards strictly on the basis of risk assumed. There is little doubt, however, that risk is the primary factor in determining returns. The market is a risk/reward system by design, and it is largely a risk/reward system in practice.

In theory, the stock market rewards only market risk—the risk associated with stocks generally—since the risks associated with individual stocks can be diversified away. Nevertheless, we have seen that certain categories of stocks have had strong (albeit erratic) tendencies to yield returns far higher than their market risk can explain. We have also seen that these categories all seem to be based on characteristics and qualities that make most investors leery. We've referred to these negatives as *perceived risks*. The extent to which they represent actual risks is hotly debated in academic and financial circles and may be more a matter of semantics than anything else. It is clear that anyone attempting to exploit them will have to endure both more discomfort and more real risk than someone with a diversified portfolio spanning the entire spectrum of common stocks.

Once you recognize the market for what it is, investing is much less complicated and worrisome than most people make it, because the stock market game is really quite simple. It is structured to reward risk taking and effective risk management. The key to successful investing is to understand risk and to create strategies that correspond both to that understanding and to your own temperament and circumstances.

Many people compare the market to gambling, describing the stock exchange as a casino. Well, it *is* like a casino. Risk is real, the market is much more efficient than most people would like to acknowledge, and so the outcome of each spin of the wheel—each individual stock, each investment period—is governed largely by luck. But casino operators don't need to predict the future, and neither do you.

If you are willing to engage in some intelligent but simple risk management, and if you view investing not as a quarterly or annual contest but as a long-term endeavor, the market is practically a sure thing. So, yes—it is a casino, but with a little effort, you need not be in the position of a gambler. You will be in the position of the house, with the odds in your favor.

Bibliography

This list includes works cited or referred to in the text. The *Financial Analysts Journal, International Economic Review, Journal of Business, Journal of Finance, Journal of Financial Economics,* and *Journal of Portfolio Management* are professional and academic publications and the articles that appear there tend to be technical and mathematical. They are useful for serious students of the market, since they form the underpinnings of modern investment theory and practice. Many classic studies, including some cited here, have been reprinted in Lorie and Brealey, eds., *Modern Developments in Investment Management,* 2d ed. (Hinsdale, Ill.: Dryden Press, 1978). A useful, thorough, but not highly technical review of the entire field is Lorie, Dodd, and Kimpton, *The Stock Market: Theories and Evidence,* 2d ed. (Homewood, Ill.: Dow Jones–Irwin, 1985).

Allman, William F. "Staying Alive in the 20th Century: The Experts Can Tell Us What's Risky, but Most of Us Take Our Own Chances." *Science 85,* Oct. 1985.

"All Players in Stock Market Contest End Up in the Red." *San Jose Mercury News,* Dec. 30, 1984.

Ambachtsheer, Keith P. "Where Are the Customers' Alphas?" *Journal of Portfolio Management,* Fall 1977.

Anders, George. "Some 'Efficient-Market' Scholars Decide It's Possible to Beat the Averages After All." *Wall Street Journal,* Dec. 31, 1985.

Anders, George. "By the Numbers: Using Rote and Math, Wells Fargo Succeeds as a Money Manager." *Wall Street Journal*, March 23, 1987.

Appel, Gerald, and Hitschler, Fred. *Stock Market Trading Systems*. Homewood, Ill.: Dow Jones–Irwin, 1980.

Arbel, Avner; Carvell, Steven; and Strebel, Paul. "Giraffes, Institutions and Neglected Firms." *Financial Analysts Journal*, May–June 1983.

Arbel, Avner, and Strebel, Paul. "Pay Attention to Neglected Firms!" *Journal of Portfolio Management*, Winter 1983.

Arnott, Robert D. "What Hath MPT Wrought: Which Risks Reap Rewards?" *Journal of Portfolio Management*, Fall 1983.

Banz, Rolf W. "The Relationship Between Return and Market Value of Common Stock." *Journal of Financial Economics*, March 1981.

Barry, Christopher B., and Brown, Stephen J. "Limited Information as a Source of Risk." *Journal of Portfolio Management*, Winter 1986.

Basu, Sanjoy. "Investment Performance of Common Stocks in Relation to Their Price/Earnings Ratios: A Test of the Efficient Market Hypothesis." *Journal of Finance*, June 1977.

Bernstein, Peter L. "Will the Beauty Contest Ever Be Obsolete?" *Journal of Portfolio Management*, Spring 1983.

Black, Fischer. "Yes, Virginia, There Is Hope: Tests of the Value Line Ranking System." *Financial Analysts Journal*, Sept.–Oct. 1973.

Block, Stanley B. "Efficient Markets: Buzz Word of the '60s Gets Stung." *American Association of Individual Investors Journal*, Sept. 1984.

Blume, Marshall E. "On the Assessment of Risk." *Journal of Finance*, March 1972.

Boldt, Bob L., and Arbit, Hal L. "Efficient Markets and the Professional Investor." *Financial Analysts Journal*, July–Aug. 1984.

Brimelow, Peter. "Order in the Ranks: Value Line's Courtly Progenitor and the Service He's Wrought." *Barron's*, June 3, 1985.

Brown, Lawrence D., and Rozeff, Michael S. "The Superiority of Analyst Forecastings as Measures of Expectations: Evidence of Earnings." *Journal of Finance*, March 1978.

Chalk, Andrew J., and Peavy, John W. III. "IPOs: Why Individuals Don't Get the 'Hot' Issues." *American Association of Individual Investors Journal*, March 1987.

Coggin, T. Daniel, and Hunter, John E. "Problems in Measuring the Quality of Investment Information." *Financial Analysts Journal*, May–June 1983.

Consumers Union. "A Guide to Mutual Funds." *Consumer Reports*, July 1985.

Copeland, Thomas E., and Mayers, David. "The Value Line Enigma (1965–1978)." *Journal of Financial Economics*, no. 10, 1982.

Curran, John J. "Value Line's Winning Way." *Fortune*, April 18, 1983.

Dreman, David. *The New Contrarian Investment Strategy*. New York: Random House, 1982.

Edminster, Robert O., and James, Christopher. "Is Illiquidity a Bar to Buying Small Cap Stocks?" *Journal of Portfolio Management*, Summer 1983.

Edwards, Robert D., and Magee, John. *Technical Analysis of Stock Trends*. 5th ed. Boston: John Magee, Inc., 1966.

Ellis, Charles D. "A Conversation with Benjamin Graham." *Financial Analysts Journal*, Sept.–Oct. 1976.

Fama, Eugene F. "Efficient Capital Markets: A Review of Theory and Empirical Work." *Journal of Finance*, May 1970.

Fama, Eugene; Fisher, Lawrence; Jensen, Michael; and Roll, Richard. "The Adjustment of Stock Prices to New Information." *International Economic Review*, Feb. 1969.

Farrell, James J., Jr. "Homogeneous Stock Groupings: Implications for Portfolio Management." *Financial Analysts Journal*, May–June 1975.

Fisher, Kenneth L. *Super Stocks*. Homewood, Ill.: Dow Jones–Irwin, 1984.

Goodman, David A. "Price-to-Equity Screens: Low Ratios, High Returns." *American Association of Individual Investors Journal*, Aug. 1986.

Granville, Joseph E. *Granville's New Strategy of Daily Stock Market Timing for Maximum Profit*. Englewood Cliffs, N.J.: Prentice-Hall, 1976.

Greenblatt, Joel; Pzena, Richard; and Newburg, Bruce. "How the Small Investor Can Beat the Market." *Journal of Portfolio Management*, Summer 1981.

Harrington, Diana R. "Whose Beta Is Best?" *Financial Analysts Journal*, July–Aug. 1983.

Holloway, Clark. "A Note on Testing an Aggressive Investment Strategy Using Value Line Ranks." *Journal of Finance*, June 1981 (see also criticisms in March 1983 issue).

Hulbert, Mark. "Buy-and-Hold: The January Market's Winning Strategy." *American Association of Individual Investors Journal*, April 1985.

Ibbotson, Roger G., and Sinquefield, Rex A. *Stocks, Bonds, Bills and Inflation*. Charlottesville, Va.: Financial Analysts Research Foundation, 1982. Updated in *Stocks, Bonds, Bills and Inflation: 1987 Yearbook*. Chicago: Ibbotson Associates, 1987.

Jacobs, Sheldon. "High Expense Ratios: Can the Funds Overcome the Drag?" *American Association of Individual Investors Journal*, March 1987.

Jansson, Solveig. "The Big Debate Over Little Stocks." *Institutional Investor*, June 1982.

Jeffrey, Robert H. "Putting Market Timing to the Test: Is It Worth the Risk?" *American Association of Individual Investors Journal*, Sept. 1985.

Jensen, Michael C. "Random Walks: Reality or Myth—Comment." *Financial Analysts Journal*, Nov.–Dec. 1967.

Jensen, Michael C. "Risk, the Pricing of Capital Assets, and the Evaluation of Investment Portfolios." *Journal of Business*, April 1969.

Jensen, Michael C., and Bennington, George A. "Random Walks and Technical Theories: Some Additional Evidence." *Journal of Finance*, May 1970.

Jones, Charles; Rendleman, Richard J., Jr.; and Latane, Henry A. "Stock Returns and SUEs During the 1970s." *Journal of Portfolio Management*, Winter 1984.

Keim, Donald B. "Size-Related Anomalies and Stock Market Return Seasonality: Further Empirical Evidence." *Journal of Financial Economics*, June 1983.

Keim, Donald B. "CAPM and Equity Return Regularities." *Financial Analysts Journal*, May–June 1986.

Keynes, John Maynard. *The General Theory of Employment, Interest, and Money.* New York: Harcourt Brace Jovanovich, 1964.

Kinsman, Robert. "There Is a Beta Way: Measuring the Risk in Your Mutual Fund." *Barron's,* Oct. 15, 1984.

LeBaron, Dean. "Reflections on Market Inefficiency." *Financial Analysts Journal,* May–June 1983.

Levy, Robert A. "Random Walks: Reality or Myth?" *Financial Analysts Journal,* Nov.–Dec. 1967.

Lindsey, Lawrence B. "Misguided Capital Gains Levy." *Wall Street Journal,* Sept. 10, 1986.

Lloyd, William P., and Haney, Richard L., Jr. "Time Diversification: Surest Route to Lower Risk." *Journal of Portfolio Management,* Spring 1980.

Loeb, Thomas F. "Trading Cost: The Critical Link Between Investment Information and Results." *Financial Analysts Journal,* May–June 1983.

Lustig, Ivan L., and Leinbach, Philip A. "The Small Firm Effect." *Financial Analysts Journal,* May–June 1983.

McDonald, John G. "Investment Objectives: Diversification, Risk and Exposure to Surprise." *Financial Analysts Journal,* March–April 1975.

Macklin, Gordon S. "A NASDAQ Overview from an Insider's Vantage." *American Association of Individual Investors Journal,* Oct. 1985.

McMurray, Scott. "OTC Market Is Booming, but Cost of Active Trading Can Cut Gains." *Wall Street Journal,* March 12, 1985.

Malkiel, Burton G. *A Random Walk Down Wall Street.* 4th ed. New York: W.W. Norton, 1985.

Markowitz, Harry M. "Portfolio Selection." *Journal of Finance,* March 1952 (this article stimulated the development of modern investment theory).

Modigliani, Franco, and Pogue, Gerald A. "An Introduction to Risk and Return." *Financial Analysts Journal,* March–April 1974.

Niederhaffer, Victor, and Regan, Patrick J. "Earnings Changes, Analysts' Forecasts, and Stock Prices." *Financial Analysts Journal,* May–June 1972.

O'Higgins, Michael. "All-Star Strikeouts." *Barron's,* June 4, 1984.

Oppenheimer, Henry J., and Schlarbaum, Gary G. "'Father' Knows Best: Benjamin Graham's Net Current Asset Values." *American Association of Individual Investors Journal,* March 1985.

Peavy, John W. III, and Goodman, David A. "The Significance of P/Es for Portfolio Returns." *Journal of Portfolio Management,* Winter 1983.

Perritt, Gerald W. "[Mutual Fund] Expenses: Watch Your Pennies." *American Association of Individual Investors Journal,* March 1985.

Pines, Harvey. "A New Psychological Perspective on Investor Decision Making." *American Association of Individual Investors Journal,* Sept. 1983.

"Points of View: An Interview with Dean LeBaron." *American Association of Individual Investors Journal,* Sept. 1984.

Pope, Alan. "Distributions: A Taxing Effect on Mutual Fund Returns." *American Association of Individual Investors Journal,* Oct. 1984.

Reinganum, Marc. "Abnormal Returns in Small Firm Portfolios." *Financial Analysts Journal,* March–April 1981.

Reinganum, Marc. "Portfolio Strategies Based on Market Capitalization." *Journal of Portfolio Management,* Winter 1983.

Renshaw, Edward F. "The Anatomy of Stock Market Cycles." *Journal of Portfolio Management,* Fall 1983.

Roll, Richard. "*Vas ist das?* The Turn-of-the-Year Effect and the Return Premium of Small Firms." *Journal of Portfolio Management,* Winter 1983.

Rose, Robert L. "Tracking the Trades of Corporate Insiders Doesn't Always Give an Edge to Investors." *Wall Street Journal,* December 19, 1985.

Samuelson, Paul. "Challenge to Judgment." *Journal of Portfolio Management,* Fall, 1974.

Schneller, Meir I. "Are Better Betas Worth the Trouble?" *Financial Analysts Journal,* July–Aug. 1983.

Scott, Maria Crawford. "Diversification: It's About Time." *American Association of Individual Investors Journal,* Sept. 1984.

Scott, Maria Crawford. "Points of View: An Interview with Stan Weinstein." *American Association of Individual Investors Journal,* Nov. 1984.

Scott, Maria Crawford. "Everything You Always Wanted to Know About 12b-1 Plans—and More." *American Association of Individual Investors Journal,* Mar. 1985.

Scott, Maria Crawford. "Fund Distributions: A Search for the Source." *American Association of Individual Investors Journal,* Nov. 1985.

Sebastian, Pamela. "Funds That Buy Into Small Firms Aren't for Timid." *Wall Street Journal,* May 29, 1985.

Sharpe, William F. "A Simplified Model for Portfolio Analysis." *Management Science,* Jan. 1963.

Sharpe, William F. "Capital Asset Prices: A Theory of Market Equilibrium Under Conditions of Risk." *Journal of Finance,* Sept. 1964.

Sharpe, William F. "Risk, Market Sensitivity and Diversification." *Financial Analysts Journal,* Jan.–Feb. 1972.

Sharpe, William F. *Investments.* 2d ed. Englewood Cliffs, N.J.: Prentice-Hall, 1981.

Sharpe, William F. "Factors in New York Stock Exchange Security Returns, 1931–1979." *Journal of Portfolio Management,* Summer 1982.

Stern, Richard L., and Bornstein, Paul. "Why New Issues Are Lousy Investments." *Forbes,* Dec. 2, 1985.

Tobias, Andrew. *The Only Investment Guide You'll Ever Need.* New York: Harcourt Brace Jovanovich, 1983.

Wagner, W.H., and Lau, S.C. "The Effect of Diversification on Risk." *Financial Analysts Journal,* Nov.–Dec. 1971.

Glossary

Alpha. A measure of the return on a security not attributable to its riskiness. Alpha is derived from the equation in the *Capital Assets Pricing Model (CAPM)*. In an efficient market, the expected value of alpha is zero for all securities. In hindsight, most alphas are positive or negative. The attempt to identify individual stocks that will outperform or underperform the market is thus an attempt to predict future alphas.

Beta coefficient. Usually just called "beta," this measure is a multiplier that relates returns on a stock or portfolio to returns on the market as a whole, whose beta is 1.0, by definition. For example, a beta of 1.4 implies that a stock exaggerates the market moves by 40%. The S&P 500 stock index is usually used as the measure of the market as a whole. Beta measures the degree of *market risk* in a stock or portfolio, but it measures only the extent to which returns track the market, not their consistency. If the market is efficient, and under CAPM, beta fully determines the expected return on an investment in relation to the market. Both beta and alpha are estimated from a statistical analysis of past price movements.

Book value. The remainder after deducting all liabilities from a company's assets. It is essentially the net worth of a company. Book value is usually expressed on a per-share basis. Book value is an accounting number and is not directly related to the market price of a stock.

Capital Assets Pricing Model (CAPM). A model in which individual security returns are explained solely by the return on the market, the relative riskiness of the individual securities as measured by beta, and a random variable whose expected (and average) value is zero. It is a complete expression of the returns from stocks if the market is efficient.

Efficient market. A market in which current stock prices accurately reflect all information that is relevant to stock values and in which new information is rapidly and accurately reflected in stock prices. In such a market, investors cannot achieve higher returns through the analysis of existing or arriving information. Rather, they will receive 1) fair returns for the amount of market risk assumed, and 2) unpredictable returns (positive or negative) based on luck and the amount of *specific risk* incurred.

Excess return. This term is used in different ways and must be understood in context. First, it is often simply the difference between the return on a stock or portfolio and the return available on a risk-free asset, such as a Treasury Bill. Second, it is sometimes used to denote return in excess of a common measure of the market, such as the S&P 500. Finally, it sometimes means the return in excess of what can be attributed to market risk assumed.

Expected return. The weighted average of all possible return outcomes: the possible returns weighted by their probabilities of occurring.

Intrinsic value. The "true" value of a security. In effect, it is the value we would place on a security if we had perfect foresight of everything bearing on that security's value.

Liquidity. The extent to which a market can absorb purchases or sales without large changes in prices. There is no standard measure of liquidity.

Net asset value. This is identical to book value in an accounting sense. Investors commonly encounter this term in connection with mutual funds, where net asset values per share are computed and published daily and are the bases of purchase and redemption prices.

New issue. Any stock sold by a corporation for the first time. This can be a new issue of the same class of stock that has been issued previously, so a new issue is not technically the same as an "initial public offering." But in common parlance, that is what is usually meant by a new issue.

Present value. A future value or stream of payments that has been discounted at an appropriate rate of interest to establish its worth today.

The discount rate will depend upon credit market conditions (reflecting the time value of money) and risk factors applying to the asset.

Random walk theory. A random walk is a process in which successive movements are independent so that future movements cannot be predicted from past ones. In the stock market, the random walk theory states that past trading patterns cannot be used to predict future ones. This is often expanded to state that no information can be used to predict future prices.

Risk. The uncertainty or variability of the outcomes of actions or situations.

Risk—market. The risk associated with being a stockholder in general. It is the risk associated with just being in the market, regardless of which stocks are held. Market risk is usually measured by beta, a relative rather than absolute measure. Also commonly referred to as "systematic risk."

Risk—specific. The risk associated with a particular stock or stock group. In an efficient market and under CAPM, no returns accrue to specific risk. Specific risk can be reduced or eliminated through diversification without reducing expected returns. Thus it is often referred to as diversifiable risk. It is also often called nonmarket or unsystematic risk.

Risk aversion. The desire to avoid unnecessary risk. Rational investors will seek the highest possible returns for a given degree of risk or the lowest possible risk for a given level of expected returns.

Risk-adjusted returns. Portfolio returns that have been recalculated to reflect the amount of risk incurred to achieve them, usually on the basis of their betas. Risk-adjusted returns are a way of standardizing return data. They are used to investigate possible market inefficiencies and to compare the performance of different investors, especially in the institutional field.

R-squared. A statistic that shows the extent to which two variables move together. Specifically, it shows what percentage of the movement in one variable can be explained by the movement of the other, assuming there is a causal relationship. In the context of the stock market, R-squared measures the extent to which movements in the general market explain the movements of a given stock or portfolio. It thus measures what proportion of total risk is market risk.

Standard deviation. A statistical measure of dispersion or variability in figures that are distributed approximately normally (i.e. symmetrically). Standard deviation is the usual measure of total risk in a stock, portfolio, or the market as a whole. Standard deviation is an absolute measure. The *coefficient of variation* is the standard deviation divided by the mean, turning it into a relative measure that is useful for comparisons.

Wealth ratio. The terminal value of an investment divided by its initial value. From a knowledge of the wealth ratio and the length of the term, rate of return can be calculated.

Weighting. The relative importance of each of a group of figures that are combined into some index, average, or statistic, for example the importance given to each stock in creating a stock market index.

Index